HEALING THE WOUNDS

D1740211

Oñati International Series in Law and Society

A SERIES PUBLISHED FOR THE OÑATI INSTITUTE
FOR THE SOCIOLOGY OF LAW

General Editors

William L F Felstiner   Professor Johannes Feest

Board of General Editors

Rosemary Hunter, Griffiths University, Australia
Carlos Lugo, Hostos Law School, Puerto Rico
David Nelken, Macerata University, Italy
Jacek Kurczewski, Warsaw University, Poland
Marie Claire Foblets, Leuven University, Belgium
Roderick Macdonald, McGill University, Canada

Titles in This Series

*Social Dynamics of Crime and Control:
New Theories for a World in Transition*
Edited by Susanne Karstedt and Kai-D Bussmann

Criminal Policy in Transition
Edited by Penny Green and Andrew Rutherford

Making Law for Families
Edited by Mavis Maclean

Poverty and the Law
Edited by Peter Robson and Asbjørn Kjønstad

Adapting Legal Cultures
Edited by Johannes Feest and David Nelken

Rethinking Law Society and Governance: Foucault's Bequest
Edited by Gary Wickham and George Pavlich

Rules and Networks
Edited by Richard Appelbaum, Bill Felstiner and Volkmar Gessner

Women in the World's Legal Professions
Edited by Ulrike Schultz and Gisela Shaw

Healing the Wounds

Essays on the Reconstruction of Societies after War

Edited by

Marie-Claire Foblets

and

Trutz von Trotha

Oñati International Series in Law and Society
A SERIES PUBLISHED FOR THE OÑATI INSTITUTE
FOR THE SOCIOLOGY OF LAW

·HART·
PUBLISHING

OXFORD AND PORTLAND OREGON
2004

Published in North America (US and Canada) by
Hart Publishing c/o
International Specialized Book Services
5804 NE Hassalo Street
Portland, Oregon
97213-3644
USA

© Oñati IISL 2004

Hart Publishing is a specialist legal publisher based in Oxford, England.
To order further copies of this book or to request a list of other
publications please write to:

Hart Publishing, Salter's Boatyard,
Folly Bridge, Abingdon Road, Oxford, OX1 4LB
email: mail@hartpub.co.uk
Telephone: +44 (0)1865 245533 Fax: +44 (0)1865 794882
WEB SITE http//:www.hartpub.co.uk

British Library Cataloguing in Publication Data
Data Available

ISBN 1-84113-468-6 (cased)
ISBN 1-84113-469-4 (paper)

Typeset by Olympus Infotech Pvt, Ltd, India Sabon 10/12 pt
Printed and bound in Great Britain by
Lightning Source UK Ltd

Abstracts

Legislation and Decentralisation in Uganda: From Resistance Councils to Elected Local Councils with Guaranteed Representation

DIRK BEKE

THE PROCESS OF legislation related to the decentralisation and local governments in Uganda shows an interesting correlation between legal evolutionism and legal instrumentalism or legal engineering. The Local Resistance Councils (LRCs) were progressively established in an informal and 'revolutionary' way by Museveni's troops in the newly conquered area. After Museveni seized power in Kampala, new laws legalised and reshaped the LRCs into elected Local Councils. The new legislation confirms the 'no-party system' but at the same time imposes remarkably strict rules for guaranteed representation of women, youth and disabled people in the councils. On the one hand we notice that decentralisation is used by the central government to pass on responsibilities, including financing, to local administration. On the other hand, there are important signs that the mainly top-down process of formal decentralisation has generated local dynamism. The use by the regime of decentralisation for the purpose of both the creation and the control of a local sphere of power, has established new administrative structures which — intended or not — have created new possibilities for local participation by countervailing powers. The provisions on the role of traditional leaders reflect an ambivalent but strategic approach to cope as well with the social and cultural realities, the government's interests and the claim for democracy at the local levels.

Law, Violence, and Peace Making on the Island of Ambon

KEEBET VON BENDA-BECKMANN

F OR TWO AND a half years waves of violence have raged through the Moluccas, coming close to civil war. This chapter tries to understand the complexities of the underlying conflicts that have given rise to this outburst of violence on the Central Moluccas. It is argued that the conflicts combine elements of class, a highly authoritarian and corrupt state, ethnicity, the urban-rural divide and religion and active political and material support from outside the region and from abroad. Central Moluccan society is characterised by weak centralised leadership, and it is argued that customary constraints on cycles of violence have been severely weakened. Any attempt to create ways to peace that only concentrates on leaders and does not pay specific attention to the role of young adults can create a highly unstable peace at best, and is more likely to fail.

The Search for New Sources of Legitimacy in Indonesia after Suharto

JOHN BOWEN

V IOLENCE CONTINUES TO rage in Indonesia, either as the result of conflicts between immigrant and long-resident groups or, in the case of Aceh, as the escalation of a long-term conflict over autonomy between local people and the government. The paper considers alternative sources of legitimacy for resolving these conflicts and creating new forms of law and of local and regional government: adat, Islam, and norms of equal rights. Noted is the recent turn from searching for indigenous forms of government and justice, to looking elsewhere for models of conflict resolution and the rule of law.

The South African Truth and Reconciliation Commission: 'The Truth will Set You Free'

WILLEMIEN DU PLESSIS

S OUTH AFRICA HAS a long history of violence and disregard for human rights. In the process the government of the day believed they were above the law, and many gross human right violations were committed in the name of law and order while the real issue was the enforcement of apartheid. The negotiated Interim Constitution provided for the possibility of a truth and reconciliation commission, and this was done in terms of the Promotion of Truth and Reconciliation Act of 1995. The Act provided inter alia for a Truth and Reconciliation Commission under the chair of Bishop Tutu, an amnesty committee consisting of lawyers, a committee for gross violations of human rights and a committee for redress and rehabilitation. The Commission investigated violations not only by the previous government but also of the different freedom groups such as the ANC, PAC and AWB. The report of the Commission was met with mixed reactions. Both the ANC and the National Party tried to prevent the publication of the report. Some people complained that it contained some untruths; others were glad that the story was written. The work of the Commission is finished but not that of the amnesty committee. Whether the whole process brought about reconciliation is a question that only time will answer. It did, however, bring information to the fore that was not readily available in South Africa. To the advantaged, the truth as unveiled by the commission came as a shock and a revelation; to the disadvantaged it was a confirmation of what they have fought against all these years. The Commission was a necessary start in the healing process, but if socio-economic reform does not form part of the process, the good effect of the healing process, might be lost again.

Roads to Peace: From Small War to Parasovereign Peace in the North of Mali

GEORG KLUTE AND TRUTZ VON TROTHA

IN THE 1990s Mali experienced the Second Tuareg Rebellion. The rebellion also led to a war among the rebel movements. Aside from providing a short history of the rebellion, the article studies the search for peace in both wars and their relationships to one another. The article is based on many years of fieldwork and gives special analytical attention to the local level of peace processes. Its main thesis is that the route to peace is a road to rule. In West Africa it means that the contemporary search for peace is linked to the rise of a new type of domination, which the authors call 'parastate rule'. The article emphasises that demobilisation and reconstruction programs of the international donor community not only strengthen the rise of local forms of parastate rule like in the case of the Ifoghas parasovereign chiefdom but might become themselves forms of parastate rule.

Concepts of Violence and Peace in African Languages

WILHELM JG MÖHLIG AND RÜDIGER KÖPPE

I N OUR CONTRIBUTION, we discuss the question whether the African societies that experienced violence and war in the recent past are willing or even capable to be healed from their traumata induced by that experience. Our discussion is based on a semantic-pragmatic approach taking into account texts and vocabularies on violence and peace of several African societies that, according to their cultural background, differ widely.

In the field of what we name 'culture of violence' we find three types relevant to the questions raised in the beginning. Firstly, we distinguish an *elaborated type* exemplified by the Kavango peoples on the border between Namibia and Angola. Secondly, we identify an *elevated type* exemplified by the Rendille of North East Kenya. Thirdly, we define a *basic type* exemplified here by the Swahili of the East African coast.

We draw the conclusion that societies belonging to the basic type like the Swahili appear to be conceptually well equipped to overcome incidents of external or internal violence on their own. Also, cultures belonging to the elevated type like the Rendille, according to our findings, have a great chance to counterbalance situations of at least external violence, since they possess the necessary social and cultural instruments for that. Only with respect to the elaborated type of culture of violence, we estimate the prospects of 'healing' the effects of internal or external violence, as rather low, since societies like the Kavango peoples have no conceptual disposition to accept voluntarily healing impulses from outside, unless they are forced to do so.

The 'Peacemakers' Dilemma': The Role of NGOs in Processes of Peace-Building in Decentralised Conflicts

DIETER NEUBERT

THE NEW DISCUSSION over peace-building places high expectations on the ability to regulate and solve violent conflicts and wars. Peace-building is seen as a three-phase process, which includes conflict prevention and de-escalation, crisis management and end of combat (negative peace) and, finally, consolidation of peace (positive peace). This notion of peace-building places emphasis on the idea that stable peace can only be reached when both political and development issues are addressed. In line with the current trend, NGOs are seen as important actors in the process of peace-building. This optimistic development-oriented view carries some important weaknesses. Firstly, the complex and diversified structure of an ongoing conflict does not seem to be taken sufficiently into account. Secondly, the change from negative to positive peace constitutes a dilemma for peacemakers. The promotion of a stable peace-order (based on human rights and the rule of law) will diminish opportunities for military leaders and fighters and warrant their resistance. A peace agreement that follows the interests of military leaders and fighters risks violating human rights and the rule of law and counteracts steps towards a stable peace-order. Thirdly, NGOs might play an important role in this process. However, the main agreements and steps in the process of peace-building need security and political guarantees as well as to be founded on well functioning state structures under the rule of law. In this sense, then, NGOs can only play a supplementary role. When these contradictions are taken into account the expectations raised by the current peace-building enterprises appear much too high and unrealistic.

Peace and Aid: The 'Programme Mali Nord' and the Search for Peace in Northern Mali

HENNER PAPENDIECK AND
BARBARA ROCKSLOH-PAPENDIECK

T HE MALIAN-GERMAN bilateral 'Programme Mali-Nord' was created in 1993 to accompany the peace process in Northern Mali. The two authors have managed this program since its beginning. They describe their thoughts and strategies since the summer of 1993. The funds (fifty million Euro over a period of ten years) are being invested to recreate the public infrastructure and create a viable economic basis for the peaceful cohabitation of the various ethnic groups in the zone of intervention.

Around 40,000 Tuareg and Arabs had fled the Timbuktu region to refugee camps in the East of Mauritania. The black population, mainly Bellah (around 60,000), had left the zone to take refuge near the army camps in the larger cities. The German contribution was used to help reconstruct this zone largely flooded by the river Niger, almost inaccessible for many months of the year. Only local populations know which means of transport or production to utilise at which time of the season (during the rains, during the drought, during the floods). All activities were therefore — and for many other reasons — based on local knowledge.

The authors are often being asked: How do you have to go about it? What conclusions do you draw from your experience? The generally applicable policy conclusions are simple and self-evident. The secret lies in the particularities. The chapter is designed to describe some of them.

The chapter discusses the approach, the first orientation, the work for reconciliation, the creation of the physical network and the role of inter-community meetings. The largest part is consecrated on the economics of peace and the revival of the local economy.

Some of the lessons drawn from this experience: Peace did not come from outside, but from inside Mali. Leaders of civil society negotiated the pace, and they knew how to settle the issues. Peace did not come in one spectacular spurt. It had to conquer the terrain slowly. The warmongers subsided when they found themselves in a minority.

Democracy and Ethnic Conflicts: The Politics of Ethnicity and Conflict Resolution in South Asia

JAKOB RÖSEL

HOW CAN INDIA (a consolidated democracy), Sri Lanka (an ethnic democracy split by civil war), and Pakistan (a democratic failure) prevent or contain ethnic conflicts?

The chapter attempts to demonstrate that in these multiethnic societies broad-based processes of democratisation are not sufficient to prevent ethnic conflict: democratisation might even contribute to the politisation and radicalisation of ethnicity and its demands for respect and power. Beyond the primacy of democratisation there is the need to implement a genuine cooperative federalism and to embrace and defend the idea of the secular state.

Comments on the Construction of Political Order: Social Contract Theories and Anthropological Observation

GORDON R WOODMAN

T HE MOST SHOCKING instances of widespread violence are often associated with efforts of social groups smaller than the state, defined by ethnicity or otherwise, to maintain their internal coherence and their own laws against other groups. Remedial measures are rightly seen as requiring the re-establishment of an effective state law with a wide base of social acceptance. In the classical view the social contract on which state law is based is a consensus between individuals. This underestimates the importance of the universal, inevitable existence of smaller groups. Violence is perhaps to be prevented primarily by the formation of effective states within which smaller groups co-exist, contributing to the individual's sense of self-identity but so ordered as to minimise incompatibility between state and non-state laws.

List of Contributors

Dirk Beke is Professor of Law at the University of Ghent and the Institute of Development Policy and Management of the University of Antwerp (Belgium). Email: Dirk.Beke@rug.ac.be

Keebet von Benda-Beckmann is co-director of the Project Group on Legal Pluralism at the Max Planck Institute for Social Anthropology in Halle (Germany) and Professor in Anthropology of Law at Erasmus University Rotterdam (The Netherlands). Email: kbenda@eth.mpg.de

John R Bowen is Dunbar-Van Cleve Professor in Arts and Sciences at Washington University (St Louis, USA). Email: jbowen@artsci.wustl.edu

Willemien du Plessis is Professor of Law at the Potchefstroom University (South Africa). Email: rmrwdp@puknet.puk.ac.za

Marie-Claire Foblets is Professor of Law and Anthropology at the Universities of Leuven, Brussels and Antwerp and a member of the Flemish Royal Academy of Sciences. Email: marie-claire.foblets@ant.kuleuven.ac.be

George Klute is Professor of Anthropology at the University of Bayreuth. Email: georg.klute@uni-bayreuth.de

Rüdiger Köppe is a publisher (Rüdiger Köppe Verlag, Cologne) and a lecturer in African traditional law at the University of Cologne (Germany). Email: info@koeppe.de

Wilhelm JG Möhlig is Professor Emeritus in the Department of African Studies at the University of Cologne (Germany). Email: ama13@rrzk.uni-koeln.de

Dieter Neubert is Professor for the Sociology of Development at the University of Bayreuth (Germany). Email: dieter.neubert@uni-bayreuth.de

Henner Papendieck, an economist, is the owner and director of Consulting-Firma Dr Henner Papendieck, Büro für Wirtschafts- und Sozialforschung (Berlin), and directs the Malian-German 'Programme Mali-Nord'. Email: henner.papendieck@t-online.de

Barbara Rocksloh-Papendieck, a sociologist, is co-director of the Malian-German 'Programme Mali Nord'. Email: malinord@afribone.net.ml

Jakob Rösel is Professor of International Politics at the University of Rostock (Germany). Email: jakob.roesel@wisofak.uni-rostock.de

Trutz von Trotha is Professor of Sociology at the University of Siegen (Germany). Email: samlowitz@soziologie.uni-siegen.de

Barbara Truffin is a member of the Center for Cultural Anthropology of the Free University of Brussels.

Gordon R Woodman is Professor of Comparative Law at the University of Birmingham (UK). Email: g.r.woodman@bham.ac.uk

Contents

1

In Search of Peace. History, Basic Narrative, the Future of War, and the Rise of the Local. An Introduction with a Short Overview of the Contributions

TRUTZ VON TROTHA

TWO EXPERIENCES COME together in the subject of this book. One is a European experience, the other a global one.

The *European* experience has many aspects and is not only a product of the 20th century, which was uniquely horrendous in the history of the world up to now. We shall consider only two of these aspects here. The first is the experience that peace and reconciliation are possible, even after the most terrible injustices and the most horrifying atrocities. For the generation which experienced the Second World War, and for the post-war generation, this is perhaps the most important optimistic experience. This is true in particular of the Germans. It is also a part of the experience that peace and reconciliation can be brought about comparatively quickly. However, this is possible only under special conditions, and only at the cost of enormous sacrifices on the part of those who were the *victims* of the war. And both experiences lead to an insight which many people must find extremely bitter: it is a fact that reconciliation and peace are primarily due to the efforts of those who have suffered, not of those who have caused suffering.

The second side of the European experience which must be emphasised leads us directly into the more narrow theoretical context of the subject of this book. A key for and against reconciliation and peace is the 'semantics of history', which is a special feature of each political culture. The past is always woven into the pattern of meanings of political culture, in the form of the history of institutions, the socialisation of the actors, the problems which are wrestled with, the language, and ideas, values and norms. Generations are therefore also orders of generational historical semantics. For better or for worse, in Germany today this can be seen in the fact that National Socialism is historicised in political discourse and has sunk into oblivion in people's day-to-day awareness, in line with the Tamajaq saying: 'Wa okayan, okayan. What is past, is past'. This includes the fact that political acts and the conflicts of political culture are shaped by constructions of the past. Present-day social action is justified and legitimised by such constructions. In this sense we can understand political culture as a dispute over constructions of the past. In particular this applies to those societies which Claude Lévi-Strauss calls 'hot' societies. Here an important role is played by that order of meanings which I call the 'basic story' ('Basiserzählung').

The basic story is that construction of the history of a society and culture, which contains the dominating legitimatory construction of the past. In disputes over constructions of the past, the basic story is an inevitable point of reference. It is the benchmark of the collective political self-image of a society. Political identity must contain a model of the past. The basic story is the cultural and political institutionalised version of this past. For Germany after the Second World War the basic story was the history of National Socialism. National Socialism and the need to 'come to terms' with it supplied the basic legitimation for the political system and defined the fundamental norms of political actions. 'Coming to terms' with it meant above all the way in which people dissociated themselves from Nazism while using it to explain, criticise and justify events in the present. For the Federal Republic of Germany, the National Socialist past set the boundaries which have to be drawn by any society and culture which has implemented a radical change in its political system. I therefore call it the 'basic story of separation' ('Basiserzählung der Abgrenzung').

This German experience shows that for the promotion of peace it is of no small significance that a basic story be found on which the former warring parties can agree and which helps in defining separation from the past. The new beginning also needs a new basic story in which the break with those things and those people who were the chief actors in the conflict is implemented. However, political cultures probably differ greatly from each other in respect of how great the effective separation is and especially how much separation they are capable of sustaining; it would be interesing to compare Germany, Austria, Japan, Chile, or the Iberian Peninsula after Salazar and Franco in this respect. The elites play an important role here, for the basic story is shaped by the elites. They set the themes. They exercise the effective, if not the exclusive, power of definition. Added to this is the importance of time. As in all conflict resolution processes, time in particular plays a key role. Peace is the gaining of time. Whoever gains time, also gains agreement on the basic story.

The *global* experience consists of an inestimable number of violent conflicts in many regions of the world, representing a new form of war which necessarily involves changes in our ideas about how to bring about peace.

The most important contemporary theoreticians of war, from Philipps Huntington through Hans Magnus Enzensberger and Martin van Creveld to John Keegan and Herfried Münkler, are all remarkably in agreement on one point: the Clausewitzian world is declining; the modern conventional war, the Clausewitzian war, is history.

The kind of war which developed in the modern age is tied to the nation state which has a legitimate claim to a monopoly on the use of force; it is, as van Creveld aptly puts it, a 'trinitarian war'. The trinitarian war is conducted by states against other states in the 'interest' of the state; it is based on the differential unity of state, army and 'people'; it is the means to an end or, to use Clausewitz's famous formula, 'a continuation of political activity by other means'. The Clausewitzian world is a world in which there are 'soldiers' and 'civilians', the 'front' and 'home'. It is determined by military 'strategy' and is the playground of 'strategists', whose status has steadily risen in the course of the last 350 years. It is a world of general staffs and an armaments industry which produces ever more destructive and ever more expensive weapons systems. The trinitarian war has its own conventions, which are in part highly formalised such as the Geneva Convention; it makes a strict distinction between war and crime, and not least for this reason, and despite the unchanged bloodiness of its face, claims to be 'civilized'.

This Clausewitzian world is currently abdicating and making room for another world. In this world 'states' are no longer the dominating political power structure; the form of war is changing correspondingly. In the eyes of van Creveld and Enzensberger the state unit is breaking up into a variety of violent actors; this non-uniformity of the actors is reflected in the decentralised forms of war.

The most radical among the four theoreticians of war we have mentioned is the Israeli military historian, van Creveld. According to him, the 'future of war' (which is the German title of his book 'The Transformation of War') lies in 'low intensity warfare'. This kind of war is no longer the affair of state goverments and their armies. In their place appear police-like armed units, security services and secret services, groups and organisations of religious, political and social fanatics ready to resort to violence, 'militias', bands of mercenaries, or just gangs of thugs, led by the condottiere of the 21st century, consisting of militant charismatics, militia 'generals', 'drug barons', 'warlords' of various kinds. They conduct wars in which the soldiers no longer wear uniforms and there is no meeting of armies in open battle. There is no longer a 'front' and a 'hinterland'. The armed organisations fight in urban agglomerations and in difficult, inaccessible regions. Rival organisations hunt each other with complete disregard for national borders. The weapons of the 'combatants' are 'primitive' and cheap, even when they appreciate the latest technologies in communications, surveillance and weapons engineering. It is a war which makes no distinction between soldiers and civilians, and even less so between the 'guilty' and the 'innocent' — all are 'guilty' who do not belong to the 'combatants', support them, or at least let them have their way. The distinction between crime and war becomes blurred; crimes are frequently disguised as war, and in other cases war is treated as if conducting it were a crime. Whether ostensibly or genuinely, the combatants fight for religion and quasi-religious ideologies, for the 'rights of the people' or 'national liberation', but above all for power, gain, booty and women. The forms of war and its conventions will have much in common with wars in medieval and early modern times. But as a rule, more so than in the past, there is no decisive victory and no ultimate defeat; there are victories and defeats, now the one party and now the other getting the upper hand. As in civil wars, there comes a time when no one knows any longer exactly how and when the war began; the violence finally comes to an end, to be replaced by a peace which no one can build on.

For the practice of peace, this kind of war and the kinds of conflicts which are fought out in these wars, have far-reaching consequences. We shall consider here only two aspects.

Violence may be directed against immediate neighbours, for which reason these wars are often and misleadingly called 'civil wars'; the term 'civil war' is misleading because it suggests that the state unit is the frame of reference, even though such a reference plays no role either in respect of the actors or of the classification 'guilty' and 'innocent'. Or the combatants may attack an 'enemy' with whom they are not at war as understood in the former Clausewitzian world. The date of September 11th 2001 shines out here like a beacon; it is the writing on the wall.

In the first case 'peace' means that peace must take into account and even try to resolve all the immense difficulties which accompany civil wars; these difficulties include the genocidal traits of civil-war-like conflicts and thus the boundless hatred produced by such wars. In the second case there are no addressees who could conclude a peace agreement; with warring parties that are called terrorists, such as in Chechnya or in the conflict between the US and that Afghan by choice, Ben Laden, there is only the criminal court in the case of constitutional states, while in the case of non-constitutional states — and typically these are the majority — the enemy is simply killed or tortured to death in jails and camps.

These are wars which are fought in order to gain recognition. But how is it possible to satisfy the desire for recognition, which is fundamentally insatiable? How can peace be brought about in wars where, as Enzensberger comments, there is no classic justification, not even a need to justify violent acts, because hatred and violence themselves are the justification for denial of recognition? The ideologies of the 'combatants' are mere set pieces from the second-hand shops of failed political ideologies and of political sectarianism. These are wars of young men living a masculinity which has lost sight of the difference between courage and cowardice. They are young men who prefer to let out their anger on the defenceless and tear down all distinctions, especially those between men on the one hand and women and children on the other. How can peace be attained if the 'combatants' do not care about themselves, and therefore do not care about anybody or anything? How is peace possible with actors who celebrate the culture of hate and are celebrated by a culture of hate?

There are solutions for wars that are fought in order to obtain recognition. An important lesson can be learned here from the solution worked out for South Tyrol in Italy. In June 1992, when the general secretary of the UN announced the end of the dispute between Austria and Italy over South Tyrol, this marked the peaceful settlement of a conflict which had dragged on for almost two hundred years. There were bomb attacks in this conflict, which escalated dramatically in the 'Night of Fires' on June 11th 1961. But there were also negotiations, which lasted for decades, and which finally led to an agreement on autonomy status for the province of Bolzano — South Tyrol, which granted the German minority in the Italian state extensive protection of its language and culture and considerable rights of political and administrative self-administration. If today minority and independence movements travel to South Tyrol, as a delegation of South Moluccans did in March 2000, then this allows us to hope that peaceful resolution of conflicts is possible for the 'new wars' of the post-Clausewitzian era and that such processes may even be able to prevent some of these wars. Nevertheless, our experience in the foreseeable future will be that 'wars of recognition' tend towards a very fragile peace — from Northern Ireland and the Basque Provinces to Sri Lanka.

These and other problems mean that finding solutions to the question of how to bring about peace is bound to be extremely difficult. In this book the authors examine various solutions and show that the search for peace requires great patience and much imagination. However, based on the observations and empirical theories in this book, my understanding is that, unlike the peace which ended the 'trinitarian war' (Martin van Creveld) of the nation states, peace in the new wars is less easy to make. It depends to a much greater degree on local conditions and the given 'culture of violence' in each case. It must not lose sight of the more or less local power processes in which the warring parties are involved. A 'diktat of the victor' has less importance, because there are neither clear victors nor is it easy to enforce a diktat. Peace is at the end of a road along which, from the point of view of the warring parties, one of the parties has succeeded in gaining the upper hand in the armed struggle, turning it into a process for forming a government and taking advantage of the precarious peace to create a new, comparatively stable power structure.

The international community can play an important role in this process, institutionally, particularly in the form of NGOs, and economically, through more or less deliberate financial subsidising of the creation of new government institutions. Such external interventions not only require a great deal of imagination and common sense, as well as enormous politico-social 'tact', but they remain tied to the highly localised nature of the war and the power conflict. This localisation of peace processes will be a bitter mentor for all the new military and political would-be peace-makers who like to use terminology taken from the arsenal of virile, bragging administrative jargon. 'Rapid deployment forces' will either have to 'rapidly' take to their heels, like the US Americans in Somalia, or will have to settle in permanently, as has been impressively documented by the course of intervention from implementation forces (IFOR) and stabilisation forces (SFOR) to the Kosovo 'occupying power' (KFOR) in ex-Yugoslavia — and as continued in Afghanistan. Moreover, KFOR appears to have become one among several local actors, and has proved to be driven by the actors and logics of local power processes, rather than being a powerful and decisive actor on behalf of NATO and the international community of states. 'Rapid deployment forces' want to turn the world into a 'global village' and peace into a matter of global military alliances. But the search for the end of the new war will show that today, as never before since the rise of the nation state and the 'trinitarian war', peace will again be decided in 'villages'. Their 'globality' is limited to efficient international arms smuggling and clever handling of the mass media by actors who are either 'local heroes' or mercenaries in the service of local heroes. Like the logic of the post-Clausewitzian war, the logic of peace will also be a logic of local and regional power.

A SHORT OVERVIEW OF THE CONTRIBUTIONS*

The contributions to this publication are divided into three parts. *Gordon Woodman* starts with some thoughts about the theory of peace. He reformulates the question about the reconstruction of peace into the classical modern question: what are the foundations for a peaceful order. He finds his answer in the communitarian idea of the social contract. The basis of this new social contract is no longer the individual but the community. The latter is only to be found in the multiplicity of communities which are highly fragile and autonomous social fields. The task which the establishment of peace has to solve is, according to Woodman, to change these fields

---

*Translated from German by Heather Kempson, Zwalm, Belgium.

into secure, semi-autonomous fields — whereby Woodman adopts and generalises Sally Falk Moore's famous concept of law.[1] The challenge of legal ethnology is to help resolve inter-community conflicts. Woodman considers that legal ethnology, as a result of its decade-long involvement with conflict resolution mechanisms, is particularly suited to this task.

Rüdiger Köppe and *Wilhelm JG Möhlig* present a cultural theory of the establishment of peace at whose heart lies the concept of 'cultures of violence'. By means of semantic field research methods they investigate the semantic inventory of the concepts of war and peace in three southwest East African peoples (Kavango, Rendille and Swahili). Using both qualitative and quantitative analyses they classify these three peoples into a 'fundamental' (Kavango), 'elevated' (Rendille) and 'sublimated culture of violence.' These cultures of violence correspond with various social structures whose differentiation and hierarchisation increase from fundamental to elevated to sublimated cultures of violence. The basic theses of Köppe and Möhlig are directly linked with the results of classical research into the connection between culture and dispute regulation. These results record a close connection which exists between the degree of observable violence and the meaning of a cultural pattern which peace, agreement and conflict resolution uphold. The hypotheses of Köppe and Möhlig are as follows: peace cannot be 'made' — and certainly not from outside. Peace is the result of processes which are connected to the cultures and the social structures of the societies involved and their inherent cultures of violence. If in the case of fundamental cultures of violence, it is always extraordinarily difficult to create a stable peace, then the chances of creating peace increase from elevated to sublimated cultures of violence.

Dieter Neubert develops a conflict sociological theory of the role of Non-Governmental Organisations (NGOs) in peace processes. The theory distinguishes between 'negative' and 'positive' peace, ie between the end of hostilities and the consolidation of peace, and is based on a multi-dimensional typology of violent group conflicts. This typology permits the determination of the problems of peace dependent on the types of group conflicts and the differentiation of the requirements and limits of the activities of the NGOs in peace processes. Neubert's actual results include: in decentralised conflicts NGOs have very limited possibilities of exerting any influence and their resources in fact become part of violent conflict — here Neubert underlines the observations and considerations of François Jean and Jean-Christophe Rufin.[2] NGOs can usually only become active when a negative peace has already been achieved; the task of an NGO is rather more to support the decisions in favour of peace, they are not the main players but assist from

---

[1] Sally Falk Moore (1973): Law and Social Change: the Semi-autonomous Social Fields as an Appropriate Subject of Study. In Law and Society Review 7: 710–46
[2] François Jean, Jean-Christophe Rufin (ed) (1996): The Economy of Civil Wars. Paris, Hachette.

the side lines; NGOs are faced with the dilemma that the promotion of justice and observation of human rights can run counter to peace efforts.

The *second* part of the book, using empirical individual cases, deals with questions of power, structures, processes and history for the reconstruction of peace in Africa and Asia. It starts with a case study from the insider view of those who were directly responsible for concrete measures within the framework of a political peace development project. The economist *Henner Papendieck* and the sociologist *Barbara Rocksloh-Papendieck* present the project 'North Mali Programme' (NMP) which was to promote peace in the North of Mali after the Second Tuareg Rebellion and to ensure its continuation. The programme, which was financed by the Gesellschaft für Technische Zusammenarbeit (gtz) at the cost of millions of marks, is considered to be one of the most successful projects in the promotion of peace and promises, therefore, to be particularly instructive. Even leaving aside the question of success, it is projects of this kind which research into conflict and peace has to consider and for whose implementation and results it must develop understandable answers and empirical hypotheses. In the summary of their experience with the project Papendieck and Rocksloh-Papendieck emphasise the following aspects: peace cannot be enforced from outside — unless, as should be added, by a military victor. Peace came to Mali not top down from the central government; the latter did create however a framework for the NMP but did not get involved with the peace efforts of the project at the local level. The major players in the NMP are the leaders of the local communities, whom Rocksloh-Papendieck and Papendieck refer to in contemporary development aid jargon as 'leaders of the civil society'. They negotiated peace and knew how to deal with problems and resolve them. The task of the NMP was not to help these leaders materially, financially or ideally. Peace does not happen overnight and military metaphors are not inappropriate in order to describe the construction of peace: creating peace is similar to a 'conquest' in which each inch of ground has to be won. In the North of Mali the warmongers disappeared when they saw that they were in the minority. Economic measures must be orientated to the local context and aimed at regional growth; they have to be successful in the areas which, like all landowning relations in agrarian societies, could be considered to be particularly prone to conflict — 'serious conflicts require serious investment'. Quite rightly the two organisers of the NMP gained a new, important and momentous insight when they decided not to target those involved in the war (the Malian government, army and rebel movements). Instead the NMP worked together with those who neither had nor have access to weapons and other means of violence and were therefore obliged to negotiate.

In the eyes of the leaders of the NMP the leaders of the minorities are the best advisers, since normally they neither wish for nor have the opportunity to determine the fate of others.

Georg Klute and *Trutz von Trotha* continue the reflections about NMP and highlight some of its features within a theory of peace construction based on a sociological theory of power, especially of the rise of what they call 'parastate rule'. Klute and Trotha reiterate the scepticism of Köppe and Möhlig regarding the possibility of constructing peace. They show that peace is the result of a process of establishing rule, the change from an administrative to a parastatal chiefdom.

Dirk Beke resumes the important debate on decentralisation which, since the 1990s above all in West Africa through the pressure of international donor countries like Germany, has become the key in peace initiatives and attempts at creating democratic structures.[3] Beke investigated the dual effects of decentralisation in Uganda. Yoweri Museveni's National Resistance Movement (NRM) used decentralisation as a means to strengthen the control of central government and to increase its legitimacy in a system that formally does not permit any political parties. Decentralisation in Uganda was a procedure of formal top down decentralisation. But this centralist policy unleashed local dynamics. It led to new 'grass-roots' structures and participation, strengthened Non-Governmental Organisations, created new opportunities for the population, exerted pressure on the state — for example to vote NRM candidates out of office and opened up — as in Mali — new opportunities of power for numerous, 'traditional' chiefs.[4]

Willemien du Plessis reports on the impressive work of the South African 'Truth and Reconciliation Commission'. According to du Plessis the Commission has made an enormous contribution to the safekeeping of the historical facts about serious infringements of human rights which were committed between 1960 and 1990. However, this is not true for the years 1990–94. Whether the commission, which was also charged with amnesty procedures, has actually contributed to reconciliation is a question which still remains unanswered. Du Plessis emphasises the importance of the temporal dimension for constructing peace — it is well known that time heals many (but as experience shows not all) wounds. With concern du Plessis maintains that political criminality has been replaced by an exceptionally high rate of violent criminality which has marked South Africa since the end of the apartheid regime. Du Plessis is unsettling with her observations that peace can be very violent and can be limited to a change in the types of violence, and that violent criminality is a sign of peace — and additionally that statistics for violent criminality are a quantitative measure of peace. The more general perspective which du Plessis indicates with these observations,

---

[3] See also Jakob Rösel, Trutz von Trotha (eds) (1999): Dezentralisierung, Demokratisierung und die lokale Repräsentation des Staates. Theoretische Kontroversen und empirische Forschungen / Décentralisation, démocratisation, et les représentations locales de la force publique. Débats théoriques et recherches empiriques. Cologne: Rüdiger Köppe.

[4] See also the contribution of Klute / Trotha in this book.

is even more highly charged: measured against violent criminality, many apparently peaceful societies nowadays have become somewhat unpeaceful and call into question the cherished idea that there is an automatic connection between democracy and peace.

The contributions of Rösel, von Benda-Beckmann and Bowen focus on Asian experiences.

On the basis of the liberal democratic theory of peace, *Jakob Rösel* compares India and Pakistan. He documents the success of liberal democratic institutions, norms and values in India and compares India with the comparatively spectacular failure in Pakistan. Unlike India, Pakistan has always had problems with secularism, federalism and the removal of the military from politics.

Keebet von Benda-Beckmann continues the discussion using Indonesian case studies and the problematics of conflictual communities. Taking the Ambonese, whom she has been studying for years, as an example, she considers the complex violent conflicts between Christian and Moslem Ambonese. These are conflicts which, above all, are carried out by the young — as indeed almost everywhere, although this has not yet been taken sufficiently into consideration by theories of ethnic conflict despite the fact that the topic of 'juvenile gang delinquency' has been a feature of sociology, psychology and criminology since their very beginnings. The theoretical disregard for youth as the main perpetrators of violence has a practical counterpart in so far as young people are not included in conflict regulation. The disregard for young people in Ambon is, moreover, the result of 'traditional' norms, which honour age. Von Benda-Beckmann indicates the limits of the local common law for the construction of peace. In the case of the Ambonese there is no room in law for the inclusion of young people and can accordingly offer no help.

John Bowen investigates the problematics of political legitimation. His thesis is that peace can be endangered by the conflict between two legitimations which is in turn caused by conflicting globalisation processes. He takes as an example Indonesia and its bloody conflicts, especially in the regions of West Kalimantan and Maluku. According to Bowen's investigations, post-Suharto Indonesia has been characterised by two conflicting developments observable world-wide. On the road to democracy and human rights policy supported by the UN, on the one hand there has been a global generalisation of legal and arbitration institutions; these include 'human rights courts' or the South African 'Truth and Reconciliation Commission'. On the other hand, once again expressly supported by the UN, there has been a policy of recognition of indigenous populations and their cultures. In a number of postcolonial nation states these two procedures are not necessarily complementary. On the contrary, they are often contradictory since they encompass conflict between the idea of a nation state and the idea of an association of communities. This confrontation can become bloody and even genocidal when universalistic institutions fail to protect the individual citizen against violence and discrimination. According to Bowen this is precisely the case in Indonesia.

Marie-Claire Foblets and *Barbara Truffin* conclude the book with some considerations of the theory of peace and future research into peace.

I, however, would not like to close this overview without reporting on a further contribution from peace practice which enriched the conference, which gave rise to some of the articles here. As can be seen from the publication of this series, the conference took place in the extremely hospitable International Institute for the Sociology of Law (IISL) in Oñati.[5] Oñati is as beautiful and venerable as the university where the Institute is situated, a picturesque town in the heart of the wild, rugged mountain region of the province of Gipuzkoa. But Oñati is also the centre of the Euskadi ta Ascatasuna, better know under the acronym of ETA as are so many other organisations of this kind. A stroll through Oñati leaves no doubt: slogans on walls, posters and, above all, photos of the 'martyrs' on the walls and hung above the narrow alleyways between the impressive houses. Oñati is also one of the political centres of a bloody conflict and a place in which the horrors of the struggle have been translated into the memory of fighting myths. But that is one way to deal with war, terror, violent death and terrorist suffering. At the same time, with its university and the IISL, Oñati is also a place in which another kind of memory is sought. The not so far distant Guernica is the reason for this and 'Gernika Gogoratuz' is the protagonist for which Oñati time and time again has been the forum for its peace efforts. Gernika Gogoratuz is the name of the documentation centre for peace research in Guernica, which tries to give voice to the experiences of the survivors of the German attack on Guernica and thus tries to preserve them for posterity. Once again this emphasises the important role played by memory in the process of creating peace, both at the individual and collective level. *Juan Gutierrez* has been working for years at Gernika Gogoratuz. During the conference he gave a presentation about the work of the centre which was not recorded in writing — indeed neither could have been, nor possibly should have been. For, once again, peace, like war lives from the spoken word, from speech, from the essential power of the living word which resides in the power of the speaker and the fascination of proximity. Gutierrez' presentation reminded participants of this. He told us about the success enjoyed by the centre in achieving recognition for the suffering of the victims of the German attack both by the German President Roman Herzog and by the Spanish government — even in

---

[5] See Trutz von Trotha (2000): Cicatriser les violences. Les processus contemporains de restructuration idéologique, sociale et juridique de sociétés traumatisées par les guerres et les menaces d'éclatement. Abschlußbericht zur zweiten Tagung der Arbeitsgruppe europäischer Rechtsethnologen (6. Tagung des Arbeitskreises deutsch-französischer Rechtsanthropologen) in Oñati, Spanien, vom 3.4. April. In: Recht in Afrika, 2000, No 2: 231–40.

Spain such recognition was only possible after Franco. The present Gernika Gogoratuz Centre developed within the framework of these efforts. For the past eleven years it has been organising an annual, international meeting of groups who are involved in peace work. Special attention is given to a peaceful future for the Basque country. The work of Gernika Gogoratuz is supported by the town of Guernica, the Basque government and the European Union. The aim of their work is to develop a culture of peace which is based on respect for human rights and the principle that in cases of conflict the opponent may not be stripped of his dignity. This requires openness and the readiness to listen to all who are involved in conflict — not unlike the requirements for academic debate. This reminds us that the academic discipline of peace can only flourish when it is assured of enjoying that over which it formulates its theoretical thoughts.

Part I

On the Theory of the Reconstruction of Peace after War and Violent Conflict

2

Comments on the Construction of Political Order: Social Contract Theories and Anthropological Observation

GORDON R WOODMAN

1 PRELIMINARIES

T HE SUBJECT OF this volume has not been extensively examined in the literature of anthropology and law. Some of the classical writings in these fields may have important implications for the subject, which have not yet been discussed. The object of this chapter is to examine certain ideas in legal philosophy and anthropology, which, although belonging to the orthodoxies of the past, may have some practical usefulness today in relation to the subject.

At the outset it is suggested that two lines of inquiry seem likely to yield less helpful ideas than might have been expected. The first is the study of disputing processes. These have been much discussed by legal anthropologists, especially in the Anglophone world, and this topic might have been thought a fruitful starting-point in a search for the means to re-establish legality after war or serious social disruption. But the studies of disputing processes have generally sought to understand and analyse processes within established social and governmental systems, the procedures of disputing and attempts to resolve disputes being guided by continuing social norms. They have not been concerned with the total breakdown of social systems of the sort which accompanies extensive violence. The second line of inquiry is found in the literature that discusses the breakdown of the old certainties, and the contingency and relativity of belief and discourse in this post-modern world. Here also there must be doubt as to the usefulness to our investigation of this trend in modern legal anthropology. The claims it makes are stimulating, but they belong to relatively safe and comfortable exercises. They have not included studies of fearful human cataclysms.

In contrast, it may be helpful to take account of another feature of anthropological research. This is the fact, foundational to anthropology notwithstanding the embarrassment it sometimes causes to the proponents of this science, that it has historically been the study of non-western societies. It is possible that cases of extreme and widespread violence in western societies are characteristically distinct from instances of the same degrees of violence elsewhere. The instances of violence in non-western societies considered in this work have typically been accompanied by a collapse of the modern state and a dissolution of national civil society. On the other hand, the most notorious instances of extreme violence in the west have often concerned dictatorial states which have acted against their own subjects and against other states. The western episodes have occurred in circumstances where the state has existed in a fairly stable form for a long time, accompanied by a distinct national identity.[1] These circumstances do not usually exist in the instances with which we are primarily concerned here.

The issues of violence in non-western societies may be conveniently divided into two sub-fields, each of which is examined by papers in this volume. First, some studies are concerned with methods of dealing immediately with the trauma caused by violence. These may focus on individual perpetrators or victims, although with a view to social reconstruction. Second, other studies concern the methods of reconstructing for the longer term a civil society and a relatively non-violent state. Both types of study may be inspired by the same concern to alleviate suffering. Successful action in the first field, giving effective, immediate assistance to individuals, may be a condition precedent to achievement in the second, the later reconstitution of civil society. But if only the former is attempted, violence will inevitably continue or re-ignite. This paper seeks to contribute some preliminary thoughts to the second sub-field.

2   THE PROBLEM AND AN OUTLINE OF A POSSIBLE SOLUTION

The principal proposition to be considered is that the reconstitution of a state after a period of extreme disorder and violence may require the participation of communities rather than individuals. In the first stage, of assuaging the trauma, it may be appropriate to see people as responsible or injured individuals whose separate psychologies need treatment, and whose past acts need to be revealed through Truth Commissions and other immediate

---

[1] That the problem of violence in these states may be significantly different from that elsewhere in the world can be seen from a reading of the serious studies of violence and authoritarianism in the west. See for example Herz (1982), examining the states of West Germany, Italy, Austria, France, Japan, Spain, Portugal and Greece.

measures. At the next stage, in contrast to this, it may be necessary to focus on the communities to which individuals still belong.

The community discussed here, the ethnic group, tribe or 'people', does not coincide with the nation-state. It is usually smaller in membership than the state. Often the violence that has caused the damage has been committed on behalf of such communities. Nevertheless, when there are endeavours to reconstruct the shattered nation-state, the need is perhaps not to attack them, but to accommodate them in the revived order. I suggest that in the west much traditional and contemporary theorising about social solidarity has failed to recognise this. Anthropology may offer insights which will help to fill this lacuna.

The cases of violence discussed in other chapters in this volume display a common factor. Any legitimacy which the state and its law may in the past have had for the bulk of the population has evaporated. In some cases the state as an institution has disintegrated. In others it has been taken over by a group within the society that uses it as a tool for its factional purposes. But despite the failure of the state, there has not been a total failure of observance of law or social solidarity. Lesser communities often remain strong and cohesive. Frequently they are in a sense the cause of the problem, in that they have violently attacked other such peoples, either because they felt that their existence was threatened or because they possessed a communal policy of aggressive aggrandisement in relation to other communities. Arguably the problem may be not that 'law and order' have broken down, but that the law and order of these communities within the state have taken directions which are inimical to a wider peace.

If there is any truth in this diagnosis, it may provide the basis for a programme to prevent violence in future. It might perhaps be argued that peace cannot be achieved by resurrecting the inclusive state, but only by enabling each community to enjoy independence as a separate nation state. It would in that case be appropriate to support a policy of promoting self-determination for all peoples. But here the practical difficulty arises that there is rarely a suitable territory for each people, inhabited only by members of one community, and by nearly all the members of that community. If such a territorial imperative is not met, it can be achieved only by what we have recently come to call ethnic cleansing, which is likely to exacerbate the problem, not to solve it.

A territorial separation of peoples is sometimes practicable in the case of an indigenous minority. Where the bulk of such a people has been long confined to a particular territory, but where relations with the other peoples of the nation are not irretrievably hostile, it may be possible to separate the territories politically, leaving relatively small numbers of members of each group living on the land of the other group, as aliens but not under threat. An illustration of this possibility is the creation within the Canadian federation of the Territory of Nunavut. But this is unlikely often to be a solution for cases where severe violence has occurred because it offers insufficient protection to resident minorities on each side of the border.

It is also not an option to leave the state in abeyance in such an area, notwithstanding that one might well be sympathetic to this plan if the machinery of the state has been used to effect the violence. In the present period of history there does not appear to be any institution other than the state which can mediate effectively between conflicting communities, nor does it seem possible that if such were devised the world community could readily accommodate it. The need is for a form of social control which can gain, over a population which includes conflicting communities, sufficient legitimacy to enable it to channel their conflicts into non-violent forms; and in which they can be provided with sufficient incentives to do so, perhaps through the desire for preservation of the community. The only sort of institution we know of today with the possibility of meeting these requirements is the state. It appears, then, that long-term peace requires a reconstruction of the state.

This is not to overlook the fact that there can be violence — sometimes the most destructive and inhumane of all violence — in wars between states. But often this is controlled, more or less, by the current international system of law and international institutions. Frequently these are not at present successful, but there is a real possibility that they will be developed further, and by controlling the excesses of states will contribute to the international stability in which states can more effectively control violence within their frontiers.

If the best chance of salvation lies in the reconstitution of the state, we might conclude that anthropology cannot help. This science is not primarily concerned with the state. In the past it studied non-western societies whereas the modern form of state is widely seen as having developed in the west. Anthropologists have sometimes regarded state action as unwarranted interference with their subjects of study. However, their work may be of assistance in so far as they have sought to understand the dynamics of communities which have existed prior to states and which continue to exist within states, that is, of those communities which, it may be argued, hold the key to the reconstitution of the state, to the development of the multi-community state to the level at which it will acquire a general legitimacy.

3   THE ORIGINS OF STATE LEGITIMACY

In seeking the means to establish or re-establish a state it may be helpful to consider the basis of social solidarity in existing, effective states. However, today scholars avoid hypotheses about the historical origins of civil and political society, on the ground that they must be speculative and unreliable. Anthropologists find myths of origin useful material, but as indicators of ideologies, not as historical accounts. Neither do legal philosophers aim to establish accounts of the origins of state laws.

Even when theorists purport to write of the beginnings of a legal system, they in reality write of features which may have existed from the moment following those beginnings. Thus Hans Kelsen presents an account of the creation of a new legal system on the occurrence of a revolution. But he says nothing of why a legal revolution occurs. He states that it gives rise to a new Grundnorm which validates an 'historically first' constitution, which in turn validates all legal norms made subsequently and (if no subsequent revolution has occurred) continues to validate those of the present state. All legal reasoning within a particular legal system presupposes a Grundnorm, but legal science can say nothing about its basis of legitimacy. (Kelsen 1945, 110–19; 1967, 193–214.)

HLA Hart writes of the two categories of legal rules. Primary rules are rules of obligation; secondary rules are power-conferring rules, which fall into the sub-categories of rules of recognition, change and adjudication. He claims that there have existed societies with primary rules alone, but he sees the introduction of secondary rules as moving a society from the 'pre-legal' to the 'legal' world (Hart 1961, 91). After this transition it is possible to discern one fundamental rule of recognition which, like Kelsen's Grundnorm, enables every norm of the legal system to be identified as belonging to that system. In contrast to Kelsen, Hart claims to be engaged in 'an essay in descriptive sociology' (Hart 1961, vii), and he claims that the rule of recognition exists not as a presupposition, but as a practice followed by officials whose decisions as to what is the law are, in turn, popularly accepted (Hart 1961, 97–107, 245–46). This hypothesis concerning the social basis of an existing legal system is of interest. But its value is limited by the absence of any indication in Hart's work of the reasons for the emergence of this acceptance. Secondary rules are said to be 'introduced' (Hart 1961, 91–92), and a rule of recognition to be 'accepted' (Hart 1961, 97), but Hart does not suggest how or why these developments occur.

In earlier periods political and legal theorists attempted more comprehensive accounts of the origins of societies, and so of the bases of social solidarity. It may be worth considering the social contract theories of the age of enlightenment. Unlike other theories of law of the medieval and modern periods in the west, these explicitly propose accounts of the origins of government, and in so doing provide justifications of state power which seem to have some application to the states of today. There were variations on a few themes, but I would take as typical theorists Thomas Hobbes (1651), John Locke (1690) and Jean-Jacques Rousseau (1762).

Each of these theorists depicted in outline a state of nature (although they differed considerably in their accounts of this condition), and then postulated the formation of a social contract by which persons in the state of nature created by agreement some form of civil government. For each writer, the condition of the state of nature determined the terms of the social contract, and these in turn determined the extent of the powers of government at the time of writing. In the case of Hobbes, government was marked by unlimited, absolute sovereignty, every person having by the social contract surrendered their independence totally to the sovereign which they created. For Locke government had the power to perform the duty of enforcing those extensive natural rights which had not been surrendered in the social contract, and the power was exercisable only in the manner determined by the majority. In the case of Rousseau the sovereign had the power to perform the duty to give effect to the *volonté générale.*

It appears that each of the writers mentioned believed in the historical occurrence of such a palaeolithic constitutional convention for each state. Perhaps the most immediate reaction of the historian and the social scientist is likely to be incredulity at the notion. But this may not be the most important issue. Each writer was primarily concerned to demonstrate that such a compact, entered into in prehistoric times, was still in force in modern times. And for this purpose they presented arguments to the effect that the process of making or adhering to the social contract was continuing, and therefore that its terms were still binding.

A proposal to use these theories in attempts to understand issues of government generally in the modern world may be criticised on the ground that they were developed exclusively from the experience of the western state. However, the notion of contract which these writers used was not that of modern western state laws. It may have been rather a notion of a relationship which was brought into existence by an initial agreement, but which required constant renegotiation as circumstances and aspirations changed. That concept of contract is to be found in many normative orders outside state law and outside the west. It was observed famously by Stewart Macaulay in the relations between American businessmen — which he later found reflected also in the Trobriand Islands as depicted by Malinowski (Macaulay 1963, 1995).

These writers, in arguing that the terms of the social contract, as thus understood, determined the current extent of the lawful powers of civil government, made claims about the basis of the current legitimacy of civil government. They claimed that the state was brought into existence by agreement between its original members because they recognised that each of them would benefit more from its existence than they would from an anarchical condition; and that it continued to exist because subsequent members recognised this and continued to agree to its existence. Whatever our views as to the literal reality of the historical social contract, we may find that the claim as to the basis of legitimacy of governments resonates with modern views and is applicable to the human condition generally, not only to the west. Moreover, this claim could indicate a route towards the reconstruction of weakened or destroyed states today.

In this respect more modern theorists continue similar arguments. Hart, I have mentioned, asserts a general acceptance of the decisions of 'officials' who follow a rule of recognition designating other rules as legal. The 'acceptance' is apparently given by each person with an awareness that he or she is acting in the same way as most other members of society, and in reliance on that fact. John Rawls' theory of justice is developed avowedly on the basis of a notional social contract: his principles of justice are defended on the ground that they are what rational individuals would agree to in the state of nature (or, in his imagery, behind the veil of ignorance) (Rawls 1972, Chap 3).

It is at this point, I suggest, that anthropology may provide a corrective to the theories of the classical social contract theorists. Those theorists, and their modern successors, all express the state of nature, the terms of the social contract, and the implications of that contract in terms of the actions, responsibilities and the rights of individuals. The individual is the element in the constitution of the state. The writers recognise the existence of the family in pre-state society. But Locke denies that the paternal power, arising within families, can be the basis for civil government (Locke 1690, Chap VI). Rousseau asserts that the authority of the father of the family in the state of nature ceases as soon as the children become adults, and that the assembly that forms the social contract consists of adult individuals (Rousseau 1762, Book One, Chap II). Others simply speak about individuals without mention of their possible membership of groups or associations.

The classical writers had had little opportunity to learn about the social organisation of non-western peoples. A writer such as Locke might make reference to 'Indians' of North America and to Jewish history (Locke 1690, Chap VIII), but depended upon unreliable sources. Perhaps because he recognised this, he used these instances only as subsidiary evidence to support arguments developed a priori. In modern debates, Rawls' presupposition of a group of isolated individuals negotiating the terms of a civil society to which they would belong has given rise to criticism which has been an element in the recent libertarian-communitarian debate in Anglophone circles.[2] All the anthropological accounts we have now suggest that this notion of a pre-state society of isolated individuals is improbable. Every ethnography contains reports of kin structures, associations such as age groups, of clans and sub-divisions of polities. If some sort of notion of a social contract is to be the basis for justification of present government, it

---

[2] A considerable volume of writing has arisen from this debate. Most has been written with reference explicitly or impliedly to issues in western societies, but it has relevance to other parts of the world. See eg: Avinieri and De-Shalit (1992); Bell (1993); Christodoulidis (1998); Dworkin (1989); Kymlicka (1989) Paul, Miller and Paul (1997); Sandel (1998); Taylor (1989); Walzer (1983); Walzer and Miller (1995).

must be seen as a relationship between groups which themselves already constitute communities.

This gives a different character to any social contract that might be contemplated. The contract now becomes primarily an understanding between groups which already have internal relations of obligation. It entails the creation of a state and its law to coexist with other, usually smaller, communities and their laws. It is not the primal creation of human law, as the western theorists would suggest, but the creation of a new ordering for existing laws. To use a different but helpful image (from Moore 1978), it is the conscious attempt to convert a number of precariously autonomous social fields into securely semi-autonomous social fields.

There are some instances of the formation of states which are clearly at variance with this pattern. First, some states have been created by conquering communities which imposed their power on others. There is no ground for speaking of a social contract in these cases. It is far from original to suggest that the very reason for the instability of these states is their imposition by outside forces and their lack of an original or continuing social contract to sustain them. In some cases the colonial power succeeded in creating a local elite which was effectively socialised to accept the form of government which it imposed. But even in these cases the legality of the state remains in some doubt. Perhaps what is needed in these cases, in such time as may be left, is to negotiate social contracts which will enable the existing communities to benefit visibly from their acceptance of membership of the wider community of a nation-state.

Secondly, there are the cases in which states were formed when substantial members of a conquering community at some time in the past settled in an area, imposing their domination on the indigenous population. We may see this community as a state originating in the home state of the settlers, which itself may be found to have been formed by an alliance of previously relatively autonomous sub-groups within that community. But it has often happened that a state when established has imposed itself on others without their consent. This also is an unstable condition, although stability may be achieved over time by the emergence of consent and participation on the part of the originally conquered community. This was the course of early development of most western European states.

Other cases may be analysed by reference to the pattern of the state which is formed by an alliance of previously existing communities. There have been cases where such a state existed for a while, but then disintegrated, the apparatus of the state being seized by one community. There is the case, now emerging in western European states, where the territory of a state is subject to immigration by substantial numbers of members of particular, foreign communities, who may not be admitted to membership of the host state. All such cases are situations of tension which can give rise to violence, just as in the case where no state any longer exists.

4   CONCLUSION

That perspective on the social contacts on which existing states are based perhaps provides a basis for constructive engagement with the problem of extensive violence. It is noteworthy that large-scale, organised or quasi-organised processes of violence are so often aspects of war between communities. While they may include many instances of individual revenge, acquisitiveness or murderous insanity, what removes the restraints which normally limit the scope of these individual characteristics is the possibility of indulging them under the banner of communally endorsed action. Furthermore, they involve the collapse of state power or of the will to exercise power as a state. Any remnants of state power are used as tools in the communal war.

Such violence has admittedly often been fostered, and perhaps sometimes caused by social practices which have the primary function of maintaining the internal cohesion of the community. But communal cohesion is by no means undesirable; moreover, it is a fact and cannot be totally suppressed. I suggest that it should not be seen as necessarily and of its nature opposed to the state. The object should perhaps be to construct an internal cohesion, that is, a degree of legitimacy, of nation-state communities which in each case will include the warring groups. Ultimately, at a higher level one looks to a global international law. Any such construction requires a high measure of agreement, that is, of acceptance within the communities concerned.

It seems likely that legal anthropology can contribute to the solution of these problems. Anthropology, with its long tradition of understanding the Other, can bring to bear an understanding of both sides in inter-communal disputes, often disastrously lacking in the international perception of such disputes. Legal anthropology can contribute to the understanding of the internal modes of social control of warring communities. Socio-legal studies can show the possibility and implications of legal pluralism within states, according to which state law may be not weakened but reinforced by the customary laws of the communities that comprise the state's population. It may be possible to construct forms of such pluralism which will not threaten the identity of constituent communities.[3] Lawyers can bring techniques of constitution-building, provided that they are not obsessed with the model of western representative democracy where all the emphasis is on the rights of the individual. Finally, it may be worth adding that quite possibly existing states in the west, as their populations inevitably become increasingly multicultural, may survive as humane societies only if their laws also abandon claims to exclusivity in the legal field.

---

[3] There are, however, numerous instances in which this danger has not been avoided. Cf Schmid 2001.

REFERENCES

Avinieri, Shlomo, and Avner De-Shalit, eds 1992. *Communitarianism and Individualism.* (Oxford: Oxford University Press).

Bell, Daniel 1993. *Communitarianism and its Critics.* (Oxford: Clarendon Press).

Christodoulidis, Emilios, ed 1998. *Communitarianism and Citizenship.* (Aldershot: Ashgate).

Dworkin, Ronald, 1989. Liberal Community. *California Law Review* 77: 479.

Hart, HLA 1961. *The Concept of Law.* (Oxford: Clarendon Press).

Herz, John H, ed 1982. *From Dictatorship to Democracy: Coping with the Legacies of Authoritarianism and Totalitarianism.* (London: Greenwood).

Hobbes, Thomas 1651. *Leviathan, or the Matter, Forme and Power of a Commonwealth Ecclesiasticall and Civil.*

Kelsen, Hans 1945. *General Theory of Law and State.* Translated by A Wedberg. (Cambridge, Mass: Harvard University Press).

Kelsen, Hans 1967. *Pure Theory of Law.* Translated by M Knight. (Berkeley and Los Angeles: University of California Press).

Kymlicka, Will 1989. *Liberalism, Community and Culture.* (Oxford: Clarendon Press).

Locke, John 1690. *Second Treatise of Government.*

Macaulay, Stewart 1963. Non-Contractual Relations in Business: A Preliminary Study. *American Sociological Review* 28: 55–66.

Macaulay, Stewart 1995. Crime and Custom in Business Society. *Journal of Law & Society* 22: 248.

Moore, SF 1978. *Law as Process: An Anthropological Approach*, (London: Routledge & Kegan Paul).

Paul, Ellen Frankel, Fred D Miller Jr, and Jeffrey Paul, eds 1997. *The Communitarian Challenge to Liberalism.* (Cambridge: Cambridge University Press).

Rawls, John 1972. *A Theory of Justice.* (Cambridge, Mass: Harvard University Press).

Rousseau, Jean-Jacques 1762. *Du contrat social: ou principes du droit politique.*

Sandel, Michael J 1998. 2nd ed. Liberalism and the Limits of Justice. (Cambridge: Cambridge University Press).

Schmid, Ulrike 2001. Legal Pluralism as a Source of Conflict in Multi-Ethnic Societies: The Case of Ghana. *Journal of Legal Pluralism* 46: 1–47.

Taylor, Charles 1989. 'Cross-Purposes: The Liberal-Communitarian Debate', in: *Liberalism and the Moral Life*, ed. by NL Rosenblum. (Cambridge, Mass: Harvard University Press).

Walzer, Michael 1983. *Spheres of Justice: A Defense of Pluralism and Equality.* (New York: Basic Books).

Walzer, Michael and David Miller eds. 1995. *Pluralism, Justice and Equality.* (Oxford: Oxford University Press).

3

Concepts of Violence and Peace in African Languages

WILHELM JG MÖHLIG AND RÜDIGER KÖPPE

1 INTRODUCTION

1 1 Aims

WITH RESPECT TO the central topic of the workshop on 'healing the wounds of societies that have been traumatised by war', we here want to discuss what the chances of such processes are and to what extent the traumatised societies concerned are capable or even willing to be healed. We are convinced that the adequate discussion of these crucial questions requires a certain insight into the ethical concepts and systems of moral values of the people who have been victims of traumatising wars. We try to achieve this goal by means of linguistic data in combining the methods of conceptualisation[1] in the semantic fields of violence and peace with sociolinguistic methods.[2] Since this approach, particularly in its applied perspective, is new, we demonstrate it in three case studies referring to the Kavango Bantu in Southwest Africa, the Cushitic Rendille in Kenya and the Swahili of the East African Coast. By contrasting the relevant semantic systems of the three ethical systems as mirrored in their innate language systems, we intend to make prominent three types of a universal cultural domain that we call, 'the culture of violence'.[3] These types are not

---

[1] Compare eg Barsalou (1992), Geeraerts (1988) and Pederson & Nuyts (1998).
[2] In this approach we follow Ethel M Albert, Basil Bernstein and others (see Gumperz & Hymes 1972).
[3] The concept of *culture of violence* has a specific meaning. We derive the term from the wider ethno-linguistic concept of *verbal culture*, which denotes an internally structured complex of concepts and ideas expressed by language. Since there are other manifestations of culture besides language, indigenous texts and vocabularies can only serve as indicators or keys to get access to the section of culture that centres around the two conceptual poles of violence and peace.

only characterised by different semantic properties, but can also be correlated with different historical backgrounds and social settings, which we include in our analyses as contextual factors. Finally, we want to show that the answers to the questions raised above are highly dependent on the type of culture of violence to which a particular society belongs.

1 2   Methodological Approach

It appears to be a widely accepted theorem among socio-linguists and ethno-linguists[4] that languages reflect the historical, social, economical and mental structures of their speakers or, more precisely, of the speakers who have been socialised within these languages. For instance, it can easily be shown that hunter-gatherers possess a highly sophisticated terminology concerning their economic focus. People whose economic basis is cattle keeping, handicraft or commerce do not share these concepts. In analogy to this experience, we assume that the covert systems of ethical thinking and general mental attitudes concerning violence and peace are also mirrored by linguistic elements and structures. The lexicon of a given language is particularly revealing in this respect. Our empirical approach towards the internal and mostly covert ideas on violence and peace is therefore preferably focussed on the vocabularies of the peoples under scrutiny. However, not all semantic concepts of a society are expressed by individual terms or metaphors at the word level in a simple one-to-one correspondence. On the contrary, many of them, if not the majority, are expressed in a periphrastic way at the level of higher-ranked syntactic structures. To capture all concepts and ideas of a specific kind, it is necessary to extend the empirical basis to longer expressions at text level. Considering our thematic focus on concepts of violence and peace, we therefore include also historical texts and texts of verbal art in our analyses.

As already mentioned, our analytical approach is based on modern semantic field methods as developed by Lawrence W Barsalou (1992), Dirk Geeraerts (1988), Pederson & Nuyts (1998) and others. This allows us to analyse not only the fundamental conceptual constituents of the various ways of indigenous thinking but also the structures of the indigenous value systems. It is relatively new to exploit the semantic-conceptual results, as in this case, for socio-political conclusions. To bridge the two fields, we systematically interpret these results within their socio-anthropological and ethno-historical settings that have been constructed by the usual discipline-bound methods.

Since we mainly address a readership of non-linguists, these few remarks on our methodological approach may be sufficient. Where we feel

---

[4] See Sapir 1933 and many articles assembled in Fishman 1970.

it to be necessary for the understanding of our argumentation, we add more explanations of this kind.

1 3   The Key Terms 'Violence' and 'Peace'

Violence and peace, the two key terms of this study, do not form a real pair of antonyms in the sense that violence is non-peace and peace is non-violence. We rather introduce these terms as labels for practical use, ie to mark two separate, clearly antagonistic semantic fields. As a working definition[5], we propose to define 'violence' as the exertion of physical force with the purpose of injuring the bodily integrity of another human being. In a similar way, we propose to define 'peace' as the absence of any civil disturbance, that might fall under violence according to our definition, or expressed positively: as the observance of the human rights of other human beings, in particular respecting their dignity and bodily integrity. By this definition we do not want to restrict ourselves to physical violence respectively to the absence of physical violence. Our definition also includes the aspect of humiliation, as for instance rape or the denial of sanitary relief, eventually even the application of force against objects, particularly if their destruction affects the basis of living and existence.

1 4   Several Types in the Cultural Domain of Violence

At least within the African context, our findings show that there exist different modes of how the universal factor of human violence is culturally integrated in the ethical systems. Most of the characteristic features are — to our own surprise — recurrent. Between the two conceptual poles of violence and peace, a continuum of features exists. Cultures with a focus on violence are characterised as follows:

— The verbal notions of violence are plenty in number and elaborate, whereas the expressions of non-violence or peace are comparatively few and unstructured.

---

[5] In order to avoid misunderstandings, we want to underline that our definition is meant to be a philological contribution to the sociocultural phenomenon of violence. Our perspective is more that of a cultural insider than that of a sociologist. Therefore, the focus of our interest is directed on African concepts and their representations at the word or text levels. Since we are expressing ourselves *on* these phenomena in the meta language English, we need English terms that come as close as possible to the African concepts. In order to be able to compare these concepts among the cultures chosen for this study, we further need a more detailed definition of what we understand by the two key concepts 'violence' and 'peace'. Since our aim differs from the sociological approach that Trutz von Trotha proposes in the introduction to the edition of *Soziologie der Gewalt* (1997: 20), we operate with 'working definitions' that are only valid within the context of this article.

— These verbal expressions are handed down from one generation to the next like other cultural phenomena.
— In the ethical thinking of the people concerned, the use of violence holds a high rank as an expression of strength and bravery, whereas a lenient behaviour is considered as weakness and eventually as cowardice.

These features are not shared by all cultures along the conceptual continuum. For instance, in some African cultures, notions expressing violence at the word level are rare. Instead, the modes of violence are formulated at the text level. In some of these cultures, violence is considered bad or is valuated ethically different depending on whether it is directed against outsiders or insiders of the community. In some cultures we observe that violence is ritualised or ritually elevated. In the perspective of these cultures, acts that, according to our working definition, fall under violence are often not even recognised as such.

Already these few observations induce various types in the cultural domain of violence. This typology will prove to be particularly relevant for evaluating the chances of 'healing the wounds' of societies that suffered from violence. In this study, we distinguish three types in the conceptual domain of culture of violence, giving an example for each of them. These are:

— The *elaborated* type exemplified by the Kavango peoples living in the borderland of Namibia and Angola, where a war has been raging for the last thirty years.[6]
— The *elevated* type exemplified by the Rendille of North Eastern Kenya, who as camel breeders are famous for their raids on their neighbours.[7]
— The *basic* type here exemplified by the Swahili of the East African coast, are mostly urban and peaceful societies whose main concern is the prospering of their commerce and small industries.[8]

Certainly, under different aspects more types of culture of violence may be set up. However, this contribution is only meant to introduce the phenomenon as such and to show the consequences that result from a more detailed look into it for the question of 'healing' war-ridden societies.

2   THE KAVANGO CULTURE OF VIOLENCE

2 1   The Socio-Anthropological Background

The Kavango people consist of several ethnic groups, namely the Kwangali, Mbunza, Shambyu, Gciriku and Mbukushu (*see Appendix, Map 1*). Their

---

[6] The main source is our own field research carried out in the Kavango region since 1965.
[7] Sources: Schlee 1978, 1979, 1989; Pillinger & Letiwa Galboran 1999.
[8] Our empirical basis again consists of our own field research carried out since 1964.

traditional economy is based on agriculture and some small stock with a strong component of fishing and, until recently, of hunting game. Until recently, their habitat was the fertile Kavango river oasis at both sides of the international boundary between Namibia and Angola. Since historical experience evidently plays an important role for the shaping and developing of a culture of violence, we have to take into account that the Kavango peoples have been exposed to violence imposed on them from outside not only since the outbreak of the Angolan civil war some 30 years ago, but already since the slave hunting campaigns during the 16th century. It is perhaps felt to be an irony that the only peaceful period in their recent history happened under the South African regime of apartheid roughly between the years 1920 up to 1970.

2 2 The Semantic Field of Violence

In our model of the semantic field of violence, we take violence in the sense of our working definition as the conceptual core. This allows us to arrange other related concepts according to their conceptual distance from the core in concentric circles around it (*see Appendix, Diagram 1*).

In the centre of this field, we arrange only a few general items like: *nyânya* violence, cruelty, *kunyânyena* be violent, cruel towards somebody, *kuhómoka* be aggressive towards, *kuhómokera* attack somebody, *kukákukira* jump upon somebody, *kupûminana* attack one another, *kutínika* compel, coerce, force somebody.

Within the circle next to the centre, we take note that the Kavango languages differentiate between two types of violence, destructive and oppressive violence.

Under destructive violence the following items have to be subsumed: *kudípagha* to kill and its derivations: *kudípaghera* kill for somebody, *kudípaghita ná-* to kill with an implement, *lidípagho* murder, *lidípaghero* manslaughter, *kupônya* or *kuróya* to shoot dead, *kuvhúrura* to spear dead, *kupôndéka* to destroy.

Under oppressive violence fall the following more general items: *kuhépeka* pester, harass, maltreat, oppress, *kukîdita* hunt down, *kukôlita* torture, *kurârera munkôndo* rape, *kurêmeka* wound, injure, *kuróha* bewitch, *kushákana* plunder, ransack, *kutjútjupita* do physical harm to etc.

Besides these more general items, the category of oppressive violence contains many specific terms that in themselves form several sub-categories like for instance: beating, breaking, tearing, grabbing, assaulting etc. For the purpose of demonstration within this paper, we only take the example of beating. As a working definition, we want to understand 'beating' as the voluntary action with one arm or both arms, with an implement or without an implement, directed towards another person's body.

It is surprising that, in the Kavango languages, we find more than 30 different word forms where the English equivalent is always 'to beat'. These forms are not simple synonyms. On the semantic side, they contain several specifications as to the manner or kind of beating, the agent, the specific reason of beating or specific features on the side of the target. In the diagram, these are summarised at the bottom.

Although other languages like for instance English also exhibit a certain elaboration in their terms relating to direct corporal aggression — compare: 'beat, pound, strike, punch, box, slap' — the semantic elaboration of the Kavango languages in the same semantic field is by far greater (*see Appendix, Diagram 1*).

2 3   The Semantic Field of Peace

When we look at the semantic field of 'peace' in the Kavango languages, we find that, in its structural elaboration and quantity of different terms, it cannot compete with that of 'violence' (*see Appendix, Diagram 2*).

In the centre of the field, we find two items *mbîri* and *mpôra* both meaning 'peace'. The first is the 'peace of the soul', whereas the second form comes closer to the meaning of 'absence of war or violence'. There is still the compound noun *mutâpi-mpôra* meaning 'peacemaker'. We have reasons to assume that this is a neologism probably coined under the influence of Christian missionaries, since the word is structured in a way as nowadays new concepts are incorporated into the language. It is composed of the two elements *mutâpi* 'giver' derived from the verb *kutâpa* 'to give' and the noun *mpôra* 'peace'. The terms *kuhâmba* and *kutîkanita* for 'to reconcile', which includes the idea of 'compensation' appear to us to be already longer established in the culture, because they have a wider distribution among Bantu languages. Again, the terms for 'justice' *uhûngiki* and 'fairness' *uvyúki* are comparatively new forms. Overall, the field shows a comparatively simple structure with significantly fewer terms than the semantic field of violence (*see Appendix, Diagram 2*).

2 4   The Concepts within the Socio-Anthropological and History Contexts

The exploitation of the traditional semantic structure of the vocabulary reveals that the Kavango ethnic groups have cognitive systems that are dominated rather by violence than by peace.

This conceptual system directly correlates with their permanent readiness of the Kavango peoples to use violence against others or to protect themselves against acts of violence executed by others. The tools they use are not only modern weapons but also traditional weapons like clubs, spears and charms, such as curses, poison, magical rifle butts and shot-proofs. We classify this type of culture of violence as sophisticated or *elaborated*. Right from the beginning, we consider the likelihood to 'heal' such societies from their 'trauma of violence' as very low. The conceptual structure underlying this culture is so solidly built that it is resistant to any external influence.

We have asked ourselves whether this cultural feature is interdependent with or provoked by other cultural features like the social structure, economy or habitat. However, we find many other ethnic groups in Africa living under similar conditions as the Kavango peoples and yet they do not exhibit a similar sophistication of violence concepts. We therefore think that the main difference in comparison with otherwise similar cultures lies in the historical background of the Kavango peoples. For the last three hundred years at least, these people have been exposed to permanent slave and cattle raiding. We defend the hypothesis that they could only survive in that rough sea of violence by developing for themselves a culture of elaborated violence, of which — by the by — they appear to be fully aware, when asked.

3   THE RENDILLE CULTURE OF VIOLENCE

3 1   The Socio-Anthropological Background

The Rendille are semi-nomads living in the arid North West of Kenya.[9] The backbone of their economy is camel breeding. Up to now, they lead a rather traditional life, which is comparatively uninfluenced by the central government of Kenya. In the past, they were the target of intensive field research by several social anthropologists and linguists.[10] We base our analysis and arguments on the works of these scholars. In particular, we rely on the monograph written by Günther Schlee in 1978 and on the recently published dictionary by Steve Pillinger and Letiwa Galboran of 1999.

Like other camel or cattle breeding societies living in the semi-arid belt in the North of Uganda, Kenya and the South of Ethiopia and Somalia, the Rendille are considered 'wild' and 'violent'. Because of these attributions, they aroused our curiosity, so we chose them for an analysis of their concepts in the semantic fields of violence and peace.

---

[9] See Appendix, Map 2 quoted from Schlee 1989, p 4.
[10] Ooman 1981; Pillinger & Galboran 1999; Schlee 1978; 1979; Spencer 1973.

3 2   Praise Songs as Cultural Expression of Violence

The Rendille are particularly famous for their habit to organise raids on their non-Rendille neighbours. At these occasions, they kill all members of the attacked group, men women and children without any difference. The bodies of the killed women and children are left aside, but the bodies of the killed men are deprived of their genitals. The cattle and camels of the attacked ones are captured and incorporated into the raiders' own herds.

When the killers return from such an incident, they praise themselves by singing songs composed individually by each singer, called *meraat*. These are performed in front of the huts of the clan members, and, as a sort of testimony, the killers present the cut-off genitals of the killed enemies. As a reward, particularly the young unmarried girls of the clan decorate them with pearl strings and the married ladies cook special meals for them. They are hailed as heroes, although at night they have to sleep in separate huts erected especially for them, because they are considered unclean. A while later, they are ritually purified and socially promoted to a dignitary rank.

In the *meraat* songs, the successful warriors describe the circumstances under which they were able to kill their enemies and how they captured the enemies' animals. The style of these *meraat,* as the following quotation may prove,[11] is poetic and traditional in its form, revealing a decent boastfulness.

(14)   [1]Torei af-il-gate, [2]af-desano dihe,
     [3]gorat an Wamba kosokhate, [4]wambile ichekya.
     [1]I directed my spear with its mouth [point] towards the earth,
     [2]I fought with the ones with the pierced lips [ie the Turkana]
     [3]I got it [the spear] once from Wamba [place name],
     [4]I told Wambile [name of an elder] about it.

(15)   [1]Sugub midahane, [2]anka midahane,
     [3]teba kasotabin wae, [4]orah teba fajfajan, here isfajite,
     [6]bariyo sodowateka, [7]meraat kadowe.
     [1]I did not talk about thirst, [2]I did not talk about hunger,
     [3]I did not give up for one week, [4]seven suns like the knife cutting swellings,
     [5]the warriors put their heads together, [6]when it dawned,
     [7]I sang the killer's song.

These parts of the song represent the climax, when the raider reports on killing his enemies. It is noteworthy that, apart from the word *meraat* referring only to the killer's song as a genre, all the other words in these

[11] Schlee 1979:375f.

texts could be used to describe neutral or peaceful events. Thus, no special vocabulary of the semantic field of violence occurs.

The *meraat* texts form part of a longer ritual that a young male undergoes in the process of transgression from childhood to adulthood. In the value system of the Rendille, the killing of an enemy is a sort of probation and a proof that the young adult has a brave character and is capable to defend his future family and enlarge his property of camel herds.

From Günther Schlee, who for many years lived an almost insider's life among the Rendille, we know that — in the ethical value system of the Rendille — only the warriors are appreciated for their wildness and violence. In sharp contrast to this attitude, seniors are respected for their patience and indulgence. In fact, the Rendille practise warlike violence only towards outsiders, whereas towards insiders, they seek social harmony and peace.

3 3 Expressions of Violence and Peace at the Word Level

If we look into the Rendille vocabulary as a whole, we find that the terminology referring to violence and peace, unlike the Kavango case, is not particularly elaborate. There exist some more general terms like *atoollowa* be aggressive, *agiis* to kill, destroy, *lag'dada* to rape, *asarda* to rob, *ahunna* to hurt, to pierce, *amida* to molest, but special terms as to the manner, implement, agent, reason etc of a violent action are absent.

3 4 The Concepts within the Socio-Anthropological and History Contexts

The socio-anthropological setting of the Rendille culture is characterised by ritualising actual violence and incorporating it into the educational system particularly for males. There are certain ethical values connected with maleness. One is bravery and the capability to defend one's own family and the camel herds against external enemies. For the Rendille system, the concept of violence is reduced to either an ever ready property of young warriors or to the hostile and warlike acts from outsiders to which the Rendille themselves are eventually exposed. At a more abstract level, for them violence is also a ritualised matter as can be seen by the fact that killer warriors are considered as unclean. In our opinion, the ritual level is the domain where violence is actually channelled and controlled by the community.

With regard to our topic, we conclude that the Rendille example represents a culture of violence that we would classify as *elevated*. The conceptual system does not show a particular refinement of the vocabulary in the semantic field of violence. Only ritual texts or texts of panegyric literature practised in real situations of violence towards outsiders hold a high rank in the value system of the Rendille people, whereas the behaviour towards insiders is determined by harmony and peace. Experience over many decades shows us that the Rendille culture of reputed violence could so far resist to attempts of its abolition from outside. We therefore dare to predict, as long as the internal social structure of the Rendille is not completely shattered, their value system and hence their elevated culture of violence will persist. In their insider's perspective, phenomena that we subsume under violence according to our working definition are not even recognised as such. In other words, for them there is nothing to be healed. Hence, also in this case, the chances of producing a change from outside are futile.

The Rendille type of culture of violence is shared with more or less all cattle or camel herders of North East Africa. These societies have no central rulers, but are controlled by elaborate age group and clan systems.[12] Their economy of accumulating big herds owned by individuals brings it about that their often widely scattered property is not only vulnerable towards environmental factors, but also towards strangers competing with them for the same ecological niches. This fact may be responsible for the remarkable separation between their readiness of aggression towards outsiders and their desire for harmony with ethnic insiders. When one reflects on this system of two antagonistic and at a first glance irreconcilable forces within the same value system, one comes to the conclusion that in fact the ideal balance between the two is the elevation of violence towards outsiders to the ritual level. In this perspective, it becomes understandable why, for the Rendille, non-ritual violence is a marginal social phenomenon that does not need any terminological elaboration at the word level.

4   THE SWAHILI CULTURE OF VIOLENCE

4 1   The Socio-Anthropological Background

The Swahili peoples live in many ethnic groups along the East African coast from Somalia in the North up to Mozambique in the South (*see Appendix, Map 3 quoted from Möhlig 1995, p 45*). Economically they are traders and fishermen. Many of them live in urban surroundings. They share the Islamic faith and speak Bantu dialects that are genetically closely related, but not always mutually understandable. In the past, a lot of rivalry among the individual Swahili groups existed, and in the course of over seven hundred years of documented history, many internal and external wars were fought. We have chosen the Swahili as an example where evidently a long experience

[12] Schlee 1989.

with violence in the sense of our working definition exists, but where, nevertheless, the topic of violence in its linguistic manifestation appears to be highly sublimated.

4 2   Verbal art Expressions of Violence

In the absence of a sophisticated vocabulary of violence similar to the Kavango type, we have selected two different sorts of thematically relevant texts to see how topics of violence are periphrastically expressed. We here present chose but two examples, one for each genre.

The first text is part of the famous chronicle of Pate,[13] a Swahili township on the island of Pate, in the North of the Swahili area. The chronicle reports on many episodes of war, but always in very general terms, as for instance the following texts testifies:

> ... *katawala Muhammad bin Seliman baada ya babake kapijana na watu wa Shanga, kawashinda, kauvunda muji, akawatukua watu wa Shanga wakaja Pate*
>
> ... and he Muhammad bin Seliman succeeded his father and he fought with the people of Shanga and he defeated them and destroyed the city and he took away the people of Shanga to Pate.

The episode that is here described in general notions concerns a very violent situation, namely the complete annihilation of a competitor township. The violence specific terms used in the text are: 'to fight', 'to defeat', 'to destroy' and 'to take away'. The general character of these notions can be estimated by contrasting them with the terms that the Kavango people, according to the real sense of the text, would have used instead, ie 'to kill', 'to hurt', 'to ransack', 'to burn down' and 'to sell into slavery'.

The other example refers to a famous poetic text written in the Kilwa dialect of Swahili. It was published by the Oxford scholar Peter Lienhardt in 1968. In this text, we find several episodes where extremely violent situations are described. The following specimens[13] describe a situation where somebody has been murdered and two policemen are called in to investigate the case:

(280)   *Baada ya kupata hayo*
        Mnyamwezi na Jaluo,
        Viliingia vibao
        Aibu kusimulia.
        Once they had that information

---

[13] Lienhardt 1968, p 160.

the Nyamwezi and Luoo policemen,[14]
they began handing out blows
in a way I'm ashamed to tell.
(281)   *Ukipata kofi moja*
Kusimama hamna haja
Anakuzusha daraja
Viatu kukushindia.
After even one single slap
one couldn't stand on one's feet,
and they knocked you flat
on the ground
and gave their boots a turn.

The policemen who are of a different ethnic groups from up-country harass the coastal population like their enemies without choice to bring them to heel to reveal what they know about the murder case. Although the text describes a scenery of utmost violence, again, the words that are used in the text to describe this situation do not belong to the category of refined terms of violence. Instead, only the pictures evoked by the text convey this violent impression to the readers, yet in a very poetic way.

4 3   Other Expressions of Violence and Peace

All Swahili dialects have a general vocabulary relating to violence in the sense of our working definition. However, in comparison with the notions referring to peace, it does not show a particular structural refinement. In this respect, the Swahili inventory resembles the Rendille inventory. In the Swahili dialects, the antagonistic social conditions of violence and peace are mainly paraphrased at the text level, and not expressed by a refined jargon at the word level.

4 4   The Concepts within the Socio-Anthropological and History Contexts

In comparison with the foregoing examples, the Swahili word cultures as a whole share in so far a different type of culture of violence as the phenomenon of violence is expressed in an everyday language and in rather trivial terms. The vocabulary is neither particularly refined as in the Kavango case, nor is violence as such ritualised or elevated to heroism as in the

[14] During Colonial times, indigenous policemen were preferably recruited from the ethnic groups Nyamwezi and Luo near Lake Victoria.

Rendille case. The conceptual analysis of the Swahili dialects rather reveals a **basic** culture of violence where even overt violence is usually expressed in a metaphoric language at the text level. From our own experience with the Swahili culture, we know that in their ethical system violence is clearly considered morally bad.

As history shows, the Swahili value system did not prevent eventual outbreaks of violence. But whenever in the past such social accidents occurred, afterwards a social healing process of reconciliation and compensation took place. It always gave the Swahili societies a chance to return to a state of relative social harmony.

In our opinion, the Swahili type representing a basic culture of violence is clearly related with Islamic faith. The Swahili urban societies are devoted followers of the Prophet and deeply religious. Their urban way of living closely together with their neighbours like weaverbirds may strengthen this dominantly peaceful character of life.

The Swahili example allows us to draw the general conclusion that if, in a basic culture of violence, an outbreak of violence should occur, the chances of helping to heal the wounds from outside are rather promising.

5   CONCLUSION

The three African word cultures show more differences in their conceptual systems than we had thought before. Referring to the Kavango peoples, our first example, we find an elaborate system of violence concepts reflected already at the word level, while the antagonistic field of peaceful concepts is comparatively underdeveloped. We subsume this system under the category of *elaborate* culture of violence and consider the chances of influencing the people of this culture in the sense of the general question of healing the wounds of violence as extremely low.

The Rendille conceptual system of violence and peace, despite of the violent reputation of the Rendille people all over East Africa, represents a *moderate* type of culture of violence. The Rendille distinguish between external and internal violence. External violence is part of their educational system that has been inherited from one generation to the next since time immemorial, whereas internal violence is suppressed. In the perspective of the Rendille themselves, there is no need to alter this system. In fact, in the past, all attempts to this end have failed.

Only the *basic* type of culture of violence represented here by the Swahili ethnic groups appears to be open to external peaceful activities. The history record of the Swahili of over almost 700 years shows several outbreaks of violence. After a short violent period, the pendulum always swung back to peace. We are therefore confident that African societies of this sort, when traumatised by war, will respond positively to efforts of 'healing' them.

REFERENCES

Barsalou, Lawrence W 1992. Frames, concepts, and conceptual fields, in: Lehrer, A & EF Kittay (eds) *Frames, Fields, and Contrasts: New Essays in Semantic and Lexical Organization*, (Lawrence Erlbaum, Hillsdale (New Jersey)): 21–68.

Bredell, AW 1994. Bukenkango Rukwangali-English. English-Rukwangali Dictionary. (Windhoek: Gamsberg Macmillan).

Fish, Joshua A (ed) 1970. *Readings in Sociology of Language.* (The Hague — Paris: Mouton).

Geeraerts, Dirk 1988. 'Cognitive grammar and the history of lexical semantics'. In: Brygida Rudzka-Ostyn (ed) *Topics in Cognitive Linguistics.* (Amsterdam — Philadelphia: John Benjamins): 647–77.

Gibson, GC, Th J Larson & CR McGurk 1981. *The Kavango Peoples.* Studien zur Kulturkunde Vol 56. (Wiesbaden: Franz Steiner).

Gumperz, John J & Dell Hymes (eds) 1972. *Directions in the Ethnography of Communication.* (New York et al: Holt, Rinehart and Winston).

Heepe, Martin 1928. Suaheli-Chronik von Pate. *Mitteilungen des Seminars für Orientalische Sprachen* 31: 145–93.

Lienhardt, Peter (ed) 1968. *The Medicine Man. Swifa ya Nguvumali.* (Oxford Clarendon Press).

Mberema, Karl PS & Wilhelm JG Möhlig (forthcoming). *Gciriku — English — Gciriku Dictionary.* (Cologne: Rüdiger Köppe).

Möhlig, Wilhelm JG 1965. *Vokabular Dciriku — Deutsch — Französisch.* (Roman Catholic Mission: Nyangana (Kavangoland)).

Möhlig, Wilhelm JG 1995. Swahili Dialekte. In: Miehe, Gudrun & Wilhelm JG Möhlig (eds) *Swahili-Handbuch.* (Köln: Rüdiger Köppe): 41–62.

Oomen, Antoinette 1981. Gender and Plurality in Rendille. *Afroasiatic Linguistics* 8.1, 35–75.

Pederson, Eric & Jan Nuyts 1998. 'Overview on the relationship between language and conceptualization'. In: Nuyts, Jan & Eric Pederson (eds) *Language and Conceptualization.* (Cambridge University Press): 1–12.

Pillinger, Steve & Letiwa Galboran 1999. *A Rendille Dictionary. Including a Grammatical Outline and an English-Rendille Index.* (Köln: Rüdiger Köppe).

Sapir, Edward 1931. 'Communication', *Encyclopedia of the Social Sciences*, 4, 78–81.

Sapir, Edward 1933. 'Language', *Encyclopedia of the Social Sciences*, 9, 155–69.

Schlee, Günther 1978. *Sprachliche Studien zum Rendille. Grammatik, Texte, Glossar. With an English Summary of Rendille Grammar.* (Hamburg: Helmut Buske).

Schlee, Günther 1979. *Das Glaubens- und Sozialsystem der Rendille. Kamelnomaden Nord-Kenias.* Dissertation Hamburg. (Berlin: Dietrich Reimer).

Schlee, Günther 1989. *Identities on the Move. Clanship and Pastoralism in Northern Kenya.* (Manchester: Manchester University Press International African Institute, London).

Spencer, Paul 1973. *Nomads in Alliance. Symbiosis and Growth among the Rendille and Samburu of Kenya.* (London: Oxford University Press).

Trotha, Trutz von 1997. Soziologie der Gewalt, Sonderheft 37 *Kölner Zeitschrift für Soziologie und Sozialpsychologie*, (Opladen: Westdeutscher Verlag).

Wynne, RC 1980. *English-Mbukushu Dictionary*. (Avebury: Avebury Publishing Company).

Appendix

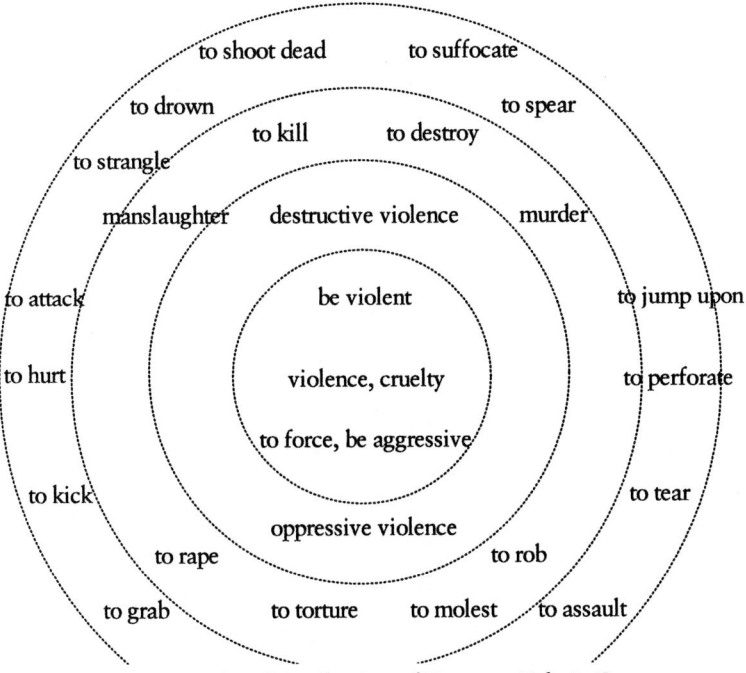

Map 1. Distribution of Kavango Ethnic Groups

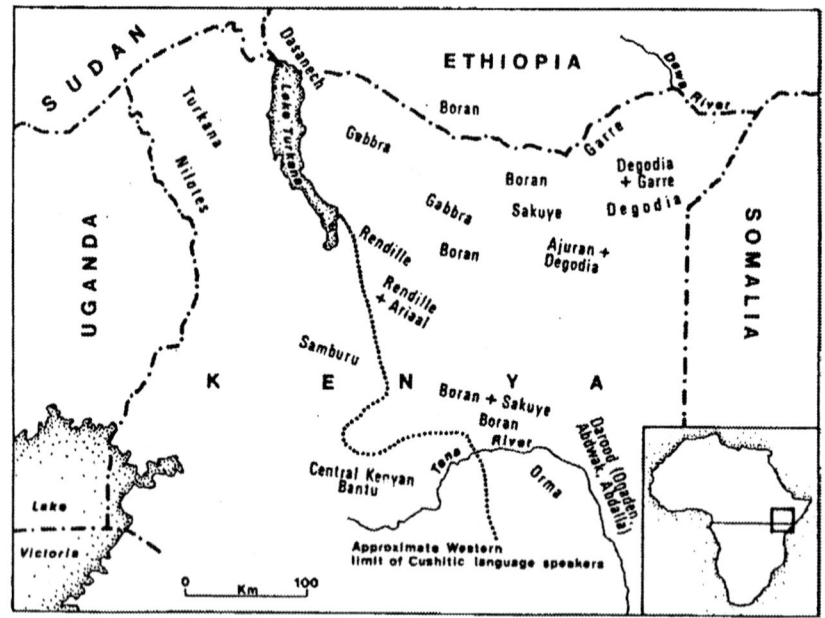

Map 2. *Distribution of Ethnic Groups in Northern Kenya*

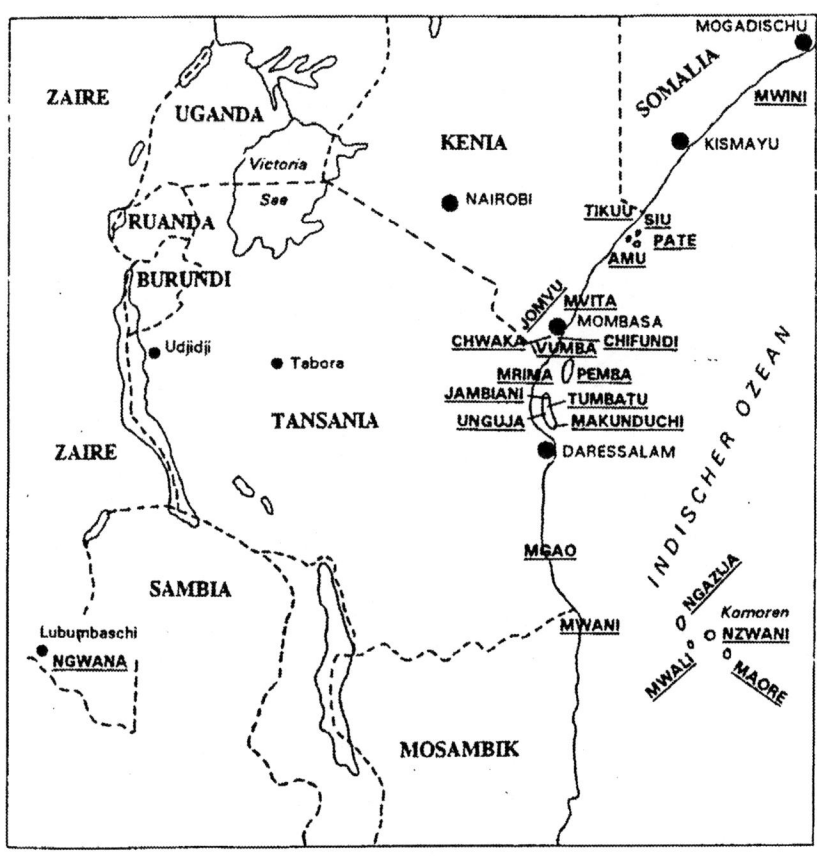

Map 3.   Swahili Speaking Communities

Diagram 1: *The semantic field of violence*

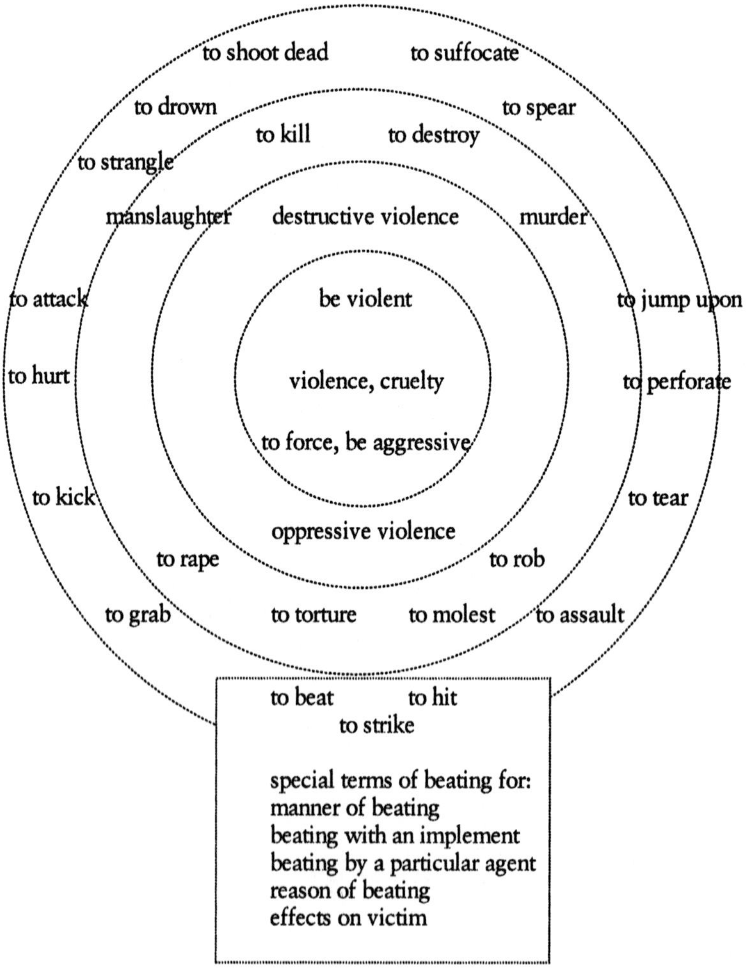

to shoot dead   to suffocate

to drown   to spear

to kill   to destroy

to strangle

manslaughter   destructive violence   murder

to attack   be violent   to jump upon

to hurt   violence, cruelty   to perforate

to force, be aggressive

to kick   to tear

oppressive violence

to rape   to rob

to grab   to torture   to molest   to assault

to beat   to hit
to strike

special terms of beating for:
manner of beating
beating with an implement
beating by a particular agent
reason of beating
effects on victim

Diagram 2:   *The semantic field of peace*

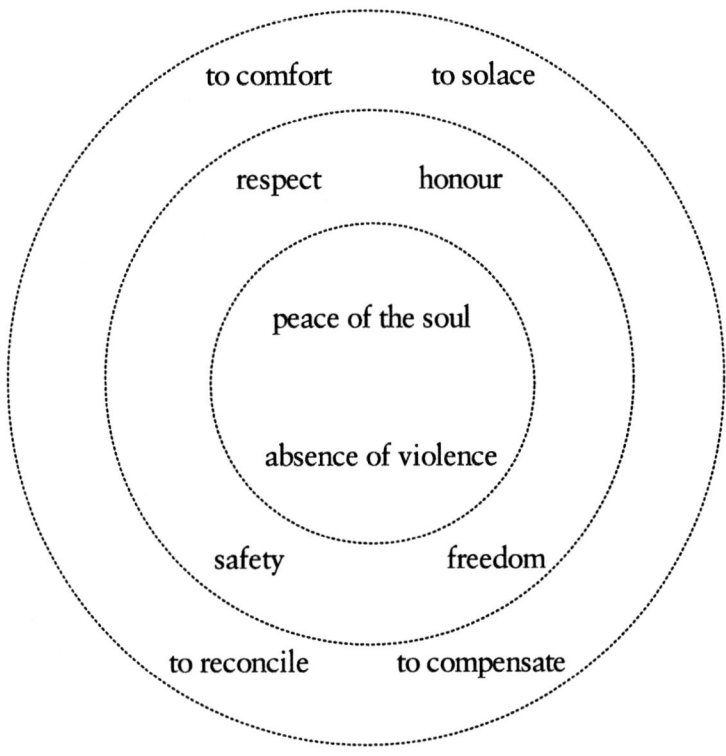

4

The 'Peacemakers' Dilemma': The Role of NGOs in Processes of Peace-Building in Decentralised Conflicts

DIETER NEUBERT

1   INTRODUCTION[1]

EMERGENCY AID IS one of the core activities of development agencies. Especially in Africa, but also in other regions of the world, emergency situations are often interlinked with violent conflicts and wars. Some of the most spectacular aid operations, such as aid for Biafra in the 1960s or aid for Somalia in 1992, were for victims of famine in war-torn countries. Until the 80s development agencies, including NGOs, had concentrated on aid and mostly did not interfere with political affairs concerned with conflict regulation. This has now changed. Since the 90s NGOs and other development agencies have discovered peace-building as a new field of activity.[2] The system of development aid faces numerous activities in conflict prevention and non-military intervention. The basic idea behind this new challenge is that development policy must be peace policy which prevents new violent conflicts and supports activities in conflict regulation (Adelmann 1997; Debiel et al 1999; Matthies 1999; Ropers and Debiel 1995; Fahrenhorst 2000; Schmieg 1997; 1998; Vogt 1999; Volmer 1999; Weiß 1999; Wieczorek-Zeul 1999). Peace-building is seen as a long-term process that includes reconciliation and healing as important

[1] I would like to thank Elísio Macamo for his comments and for making the English more intelligible.
[2] One important reason for this change is the end of the cold war. The disengagement of the superpowers from many parts of the Third World made room for new political actors and showed that local and regional conflicts were not only the outcome of the cold war but also followed their own dynamic and interests of warring parties.

means of post-conflict stabilisation and establishment of a peaceful order. According to this strategy, emergency and development aid are used as instruments to support conflict regulation and peace-building as part of a wider peace policy.

This notion of peace-policy and peace-building is deeply connected with conceptions of human rights and political participation. It expresses a desire for peace that includes justice, forgiving and the foundation of a new community. The envisaged peaceful order follows somewhat the norm set by a Western democratic, peaceful, civil society. As representatives of civil society, NGOs are seen as important actors that can promote and develop civil society in war-torn countries. NGOs and other development agencies follow, at least indirectly, the assumption that in the long run violence does not pay. Reference to human rights ensures that justice becomes a core element for a post conflict society. Violations of human rights during a conflict or a war should not be forgotten and must be pursued legally and those guilty of human rights violations must be punished. The creation of the human rights court in The Hague was at least in part a result of the lobbying of human rights NGOs.

Notwithstanding, this notion of peace-building does not apply to the reality of many current conflicts. When one looks at Central Africa, Liberia and Sierra Leone or the Caucasus what one sees is that efforts at reconciliation and healing (must) take place while violence is still on or may break out again, at any time. Partners in peace negotiations may already have been charged as war criminals.

With the new objective of peace-building NGOs and other development agencies must consider the whole process of peace-building starting with the first phase of peace negotiations up to post-conflict stabilisation. The experience of political diplomacy shows that successful peace-negotiations cannot ignore existing power structures. When these are strong enough even warlords may become important partners in peace agreements. Confronted with this harsh political reality, Western-type NGOs face a contradiction between their desire for peace on the one hand, and their orientation towards human rights and justice on the other.

A more detailed analysis should be able to show that an arrangement with the warring parties hardly follows rigid demands for human rights and justice. And yet, without such an arrangement a peace agreement can hardly be achieved. NGOs and other agencies active in conflict regulation face what I call the 'peacemakers dilemma', which consists in the quest for peace on the one hand and the desire for human rights and justice on the other. This dilemma is intensified by an observable change in the typology of conflicts. International wars and 'classical' civil wars between well-organised armies have lost their importance and represent now only a minority of ongoing violent conflicts. In Africa, only two of the current conflicts were wars between armies: the Eritrean-Ethiopian war and, to a certain extent, also the Angolan civil war (see Griggs 1995; Ali and Matthews 1999 for wars in Africa). The majority of violent group conflicts in Africa and in other parts of the world have become increasingly complicated as the number of not clearly defined warring parties and armed forces of different type have increased. Peacemakers often face decentralised violent group conflicts that cannot be tackled with classical diplomatic instruments.

Against this background the role of development organisations and especially NGOs in peace-building can be analysed in realistic terms. This will be done in five steps. A 'typology of conflicts' (1) and the 'phases of peace-building' (2) provide the framework for the analysis of the role of NGOs in peace-building focussing on 'advantages and tasks for NGOs' (3) and their 'limits, contradictions and problems' (4). The 'perspectives for NGOs for peace-building in decentralised conflicts' (5) present a plea for case-specific objectives and elements for a combined strategy that aims at a change in the local cost-benefit ratio of conflicts.[3]

2   TYPES OF CONFLICTS

The chances of and problems for the reconstruction of a peaceful order depend on the type of conflict and the actors involved in it. What is needed at the outset is an overview of these conflicts in order to underline the typical elements of different types of violent group conflicts and actors. This typology follows organisational criteria of differentiation with a focus on types of warfare and actors. The 'reasons' for conflict and the ideological basis of the groups are not seen as the main criteria for the typology. 'Class', 'nationalist', 'ethnic' or 'religious' conflicts might be issues in different types of conflicts but are not seen as factors defining the type of conflict. In simple cases the type of conflict is defined by a homogeneously structured set of actors with specific political objectives who are involved in specific types of warfare on the basis of specific resources and, in the main, with similar internal structures in terms of professionalism, authority and command-structure as well as links between fighters and the population.

---

[3] This paper focuses on the role of NGOs. At the same time it should be borne in mind that NGOs and other governmental or supra-national development agencies follow, in principle, a similar general concept of peace-building; NGOs and other development agencies widely overlap in their tasks and activities. The difference between NGOs and other governmental and supra-national development agencies lies mainly in their political role (see part 4, section on: 'Problems of NGO activities in general'). Therefore, the analysis of the NGO concept of peace-building, of their tasks and activities and of the 'peacemakers dilemma' applies to most of the governmental and supra-national development agencies, too. However, the analysis of the NGOs' political role cannot be transferred to the situation of other development agencies.

For the sake of intelligibility I would like to present these simple cases as ideal types of violent group conflicts linked to typical actors (*see Appendix, Table 1*). We should, however, bear in mind that these simple cases are rarely found in their pure form in reality. Indeed, often they overlap and mix with one another.

For a long time, the main differentiation of conflicts has been between international and national (civil) wars. The current situation in the Third World and in the former communist block, however, shows a multitude of conflict types, including guerrilla wars and war-lordism without any discernible national focus (von Trotha in this volume; Waldmann 1998a). The main dividing line that can be drawn is between centralised bi-polar violent group conflicts (wars) and decentralised multi-polar violent group conflicts (for which the shorthand 'decentralised conflicts' shall henceforth be used). While in bi-polar centralised wars the focus is on the control of an entire state with national territory in decentralised multi-polar violent group conflicts the actors follow a variety of objectives, which more often than not include the accumulation of wealth and control over a limited and not clearly well defined local territory.[4]

From the current conflicts we can distinguish five types:

— International wars between nation-states fighting for control over a state and territory.
— 'Classical' civil wars between political factions on a national level inside a nation-state fighting for political control of the state and territory. Usually one of the factions is the national government while the other is the opposition (the opposition may fight for the control of the entire state or for secession).
— Local inter-community conflicts between local warrior and defence communities or between urban communities (eg ethnic, religious) aiming at the accumulation of wealth, honour, fame, assertion of identity or control over a limited local territory and self-defence.
— Warlordism with political and economic entrepreneurs whose power is based on the violence of armed forces of different sizes (warlords) fighting for wealth accumulation, political influence and sometimes for the control of a limited local or regional territory.
— A special case are international or global terrorist networks. Whereas, terrorism as such constitutes a type of fighting or violence commonly found in other conflicts, especially in civil wars, global terrorist networks constitute a specific type of actors. They fight for the destruction of international or global structures like 'world capitalism', 'imperialism', 'the West'.

---

[4] On decentralised conflicts see: Bendrath 1999; Bollig 1996; 1999; Buijtenhuijs 1996; *Die Herren des Krieges* 1995; Elwert 1999; Klute 1999; Klute and von Trotha 2000; Reissner 1998; Richards 1996a; 1996b; Strecker 1999; Waldmann 1998b; 1999.

— Additionally, one should mention mercenary and security companies that are not linked to any special conflict type. They are out for profit maximisation on a contractual basis and are mostly used to protect and control small defined local sites (mines, oilfields, government buildings). They appear in any type of conflict in which clients are willing to pay for their services, especially in the area of security.

These types should assist us in analysing more complex real situations. Actors may change their nature from oppositional armies to warlords or from local defence communities to oppositional armies in a civil war. The point to emphasise in this respect is that these changes will transform the actors and the type of conflict they are involved in (Waldmann 1998b; 1999). Additionally, in real conflicts we often find all these types of actors at the same time in a complex conflict. The conflict as a whole may represent a national war, elements of a civil war and elements of a decentralised violent group conflict, all at the same time, eg the conflicts in the African Great Lakes region. This typology will only help in identifying different types of actors and conflicts in these complex situations.

Centralised bi-polar conflicts show the typical elements of classical war with battles between armies, heavy military hardware, often including high-tech weaponry (jets, helicopters, modern radio equipment, computer guided missiles). In civil wars guerrilla tactics, raids and terrorist acts may occur and often simple weapons are used. Fighting is financed from taxes and other government income, including the control over natural resources in the national territory and donations by the people (in a civil war the opposition tries to create independent territories with its own national structures). Sometimes in civil wars looting may become a resource to be used in the fighting. Armies consist of full-time fighters who are partly professional soldiers, all of whom are mostly supplemented by conscripts or volunteers. The army is based on a centralised military hierarchy and follows a co-ordinated strategy. The links between fighters and the population are usually strong, because the army fights for and defends 'its' population. Whereas in national armies the population is defined in nationalist terms, in civil wars the population might be defined in terms of ethnicity, religion or class. In civil wars the centralised structure of an army may not yet be established and small fighting units may actually employ guerrilla tactics. This is, however, seen as only a temporary tactic until such a time as the armed opposition judges its own forces to be strong enough to challenge the government army openly.

Decentralised conflicts, for their part, follow different patterns. Instead of battles between armies what is more common are raids and defence against attacks. Warlordism and urban communal groups also use terrorism or kidnapping. Attacks are not only against enemy fighters but ever so often aim at civilians. The weaponry used in such conflicts is mostly light and simple. One avoids engaging the armed forces openly. Furthermore, the main resources for fighting are loot and, especially in the case of warlords, protection money, smuggling, drug trafficking, kidnapping and control over natural resources (diamonds, oil). Instead of big and well-structured armies we find smaller fighting units with weak co-ordination.

Local warrior and defence units are made-up of part-time fighters, who often are volunteers. The internal structure and hierarchy of their fighting units varies according to the local political organisation and culture (for different local cultures of violence see: Möhlig and Köppe in this volume). In any case, the links between fighters and the population are strong. The former defend their community and the community is the forum that awards honour, fame or respect. We should note that local warrior and defence units may consist of 'traditional' nomad communities (Turkana–Pokot conflict) as well as of communal (mostly ethnic or religious) groups living together in a town or city (Christian–Muslim conflict in Northern Nigeria).

Warlord-like fighting units may consist of part-time fighters or professionals. Recruitment varies widely from volunteering to forced conscription. The internal structure is based on a strict hierarchy which, however, tends to split-up after internal conflicts. Links to the local population are usually weak.

International terrorist networks act at selected points but the indirect impact of their actions, especially fear, is aimed at the global system (eg capitalism, the West) as such. Their main resources are donations from followers, booty and sometimes ransom money. Fighters are part time and full time and may have special training. Their internal structures vary, but a strong element of decentralisation and autonomy of the units is quite typical. Terrorist networks are based on conspiracy and, therefore, open and direct links to the population are not shown. However, they need to have a network of direct supporters. In the long run, they need some resonance from (their) public.

In the special case of mercenary and security companies there is a highly professionalised business entreprise based on contractual payments with full-time professionals using mostly high-tech weaponry and communication facilities. Their focus is on ensuring the security of economically and politically important sites. The military professionalism of these groups includes a strong and efficient internal hierarchy. As business entreprises their sole allegiance is to their customers (companies, governments) with almost no relationship with the population.

All actors share a common set of values linked to fighting. These include the values of strength, bravery and loyalty to their own fighting unit. In spite of the different constellation of interests in different types of conflict fighters also long for honour, fame and respect. Nonetheless, attitudes towards war and fighting differ from fighting as a way of life or as a means of identity construction and fighting as a necessary evil or as a threat (Möhlig and Köppe in this volume; Richards 1996a; Weimer 1998, 191). The 'ethics of war' that regulate behaviour towards enemies and civilians differ even more. The Geneva Convention was designed as a regulation of bi-polar centralised wars. In international and civil wars parties usually claim acceptance of these rules. However, in reality the rules are often broken or ignored, as the high number of war crimes shows. Especially in civil wars fighting tends to be brutal, civilians are often victims of attacks, war crimes occur frequently and even anomie may be the result (Waldmann 1998a, 18–22). Many decentralised conflicts do not even go through the motions of accepting the Geneva Convention. Like 'classical' civil wars, they are often brutal and hit especially civilians. While warlordism can be said to fit into the frame of extreme brutality and is often accompanied by anomie conflicts between local warrior and defence communities vary widely. On one end of the spectrum there may be feuding based on local regulations and linked to local instruments for peace-building and reconciliation. On the other end, however, there may be conflicts where enemies are not even seen as human beings.

Seen from an outsider's perspective, international terrorist networks have no or only minimal 'ethics of war'. However the combatants often claim their specific code of ethics. Mercenary and security companies differ widely as far as the acceptance of rules is concerned. Some of them follow law and order strictly while others use the absence of state power and legal control for all types of unscrupulous actions.

On the level of the 'ethics' of war in all types of conflicts all types of actors may commit extreme war crimes such as rape, torture and pogroms.[5] The ongoing violations of the Geneva Convention in all types of conflicts by all types of actors show that while types of conflict may differ there is, in fact, no 'regulated' conflict as such.

The strategies and the problems for peace-building have to acknowledge the existence of different types of actors and conflicts. The success chances of peace-building in a special case depend, however, on the persons and groups involved. The generalisations made here are only an attempt at indicating structural differences between types of conflicts and actors, which, while not determining the development of a specific case, should not be ignored.

---

[5] Genocide in the strict sense of the term (' ... acts committed with intent to destroy, in whole or in part, a national, ethnic, racial, or religious group, as such ... ', UN Genocide Convention) needs a certain level of organisational capability. Therefore, the most severe cases of genocide are committed by governments or well-organised political factions during war and even during peace (like in fascist Germany).

3   PHASES OF PEACE-BUILDING

Peace-building is a process that includes much more than just an end to fighting. One can usually identify three phases:

a)   Conflict prevention and de-escalation
b)   Crisis management and end to fighting leading to negative peace (ie absence of fighting).
c)   Consolidation of peace leading to positive peace (ie stable peaceful order).

These phases constitute a kind of circle. When a conflict has already started, the first step in peace-building is crisis management followed by consolidation. The prevention of a new conflict and de-escalation can only become important as long-term tasks when the moment has come to consolidate and make positive peace stable. While this paper takes as its cue already existing wars, the actual focus here is on the conditions necessary for the creation of negative and positive peace.

3 1   Negative Peace — the End of Warfare

Usually, it is assumed that all parties look for ways of bringing a war to an end. Unfortunately, it is not as simple as that. First of all, in a war it is victory that counts, not just an end to the war. When victory is no longer a realistic option what the parties to the conflict try at first is not to loose the war. In the period after the Second World War all the way up to 1992 more than half of all wars ended with the victory of one side (Ferdowsi 1998, 64). Without victory protracted war is the more likely scenario.

Secondly, in protracted wars in particular there are groups with a vested interest in their continuation. For those who use violence permanently violence usually 'pays', either economically or politically. I shall call those engaged in violence 'violence actors'. In other words, they are social actors linked to other groups profiting from a war (war profiteers) like arms dealers, entrepreneurs controlling important markets for limited goods (eg often fuel, food), black market entrepreneurs, or smugglers. In a sense they constitute a 'war constituency' (Lederach 1995; Weiß 1997).

Fear of defeat and the interests of the war constituency are a driving factor for a self-enforced dynamic of violence (Elwert, Feuchtwang and Neubert 1999a) and the continuation of a war. When steps are taken to put an end to this dynamic of violence and turn it into a peace process violence actors play a crucial role. They have a simple, practical veto power. To wit, often a single, well-targeted violent act can stop a peace-process, since violent acts can and often do provoke a violent retaliation — causing thereby a rekindling of hostilities. Given the strong position enjoyed by violence actors any peace settlement must strive to include the relevant ones among them. They are the ones who decide to stop the fighting. Should violence actors decide to put an end to the fighting and opt for peace, peace-building must consider their cost-benefit-ratios as well as their motivation for a negotiated settlement (Krumwiede 1998; Calic 1998). I shall call this the 'realpolitik'-approach (in the sense of radical non-normative pragmatic politics). To put it differently, all powerful violence actors become important partners in peace-negotiations irrespective of their political positions and their role in the war.

According to Zartman (1985, 231–51; see also Krumwiede 1998, 42–4) negotiations only take place when a conflict is 'ripe' for resolution. Prerequisites are a military deadlock as well as the existence of a formula for political compromise. Further influencing factors are limited, costly or risky military options, dwindling economic resources and, depending on the type of conflict, fading popular support for the war.

The peaceful order itself must be attractive to violence actors. This includes, firstly, security guarantees for the fighters, failing which they may not lay down their weapons. Secondly, the peace order must offer promising political and economic prospects for violence actors (eg participation in the government, access to national resources, support for new enterprises). Therefore, peace settlements after protracted warfare are rarely about the fundamental political and ideological questions that were originally part of the conflict. What dominates is the interest of military leaders and fighters in securing their position in political, economic and legal terms.

3 2   Positive Peace-building and Consolidation of a Peaceful Order

The next step after the end of warfare is the creation of positive peace focusing on building and consolidating a stable peaceful order. This includes different actions and objectives (Kühne 1998):

— Reduction of the number of fighters including demobilisation, disarmament and the reintegration of soldiers into civilian life.
— Installation of post-conflict governance including the reconstruction of public order and security, law enforcement, and monopoly of violence as well as political reconstruction.
— Technical reconstruction of infrastructure, clearing of war damages, and economic stabilisation.
— Legal and psychological reconstruction including the regulation of war crimes, war damages, looted or illegally acquired property and reconciliation.
— Management of reconstruction activities through the co-ordination of aid and reconstruction activities.

Western conceptions of post-conflict peace-building go even further. As far as these are concerned, a stable peaceful order includes not only a monopoly of violence but also the rule of law, social justice, political participation, a constructive non-violent conflict culture and the control of affects. (Senghaas 1994, 17–49 argues for a so-called civilisation hexagon drawing from Norbert Elias.) In keeping with these conceptions sustainable peace requires a democratically legitimated monopoly of violence and a key role for the state in the maintenance of public order.

3 3   Contradictions of Peace-building

The orientations and strategies of both negative and positive peace are mostly presented as a sequence of steps that follow one after the other. However, the strategies for successful negative peace contradict the wider objectives of positive peace. Human rights and justice NGOs (and other development agencies) are trapped in the 'peacemakers' dilemma'.

To agree on negative peace military leaders and fighters want incentives, which include at least personal security guarantees, political recognition and economic options for the former military leaders and chances for a successful reintegration of the latter. Security for fighters and military leaders prevents the legal pursuit of war crimes. An amnesty encourages a 'culture of impunity' that gives legitimacy to, or at least tolerates crimes committed during warfare. Under such circumstances it is often feared that the rule of law and human rights might be off to a bad start. Political recognition for military leaders usually includes access to leading political positions and economic options (control of natural resources, access to licences or to economic support programmes). Demobilisation is usually achieved through the integration of part of the ex-fighters into the security forces as well as special demobilisation programmes for the rest. In this type of peace agreement violence actors are rewarded and privileged so that one gets the impression that violence pays. As long as those charged with war crimes are not only amnestied but also rewarded reconciliation and healing will equally be seen to be off to a bad start.

The ideal of a new peaceful order following the notion of law and justice can hardly be achieved in the context of a peace agreement between two strong warring parties. Even when some measures of punishment are envisaged they must be constructed in such a way as to affect only a minority of fighters, for, otherwise, they will not agree to a peace treaty. The South African Truth Commission is a good case in point. Violent acts committed out of political motives could be amnestied. Only those acts classified as ordinary crimes could be punished. As a result, the political leaders de facto had good chances for an amnesty and only the lower officer ranks and the rank and file risked criminal proceedings (on the Truth Commission see: du Plessis in this volume).

The situation after a military victory, as it were, the peace of the victor (Elwert, Feuchtwang and Neubert 1999b, 21), differs from the situation just described. The victor dominates through military power and may, which he often does, dictate the peaceful order. Therefore, it is easier to constitute a peaceful order that includes legal consequences. However, the consequences are defined from the perspective of the military victor and may exempt the victorious army. Depending on the new political and legal order the peace of the victor may create more or less legitimacy, social and political injustice with new sources of potential conflict. The question is not so much whether public order will be reconstructed but rather whose and what order it will be.

3 4 Type of Conflict and Chances for Peace-building

A mere consideration of the violence actors' cost-benefit ratio does not guarantee peace negotiations that will result in actual peace. Successful peace-building is based on core preconditions that are not easy to meet.

For negative peace to ensue peace-building requires:

— Recognisable conflicting parties, in the absence of which negotiations cannot take place.
— Military and political leaders that can negotiate and implement peace. This means that they must be able to control the military actions of their fighters, especially with regard to ordering an end to the fighting and demobilising.
— Leaders who are motivated to negotiate a peace-agreement, which considers specific security interests and political and economic incentives for peace and especially links to the population.

For positive peace to ensue peace-building requires:

— Leaders and fighters who will accept post-conflict governance arrangements (including a monopoly of violence not controlled by themselves).

These preconditions for peace-building and the way negotiations can be organised vary according to the type of conflict (*see Appendix, Table 2*).

Recognisable political parties with leaders able to negotiate are easier to define in centralised bi-polar conflicts. In civil wars sometimes the parties lack organisational strength. In multi-polar decentralised conflicts the conflicting parties are not clearly defined, instead they often change and are weakly organised. Leaders who could negotiate may be available but their strength varies according to the situation.

The control over military action for the purpose of bringing the fighting to an end, demobilise and accept the monopoly of violence is strongest in international war and is also to be found in classical civil wars (albeit sometimes disputed). But even in 'classical' civil wars the orders of the leaders may need the consent of the fighters. In local inter-community conflicts the control of fighters and the compliance with orders is seldom strong and varies according to the local political organisation. Warlordism and international terrorism usually do not have a reliable order as a basis of military control. Leaders need the consent of their fighters or risk a split of the group.

Motivation for peace negotiations leading to a negative peace and the chances that a given peaceful order will be accepted to establish positive peace are somehow linked. They are both influenced by the same factors (security interests and incentives for peace). The 'peacemakers' dilemma' is not constituted by a change in the motivation and attitude of combatants and leaders, but by a change in the peacemakers' demands from a mere end of fighting to a stable and just peaceful order. The warring parties' ability to follow this new demand is mainly influenced by the type of linkage between leaders and fighters on the one side and the population on the other.

In cases where linkages between military leaders and fighters with the population are nearly absent security interests and incentives are defined from the perspective of leaders and fighters, only. The population's interests are mostly ignored. This holds true for most cases of warlordism and for cases of international terrorism. Under a situation of warlordism the fighters often are cut-off from civilian social networks and practice war as a way of life.[6] Under such circumstances demobilisation means a completely new life, including the kinds of hardship faced by a farmer, craftsman or petty-trader. This applies to full-time terrorists in a similar way they have to move from their clandestine network back into regular life. (However, their professions may differ from those of the fighters in warlord conflicts.)

In international war, civil war and local inter-community conflicts military leaders and fighters are closer to the population. Fighting is at least partly justified by the protection of people's interests. The families of leaders and fighters are part and parcel of the population. For this reason they may wish to avoid enemy attacks against the population. Political and economic advancement for the population may be an incentive for leaders and fighters to agree to a peace-settlement. However, the population's influence on leaders depends on the political system. The population's attitude towards peace may vary; civilians often opt for peace, but after intense

---

[6] Eg child soldiers Richards 1996a; 1996b; on the role of reintegrating fighters back into society see: Klute and von Trotha in this volume.

fighting a high degree of hatred and mistrust in the population can also hinder peace-building. As far as ex-fighters are concerned demobilisation and integration may mean the return to a life they already know with all the advantages and disadvantages it entails.

Given a situation where a peace agreement is seen as an option for the warring parties (ie a conflict ripe for resolution) bi-polar centralised conflicts offer the best chances for peace negotiations and their implementation. They fit into the frame of classical diplomatic peace negotiation. Once the conflict is ripe for resolution both sides may be represented by leaders who are able to negotiate and implement a formal peace settlement.

Local inter-community conflicts are open for peace talks but need different political instruments than the usual diplomatic repertoire developed for the settlement of bi-polar centralised conflicts. The conflicting parties may not be well-defined, formal leadership positions and means for the implementation of an agreement may be missing. An important part of the peace settlement is the identification of leaders and even the creation of structures of representation including support for leaders interested in peace.

Peace-building in situations like warlordism and international terrorism present the biggest challenge. Warlords and fighters have based their whole lives on violence. Even if leaders are willing to agree to a peace settlement groups of fighters may split away and rekindle violence. In international terrorism due to the decentralised and clandestine nature of its structures the leaders are hard to identify. If leaders are willing to negotiate they risk being seen as traitors and others may claim leadership and the representation of the true values of the movement, underlined by new terrorist acts. Successful negotiations are unlikely. Terrorist networks more likely cease to exist than stop their activities as the result of a peace-settlement.

Finally, mercenary and security companies constitute a special case. As service enterprises they are mainly guided by their clients' interests and they have no linkage to the population. Usually the companies are internally clearly structured and executives enjoy control over their staff. As long as clients are able to pay it is mostly up to them how the company behaves. Nonetheless, there are two limitations. First, the company seeks to limit its risks in order to keep its cost-benefit ratio high; secondly, the level of compliance with the law, order and agreements with other fighting groups depends on the context and also on the company's general attitude towards law. Nevertheless, without further payment mercenary and security companies will stop their activities.

We have to be aware that current conflicts often include different types of actors and sub-conflicts. Peace-building has to be based on diplomatic activities to include the national actors and other parties with national ambitions. However, governments and political leaders often are not able to control smaller groups of allies, which may consist of either local warrior and defence communities urban communal groups or warlords and sometimes international terrorists. Additionally, local warrior and defence communities might change to warlordism with a lower sense of responsibility towards 'their' former local population. This multiplicity of motives, objectives and ratios of violence actors and the tendency to split-up and change their type is one of the reasons that makes peace-building in these complex conflicts so complicated.[7]

The current conflict landscape in Africa is dominated by decentralised conflicts. A good example is the already mentioned conflict in Central Africa. Given the extreme heterogeneity of interests in decentralised conflicts it is not likely that any peace agreement will be accepted voluntarily and implemented by all warring groups. Without strict control over all fighters leaders cannot wish peace into existence. At least small groups of fighters may see their chance for looting, honour and new political and economic rewards and they may begin to fight again. Therefore, a peaceful order with a monopoly of violence will rarely be implemented only by agreement; it has to be enforced. The creation of a peaceful order is not (only) a question of negotiated peace but of the existence or creation of a power that is able to keep the monopoly of violence in a defined territory.[8] In short, a peaceful order goes hand in hand with the establishment or the reassertion of a form of central state power. (A special case of para-statal structure is described by Klute and von Trotha in this volume.) The kind of peaceful order will depend on the type of state and its political rule. As long as the state does not yet have the power to discharge its functions it will be in need of support. Therefore, the current debate on the United Nations' role in peace-building raises the question of a robust doctrine for peacekeeping forces that enables them to control violence actively (United Nations 2000, ixf).

4   NGOS IN PEACE-BUILDING: ADVANTAGES AND TASKS

NGOs do play a role in peace-building. However, considering the wider framework within which this occurs it has to be admitted that this role is quite limited. NGOs can neither change military options that are core factors influencing the end to fighting, nor can they influence the development of state power. The specific role that NGOs want to play can be described, first, by the advantages that are claimed by NGOs and their supporters and, secondly, by the tasks and activities of NGOs in peace-building.

---

[7] A peculiarity of decentralised violent conflicts complicates peace-building even more. When instruments of peace-building are developed the risks of a new war are limited because peace may be easier to achieve. The threshold for new conflicts will be lower (Elwert, Feuchtwang and Neubert 1999b, 27).

[8] The peace agreements in Sierra Leone or in the Democratic Republic of Congo showed that agreements could be easily broken in the absence of a strong central state.

4 1 Advantages of NGOs as Claimed by NGOs and their Supporters

There is a long list of advantages that are claimed in support of the role of NGOs in peace-building (Brühl 1999, 111; Weiß 1997; Heinz 1998; Ropers 1997, 221–24; NGOs in general: Neubert 1997a, 31f; 1997b, 52):

— NGOs can act free from diplomatic constraints and face lower political risks in case of failure.
— They have a wide range of non-military options. In particular, they can act earlier than state actors and may intervene on all societal levels (top leaders, national leaders, grass-roots).
— They are (usually) oriented towards humanitarian values, towards peace and reconciliation (except some ideologically-biased NGOs) and do not focus solely on violence actors.
— They raise awareness for peaceful coexistence and are open for the socio-psychological aspects of conflicts.
— They are experienced in emergency aid and local development under extreme conditions, have (access to) local expertise, reach the people, whose interests they may even represent.
— NGOs are oriented towards long-term conflict prevention whereas state actors often focus on actual 'hot' conflicts.
— In Christian countries churches may play a leading role. They usually are organisationally strong, have churches all over the country, and enjoy a high degree of legitimacy.

The activities of international NGOs are based on the co-operation of NGOs operating nationally or locally in the South and Northern NGOs operating internationally. The international NGO-lobby uses the international public to raise funds for emergencies in the South, acts as donor or service provider for Southern NGOs or it intervenes itself, mostly in extreme emergency situations. But even in the case of direct interventions NGOs often co-operate with local organisations. NGOs from the South have specific local expertise and provide access to the local population. In extremely risky situations it is often the local staff that remains on the spot, even when expatriates are evacuated.

4 2 Tasks and Activities

The tasks named as typical for NGOs (Calließ 1996; Brühl 1999; Heinz 1998; Fischer 1999; Weiß 1997) cover all three phases of peace-building with conflict prevention and de-escalation, crisis management and end of combat and consolidation of peace. (In this respect there are a number of similarities between NGOs and other development agencies). However, the tasks are not sequentially organised even though they often cover more than one phase.

In crisis management and end of warfare NGOs perform a 'watchdog' function. They inform the international public on conflicts and the extent of suffering, they lobby for peace and act as pressure groups which seek to bring political attention to bear on the conflicts by means of placing them on the agenda (both international and national). They mobilise and provide humanitarian aid using their international structures of co-operation.

In the conflict situation itself NGOs may facilitate negotiations by investigating negotiation chances and establishing contacts between conflicting parties. They work as informal mediators and provide meeting facilities. They are important actors in the so-called 'track two' activities (alongside official government and diplomatic 'track one' activities). This includes talks with leaders without a political reputation or probing informally whether negotiating strategies and options stand any chance of success — eg the peace agreements in Mozambique and El Salvador were prepared by NGO activities (Adelmann 1997; Grohs 1999; Macamo and Neubert 2004; Pfaffenholz 1998, 160–92). NGOs may offer incentives for peace negotiations like humanitarian and technical aid (eg Mozambique), build confidence between the conflicting parties or initiate public dialogue.

After the end of warfare, but still within the consolidation phase, there is a wide range of special tasks that NGOs can fulfil with a view to achieving post-conflict stabilisation and reconstruction. They mainly engage in development and aid activities like humanitarian and technical emergency aid and economic and social reconstruction, especially at the local level (promoting equal and just development), resettlement and reintegration of refugees and displaced persons, or retraining and integration of ex-fighters. NGOs may also clear mines or provide non-armed escort for persons and groups at risk. At the local level the population and local leaders often prefer NGOs to military actors because these are not seen as a potential threat to the population.

Reconciliation is one field that is seen as especially suitable ground for NGO activities. This includes coming to terms with the crimes and injustices of the conflict both at the local and national level (including the participation in institutions of justice, like truth commissions, committees for justice and peace, local arbitration, etc). NGOs offer socio-psychological care for war victims and traumatised persons.

Conflict prevention and de-escalation are just as important before a violent conflict as they are as part of the consolidation process afterwards. Typical NGOs' tasks are watchdog functions like follow-up and verification of the implementation of peace agreements, especially at the local level, or early warning on tensions and potential violent conflicts, combined with fact-finding (as prerequisites for early mediation). NGOs act as mediators in conflicts, arise over implementation of settlements and promote communication between conflicting parties.

With a longer perspective towards conflict prevention NGOs lobby for and endorse human rights, (local) democracy, rule of law and support the empowerment of minorities. They promote local structures for de-escalation and reconciliation. The concept of 'education for peace' uses methods from social work and pedagogy and promotes non-violent conflict resolution and inter-community understanding in a wide range of training courses and workshops (Hoffman 1995). It is especially these tasks in reconciliation and conflict prevention that are linked to the Western concept of a peace-order based on the rule of law, human rights and democracy.

4 3   Building of 'Peace-constituencies'

There is one concept that links most of the activities and all phases of peace-building to an integrated strategy, namely the building of 'peace-constituencies' (Lederach 1995; Pfaffenholz 2002; Rupesinghe 1995; Weiß 1999). During a protracted war, violence actors and the 'war constituencies' (see above) dominate society. In decentralised conflicts, in particular, the main actors are part of the war constituency. The war constituency includes all the fighting parties and their allies, political followers and all kinds of people who profit from the war. They may compete or fight against each other but they all have a vested interest in the continuation of the war. The usual diplomatic repertoire and informal conflict resolution activities must focus on violence actors, for their consent is needed to bring the fighting to an end. This may imply promoting violence actors politically. Under such circumstances a negotiated peace may just confirm once more that 'violence pays'.

The concept of 'building peace-constituencies' follows a rationale to create or strengthen actors who are interested in peace and give them political voice and influence. Building peace-constituencies means creating local and national networks and organisations that lobby for peace, act as pressure groups and provide structures for peaceful conflict resolution. Typical members of peace-constituencies may be businessmen interested in stable economic conditions and security, religious organisations, human rights organisations, intellectuals, or peaceful government officials. Depending on the social situation in the war-torn country peace-building may have to include support for (the creation of) a civil society.

5   NGOS IN PEACE-BUILDING:
LIMITS, CONTRADICTIONS AND PROBLEMS[9]

In spite of the high number of peace-building activities there are in actual fact only a few studies analysing the results of peace-building measures.

---

[9] For a discussion of NGOs in conflicts and peace-building see: African Rights 1994; Allen 1999; Brühl 1999; Weiß 1997; 1999; Heinz 1998; Hanisch 1996; Heinrich 1999.

These studies focus on programmes and concepts, but fail to consider their impact. Besides, the educational approach with courses and workshops for non-violent conflict resolution or interethnic community building has yet to be well researched. On a more general level of peace consolidation the (few) available examples show a remarkable NGO activity in post conflict stabilisation (Africa: Uganda since 1986, Namibia, South Africa, Mozambique).

We must admit that post-conflict stabilisation is not easy to assess. One main factor for the successful consolidation of peace is the improvement of conditions in everyday life for the population and ex-fighters. This, however, may be the result of a complex development process that cannot be ascribed to special activities and programmes. Considering what is known about post-conflict development a sound impact analysis is hardly realistic. It appears more promising to focus on the problems and limitations of peace-building as well as post-conflict consolidation.

5 1   Problems of NGO Activities in General

Despite the generally positive judgement of NGO activities we cannot ignore a number of general weaknesses and problems with regard to NGOs, which influence their performance in peace-building (Brühl 1999; Weiß 1999; Heinz 1998; on NGOs in general see: Neubert 1997a; 1997b). An often mentioned problem is the lack of co-ordination: Activities may overlap and concentrate in special areas while leaving out other areas. The discussion on emergency aid shows the competition and rivalry between NGOs and other organisations and inside the NGO community. The issues are access to funds, official donors, or donations.[10] In negotiations between the warring parties mediators may follow different objectives or strategies that may reduce efficiency. There are often differences between official (state, multilateral) and informal NGO mediators, but also differences between different informal mediators.

The role of NGOs in society is ambiguous. While they claim to represent or to speak on behalf of civil society the basis for their legitimacy is often not clearly defined. Indeed, who is represented by NGOs? Except for churches and a few other NGOs with strong grassroots support NGOs often do not have a strong membership or a special constituency. Additionally, NGOs rely on donors for their activities and frequently adapt their position, at least partly, to suit donors' objectives and strategies.

---

[10] In this competition the prestige linked to media coverage plays a crucial role. NGOs whose work is presented positively in the media or who comment on the situation on TV-programmes have better publicity that facilitates access to resources.

The system whereby donors fund NGOs may lead to a dilemma centring on outside support: support for national and local NGOs without own resources creates dependency. Donors may willy-nilly export Western concepts and programmes in spite of specific local needs and orientation. The result may be the likelihood of creating supply-led activities and structures.

NGO local partners are not necessarily efficient. And the higher the element of self-organisation of local partners the more a contradiction emerges between donors' demands for professionalism and the demand for adapting to local needs and capabilities.

The question for NGOs implies a fundamental difference between NGOs and other organisations in the international system of development and aid. This overemphasises the peculiarity of NGOs. As far as concepts and post-conflict activities are concerned no striking differences between NGOs and state or multilateral aid organisations can be identified. Special options are fewer than the generally claimed advantages of NGOs (see above) may imply. NGOs are slightly more locally oriented. As part of civil society NGOs are not directly linked to government policy. Due to the absence of diplomatic constraints NGOs have more political freedom and more political options than state agencies in conflict situations. The heterogeneity of NGOs offers a wide spectrum of different political orientations that may create trust for actors involved in war. But even government-organisations like the German Volunteer Service (DED, Deutscher Entwicklungsdienst) and the German agency for technical co-operation (GTZ, Gesellschaft für Technische Zusammenarbeit) have promising projects for local peace-building (Fahrenhorst 2000). These are the often-mentioned programmes for post-conflict consolidation in the Tuareg conflict in Mali (financed by the German Technical Co-operation, GTZ, see: Papendieck and Rocksloh-Papendieck in this volume) and the 'islands of peace' concept used in the Sudan (German Volunteer Service, DED; Wilhelm 1999).

5 2   Special Peace-building Problems Faced by NGOs

NGOs and other development agencies involved in peace-building have to be aware of their limits. During conflicts peace-building is basically speaking a military and political task. So long as fighting goes on NGOs can only play a supporting role. Aid programmes, a watchdog role and other activities cannot provide negative peace. Even in the cases where NGOs were involved in peace-talks (eg Mozambique) political and military agreements were negotiated by politicians and military leaders (Adelmann 1997; Grohs 1999; Macamo and Neubert 2004; Pfaffenholz 1998). During peace-consolidation the importance of NGOs and other development agencies increases. Their aid programmes may facilitate economic and social development, support demobilisation of ex-fighters and promote reconciliation. But the framework for these measures is the existence of a basic public order providing for security, a monopoly of violence, a structure for the implementation of laws with a minimum of legitimacy. This public order may be supported by NGOs but its creation is mainly the task of a government. All measures for peace-consolidation focussed on the society need military and political preconditions that cannot be provided by NGOs. Peace-building is foremost a political and military task leading up to a (new) order based on a mixture of legitimacy and military power.

With regard to the protracted conflicts that are dominant in Africa we have to acknowledge that neither positive nor negative peace is existent. In decentralised conflicts, in particular, even the core preconditions for building a negative peace are absent. In this sense then the options available to NGOs for successful peace-building are clearly restricted.

Even when the core preconditions for negative peace have been met current strategies of peace-building are contradictory. NGOs are wittingly or unwittingly drawn into conflicts. This is most obvious in the case of ideologically biased NGOs like the anti-apartheid movement, solidarity movements for independence, exile organisations and Southern lobby NGOs (eg Oromo or Southern Sudan). This biased role limits or even hinders their neutrality during crisis management.

Unbiased NGOs face contradictions, too. The 'watchdog' role interferes with humanitarian aid, as the delivery of aid needs an agreement with one or more of the warring parties to guarantee security to aid agencies. This limits the distance and may influence the neutrality of NGOs. Any public statement on the conflict may be countered with the argument that the NGO in question is an ally of one of the parties. One solution is the differentiation of tasks between NGOs, where one part acts as 'watchdog' while the other provides humanitarian aid.

The internationally highly respected humanitarian aid is ambiguous, too. It has become an important political and financial source of conflict and support for warring parties. It is fair to assume that aid accepts the logic of war. In fact, the provision of aid is usually based on an arrangement with the relevant violence actors who seek approval for their power by means of military control. As far as violence actors are concerned aid becomes a means for acquiring legitimacy and frees violence actors from their duty to care for civilians. Aid itself is an economic resource that is used by violence actors in many ways (African Rights 1994; Hanisch and Moßmann 1996; Hanisch 1996; Jean 1994; Whitman and Pocock 1996). Violence actors and the war constituency may

— gain direct control of the distribution via political and military power,
— exaggerate their needs and use extra resources for the military,

— charge 'taxes' or fees in exchange for landing rights, air rights and the use of harbour or storage facilities,
— set fixed exchange rates to gain access to foreign currency,
— have income from hotels, car rental, and other means of transport,
— simply steal the resources.

Aid can be an economic core element of conflicts and access to it may become a conflict issue in itself (on the significance of aid see: Hanisch 1996, 40).

The most difficult structural problem is the 'peacemakers' dilemma' itself. The NGOs are also trapped between the local 'realpolitik' approach as a means to negotiating an end to combat conflicts and the objectives of implementing human rights, justice and prosecuting war crimes. The currently promoted mediation concept does not tackle these contradictions adequately. It ignores the 'peacemakers' dilemma' and the fact that peace-building during a conflict includes political and military tasks.

Even when mediation has a chance, perhaps because powerful actors opt for peace, the mediation models used may be culturally inadequate. They follow Western ideas and values, address individualistic interests, promote open discussion including personal relations and are implemented by impartial mediators. This may ignore local concepts of mediation dealing with groups and group interest, using formalised and metaphoric speech which underlines symbolic elements of negotiations, implemented by biased mediators and using local mediation structures (see Zartman 2000). Healing and compensation, for instance, may be more important than formal justice and reconciliation in the sense of forgiving. But attempts to use local structures run the risk of overloading and over-formalising local institutions.[11]

6   PERSPECTIVES FOR NGOS: PEACE-BUILDING IN DECENTRALISED CONFLICTS

6 1   Objectives and Challenges for Peace-building

The objective of peace-building is the result of a normative judgement in favour of peace instead of war. In many protracted conflicts considerable

---

[11] In Rwanda, a local 'court' (gacaca) should handle medium and minor crimes during the genocide. However, the 'gacaca' was no longer an important legal institution. In the current situation where victims and culprits of the genocide and new immigrants (former refugees) clash at the local level there are no legitimate structures of local authority. The 'gacaca' system risks being seen as a newly invented state structure that needs state support to secure its authority. It might not be accepted as an institution linked to the local community (Weilenmann nd; Hoywegen 2000, 25f; Reyntjens 1990; Scherrer 1996).

parts of the population support this value judgement. The NGO objective of positive peace in a legitimate and democratic political system reflects the Western conception of a peaceful and democratic society and should not assume the same widespread local support. There are regions where democracy and human rights are locally defined objectives for a peaceful order. In other regions the concept of human rights and (Western) democracy is a controversial one and in still others human rights and democracy are hardly a local political issue at all. Even in places where people may agree with the vision of peace-building leading to human rights and democracy implementation is often far away from reality.

Bearing in mind such contradictions and strict limitations of peace-building the objective has to be revised and adapted to different situations. What is needed is peace-building at different speeds and adapted objectives. In one specific situation keeping a negative peace and protection against severe human rights violations, war crimes (eg murder, rape, looting, burning down of houses) and violence may be a big step forward (on the role of protection see: Klute and von Trotha in this volume). In another situation the prosecution of war criminals, the consolidation of democracy and building of a civil society might be the minimum requirement for those involved in peace-building and for the population as well. The realistic objectives of peace-building depend on the specific case, including the aspirations of the people involved.[12]

Given the objective of peace we can ask what lessons can be learned from this analysis and develop elements of a strategy of peace-building. Peace-building is an ambiguous task fraught with contradictions. We must acknowledge that every peace-building activity carries a high risk of failure and violence actors may misuse all activities of external agencies for their own ends. A simple consequence would be non-intervention until the warring parties are weary of the war or until the conflict is 'ripe for resolution'. This would be too simple. Waiting for war-weariness would reduce peace-building activities to cases where war has already petered out and peace may come anyway. Peace-building would become nearly meaningless. While concentrating on conflicts 'ripe for resolution' may appear more promising in practice, however, peace here too is hard to come by. There is no sound indicator for when a conflict is ripe for resolution; and the chances of influencing a conflict in the direction of peace would remain untapped. Peace-building must both be bold enough to run the risk of failure while being realistic at the same time.

The starting point should be an assessment of the chances and limits of every case. This requires the identification and understanding of the type

---

[12] In situations where the people do not want peace, NGOs working for peace face a value conflict between their orientation towards peace-building and the contradictory local orientation in favour of violent conflict. Two answers are possible: to withdraw from that region or try to convince people that peace is a basic value.

(or the types) of conflict. What strategies could be applied is a question that depends on the type of conflict and the types of actors involved. For bi-polar conflicts there is already an elaborated apparatus of diplomatic and other political means and strategies. The current discussion on peace-building emerged because strategies for handling decentralised conflicts are a failure. The real challenge is peace-building in conflicts with a strong decentralised element. The problems have been named above: there is no political framework for action that provides reliable partners for negotiation; violence actors are numerous and often unstable; the leaders do not control their fighters. For violence actors violence pays and it is also a 'way of life'. Under such circumstances peace as such cannot be very attractive. The classical diplomatic strategies do not apply to this situation. Decentralised conflicts offer only limited influence for external actors. The search for diplomatic influence through alliances is complicated because actors are neither stable nor do they follow long-term political aims.

6 2   A Combined Strategy: Changing the Local Cost-benefit Ratio of Violence

We should bear in mind that there is no panacea for peace-building and we must accept that every peace-building process carries a very high risk of failure and misuse. It is against this background that I propose a strategy for peace-building in decentralised conflicts that includes NGOs and other actors. The basic principles of that combined strategy are:

— Parallel efforts of official (state, multilateral) and NGO activity.
— Combining political, military, economic and social development activities.
— Intervention at different levels (international, national, local) at the same time.
— Combining crisis management and end of combat with post-conflict stabilisation and reconstruction.
— Looking for locally adapted strategies.
— Using existing local structures for stabilisation.

In many cases it will not be realistic to expect all actors involved in peace-building to be part of a well-planned and co-ordinated strategy. The principle must not be the foundation of a wide-ranging and all inclusive initiative, but rather it should be used as a basic orientation for all actors to follow during their activities. The task of NGOs in conflict countries will be mainly in the field of localisation of activities and adaptation to decentralised conflicts. National NGOs with a broad public support, such as churches may also be involved in national peace-processes, and Northern NGOs may act as lobby organisations.

The main target to aim at is changing the local cost-benefit ratio of violence. As long as violence pays peace will be unlikely. Only when violence does not pay anymore or pays less (militarily, economically, politically) will the chances for peace-building improve. This can be achieved by following three principles:

a) Make war costly: this includes intensification of arms control and the control of smuggling. Arms trading must carry a high risk. Even if this does not stop arms trading it will at least lead to higher prices. Additionally, the marketing of resources that finance war (diamonds, oil) should be hindered. The process of marketing these resources requires international co-operation. This means, therefore, that political and economic pressure is possible. The task of NGOs will be to lobby and place the issue on the agenda of international politics. Additionally, NGOs may act as watchdogs informing on arms trade and the marketing of resources used to fund wars.

b) Make peace attractive: An important activity is building-up and supporting peace constituencies. The target is to develop small areas (islands of peace) where civilian leaders are in power and a minimum of peace is ensured. Activities include strengthening of non-military local leaders to re-conquer 'civilian' power, help them develop a local peace order (eg case of Mali, Papendieck and Rocksloh-Papendieck in this volume, 84; Klute and von Trotha in this volume), and support economic development through civilian powers. One strategy for the promotion of peace is the reliance on local religious ideas and values (justice, thou shall not kill...) (Heinrich 1997; 1999) and of local institutions for peace-making (Zartman 2000). The strengthening of linkages between fighters and the local population may influence the former to opt for peace. The special tasks for NGOs are local aid programmes and local networking activities.

c) Support potential negotiators: An agreement to end fighting needs leaders who aggregate and represent the decentralised groups and fighting units. Potential leaders have to be identified and their position should be strengthened by the prospect of post-war funds (the so-called peace dividend). The negotiation can be facilitated by the promotion and the support of links between warring groups (economic exchange, visits, contacts) (Heinrich 1997; 1999). The task of NGOs is to facilitate contacts and negotiations.[13]

This strategy is a combination of local 'realpolitik' with support for peace-constituencies. Local 'realpolitik' accepts the decentralised fighting units as potential negotiating partners in spite of their war crimes, and offers them security and economic or political rewards for peace. Support

[13] Weimer (1998) describes for Mozambique the common assessment that RENAMO fighting units were responsible for decentralised violence and anomie on the micro level. Only on the macro level was it possible to identify some elements of political objectives and strategy. The acceptance of leaders as negotiating partners promoted by the churches was the starting point for negotiation and an aggregation of RENAMO.

for peace-constituencies strengthens civilian leaders and peace oriented actors at the local level. This combined strategy is all the more effective the more fighters are linked to the society. The focus is on ending fighting and starting reconciliation; questions of justice are part of the negotiations but should not be rigidly implemented.

However, this pragmatic strategy faces clear limitations and problems. Up to now, international actions on arms control have been few, have lacked implementation and have not been very successful. There seems to be only limited international interest in embargoes on resources financing wars (diamonds, gold, oil).[14]

'Islands of peace' are attractive targets for looting. In such instances defence structures are needed. The defence units themselves are a potential nucleus for new actors of violence. The input of resources into the islands of peace and the support for peace-constituencies are an economic input into the war zone and face the risk of financing war, at least indirectly.

The hope for an end to hostilities at the local level ignores the possibility of a high level of hatred and mistrust after extreme war crimes (mass murder, pogroms, genocide). The local 'realpolitik'-approach conflicts with human rights activities or accepts those who violate human rights along with war criminals as negotiating partners. Issues of justice and human rights should be postponed to the phase of post-conflict consolidation. Only in this phase of creating positive peace will all issues of justice like human rights and the post conflict order in general be at stake. The end to the fighting should be based on compromises with violence actors without any guarantee that these fundamental questions will be tackled later.[15]

This pragmatic strategy cannot overcome the peacemakers' dilemma completely. As long as peace must be negotiated because none of the parties is able to win militarily the contradictions of peace-building have to be accepted and expectations in all peace activities can only be modest. What may be defined as a set of realistic options depends on the political situation and the stability of peace.

7   CONCLUSION

Violent conflicts are not exceptional situations. They are rather a part of reality. For actors of violence, 'violence pays'. For them peace may be a threat and not an objective or an end. An agreement to put an end to fighting that does not include the actors of violence means that all further

[14] After years of wars financed by diamonds in Liberia, Sierra Leone and Central Africa only now has a discussion on a tighter control of the diamonds trade started.

[15] The current development in Chile with the lifting of the immunity of the former president, Pinochet, shows that issues of human rights may come up again even long after a negotiated change of political system.

objectives like a stable peace-order, including a monopoly of violence or a peaceful democratic society, may be forlorn. This is when peace-building faces the 'peacemakers' dilemma'. Negative peace can be achieved when the interests of violence actors have been met, which unfortunately will include security guarantees and limitations in the prosecution of war crimes and human rights violations.

The problems of peace-building differ according to the types of conflicts. There is a wide experience with peace-building in bi-polar centralised wars. But for decentralised (multi-polar violent group) conflicts (local inter-community conflicts, warlordism, international terrorism) even strategies for the creation of negative peace are want. The development of these strategies is one of the major challenges for peace-building. We must admit that common diplomatic instruments do not apply for decentralised conflicts and that the influence of external actors on internal and especially on decentralised conflicts is limited. At the same time, external actors and their resources can become part of the conflict and be used by the local violence actors according to their interests. One way of peace-building in multi-polar decentralised conflicts is a strategy that combines the acceptance of the interests of violence actors in spite of their behaviour during the conflict (local 'realpolitik') with support for peace constituencies for wresting back civilian power.

Further consolidation of peace with the creation of positive peace is closely linked to the stabilisation of the state and needs strong government structures that can provide security and enjoy control over the monopoly of violence. Peace-building goes together with state formation and consolidation.

In a peace-building process NGOs play only a supporting role. During the establishment of negative-peace and during post-conflict stabilisation the main decisions are taken at the military and political level. During peace-consolidation the decisive actor is the government. In this framework NGOs are important as local level actors and may, on the national level, provide alternative channels for negotiations. In post-conflict stabilisation they may support aid and stabilisation programmes. Even more important can be their long-term influence in supporting the development of a civil society.

However, whatever we can expect from peace-building in general and from NGOs, in particular, must respect the shortcomings of peace-building just as we must accept that the chances for creating peace through external intervention are quite limited.

REFERENCES

Adelmann, Karin 1997. Hoffnung auf die Barfuß-Diplomaten. *E+Z Entwicklung und Zusammenarbeit 38 (10):* 264–66.

African Rights 1994. *Humanitarism unbound? Current dilemmas facing multimandate relief operations in political emergencies.* (London: African Rights).

Ali, Taisier M, Robert Matthews, (eds) 1999. *Civil wars in Africa. Roots and resolution.* (Montreal, Kingston, London, Ithaca: McGill-Queen's University Press).

Allen, Tim 1999. War, genocide and aid. In *Dynamics of violence. Processes of escalation and de-escalation in violent group conflicts. Sociologus supplement 1,* edited by G Elwert, S Feuchtwang, and D Neubert. (Berlin: Duncker & Humblot).

Bendrath, Ralf 1999. Söldnerfirmen in Afrika — Neue politische Vergesellschaftungsformen jenseits des modernen Staates. In *Friedenskultur statt Kulturkampf. Strategien kultureller und nachhaltiger Friedensstiftung,* edited by (W R Vogt. Baden Baden: Nomos).

Bollig, Michael 1996. Krieger und Waffenschieber in der ostafrikanischen Savanne. In *Krieg und Kampf. Die Gewalt in unseren Köpfen,* edited by E Orywal, A Rao, and M Bollig. (Berlin: Reimer).

Bollig, Michael 1999. Afrikanische Kriegsherrn. Überlegung zur Entstehung von Gewaltmärkten im präkolonialen und postkolonialen Afrika. In *Afrika und die Globalisierung,* edited by H P Hahn and G Spittler. (Hamburg, Münster, Hamburg, London: Lit).

Brühl, Tanja 1999. Konfliktbearbeitung durch NGOs: Chancen und Grenzen. In *Friedenskultur statt Kulturkampf. Strategien kultureller Zivilisierung und nachhaltiger Friedensstiftung,* edited by W R Vogt. (Baden Baden: Nomos).

Buijtenhuijs, Rob 1996. The rational rebel: how rational, how rebellious. Some African examples. *Afrika Focus 12:* 3–25.

Calic, Marie-Janine 1998. Probleme Dritter Parteien bei der Regulierung von Bürgerkriegen: Der Fall Bosnien-Herzegowina. In *Bürgerkriege: Folgen und Regulierungsmöglichkeiten,* edited by H-W Krumwiede and P Waldmann. (Baden Baden: Nomos).

Calließ, Jörg 1996. Die Aufgaben ziviler Konfliktbearbeitung und der Aufbau einer angemessenen Infrastruktur. *Die Friedens-Warte 71:* 395–416.

Debiel, Tobias, Martina Fischer, Volker Matthies, and Norbert Ropers. 1999. *Effektive Krisenprävention. Herausforderung für die deutsche Außen- und Entwicklungspolitik.* (Bonn: Stiftung Entwicklung und Frieden).

Die Herren des Krieges (Special issue). 1995. Der Überblick 31.

Elwert, Georg 1999. Markets of violence. In *Dynamics of violence. Processes of escalation and de-escalation of violent group conflicts. Sociologus supplement 1,* edited by G Elwert, S Feuchtwang, and D Neubert. (Berlin: Duncker & Humblot).

Elwert, Georg, Stephan Feuchtwang, and Dieter Neubert, eds, 1999a. *Dynamics of violence. Processes of escalation and de-escalation in violent group conflicts. Sociologus supplement 1.* (Berlin: Duncker & Humblot).

Elwert, Georg, Stephan Feuchtwang, and Dieter Neubert, 1999b. The dynamics of collective violence. An introduction. In *Dynamics of violence. Processes of escalation and de-escalation of violent group conflicts. Sociologus supplement 1,* edited by G Elwert, S Feuchtwang, and D Neubert. (Berlin: Duncker & Humblot).

Fahrenhorst, Brigitte (ed) 2000. *Die Rolle der Entwicklungszusammenarbeit in gewalttätigen Konflikten.* (Berlin: SID-Berlin-Berichte Nr 11).

Ferdowsi, Mir A 1998. Die Rolle externer Akteure bei der Genese und Regulierung von Bürgerkriegen. In *Bürgerkriege: Folgen und Regulierungs-möglichkeiten,* edited by H-W Krumwiede and P Waldmann. (Baden Baden: Nomos).

Fischer, Martina 1999. Friedenskonsolidierung in Bosnien-Herzegowina. Ansätze von Nichtregierungsorganisationen. *E + Z Entwicklung und Zusammenarbeit 40 (4):* 113.

Griggs, Richard E 1995. The map of war in Africa. *Internationales Afrikaforum 31:* 163–66.

Grohs, Gerhard 1999. About the role of the churches in the peace process in Africa and Central America. In *Dynamics of violence. Processes of escalation and de-escalation of violent group conflicts. Sociologus supplement 1,* edited by G Elwert, S Feuchtwang, and D Neubert. (Berlin: Duncker & Humblot).

Hanisch, Rolf. 1996. Katastrophen und ihre Opfer. In *Katastrophen und ihre Bewältigung in den Ländern des Südens,* edited by R Hanisch and P Moßmann. (Hamburg: Deutsches Übersee Institut).

Hanisch, Rolf and Peter Moßmann, eds. 1996. *Katastrophen und ihre Bewältigung in den Ländern des Südens.* (Hamburg: Deutsches Übersee-Institut).

Heinrich, Wolfgang. 1997. *Building the peace. Experiences of collaborative peace-building in Somalia 1993–1996.* (Uppsala: Life and Peace Institute).

Heinrich, Wolfgang, 1999. Förderung von Friedensprozessen durch EZ. Lokale Friedenspotentiale müssen genutzt werden. *E + Z Entwicklung und Zusammenarbeit 40 (4):* 106–9.

Heinz, Wolfgang 1998. Chancen und Grenzen externer gesellschaftlicher Vermittlungsinitiativen. Die Erfahrungen der Kirchen. In *Bürgerkriege: Folgen und Regulierungsmöglichkeiten,* edited by H-W Krumwiede and P Waldmann. (Baden Baden: Nomos).

Hoffmann, Mark 1995. Konfliktlösung durch gesellschaftliche Akteure. In *Friedliche Konfliktbearbeitung in der Staaten- und Gesellschaftswelt,* edited by N Ropers and T Debiel. (Bonn: Stiftung Entwicklung und Frieden).

Hoywegen, Saskia van 2000. *From human(itarian) disaster to development success? The case of Rwanda.* (Brussels: Centre of African Studies, Consortium for political Emergencies (COPE)).

Jean, Francois 1994. *Helfer im Kreuzfeuer. Humanitäre Hilfe und militärische Intervention. Ein Report über Völker in Not.* (Bonn: Dietz Nachfolger).

Klute, Georg 1999. Vom Krieg zum Frieden im Norden von Mali. In *Afrika und die Globalisierung,* edited by H P Hahn and G Spittler. Hamburg, Münster, London: Lit.

Klute, Georg, and Trutz von Trotha. 2000. *Roads to peace. From small war to parastatal peace in the North of Mali.* Paper presented at the conference 'Cicatriser les violences'. Oñati 3–4.4.2000.

Köppe, Rüdiger and Wilhelm J G Möhlig. 2000. *Concepts of violence and peace in African languages.* Paper presented at the conference 'Cicatriser les violences'. Oñati 3–4.4.2000.

Krumwiede, Heinrich-W 1998. Regulierungsmöglichkeiten von Bürgerkriegen — Fragen und Hypothesen. In *Bürgerkriege: Folgen und Regulierungs möglichkeiten,* edited by H-W Krumwiede and P Waldmann. (Baden Baden: Nomos).

Krumwiede, Heinrich-W and Peter Waldmann, eds, 1998. *Bürgerkriege: Folgen und Regulierungsmöglichkeiten*. (Baden Baden: Nomos Verlagsgesellschaft).

Kühne, Winrich 1998. Post-conflict peace-building: Aufgaben, Erfahrungen, Lehren und Empfehlungen für die Praxis. In *Bürgerkriege: Folgen und Regulierungsmöglichkeiten*, edited by H-W Krumwiede and P Waldmann. (Baden Baden: Nomos).

Lederach, John Paul 1995. Conflict transformation in protracted internal conflicts. The case for a comprehensive network. In *Conflict Transformation*, edited by K Rupesinghe (New York: St Martin's).

Macamo, Elísio and Dieter Neubert 2004. The politics of negative peace: Mozambique in the aftermath of the Rome cease-fire agreement. *Portuguese Literary and Cultural Studies* 10: 23–47.

Matthies, Volker 1999. Krisenprävention als Friedenspolitik. Zur Entstehung und Entwicklung eines neuen politischen Konzepts. *E+Z Entwicklung und Zusammenarbeit 40 (4):* 103–6.

Neubert, Dieter 1997a. *Entwicklungspolitische Hoffnungen und gesellschaftliche Wirklichkeit. Eine vergleichende Länderfallstudie von Nicht-Regierungsorganisationen in Kenia und Ruanda.* (Frankfurt aM, New York: Campus).

Neubert, Dieter 1997b. Development utopia re-visited. Non-governmental organisations in Africa. *Sociologus 4:* 51–77.

Papendieck, Henner, and Barbara Rocksloh-Papendieck. 2000. *Peace and aid. The 'Programme Mali-Nord' and the search for peace in Northern Mali.* Paper presented at the conference 'Cicatriser les violences'. Oñati 3–4.4.2000.

Pfaffenholz, Thania 1998. *Konflikttransformation durch Vermittlung. Theoretische und praktische Erkenntnisse aus dem Friedensprozeß in Mosambik (1976–1995).* (Mainz: Matthias-Grünewald-Verlag).

Pfaffenholz, Thania 2002. *Stärkung von Friedensallianzen.* (Eschborn: Universum Verlagsanstalt).

Plessis, Willemien du 2000. *The South African truth and reconciliation commission: 'The truth will set you free'.* Paper presented at the conference 'Cicatriser les violences'. Oñati 3–4.4.2000.

Reissner, Johannes 1998. Der Bürgerkrieg in Tadschikistan. In *Bürgerkriege: Folgen und Regulierungsmöglichkeiten*, edited by H-W Krumwiede and P Waldmann. (Baden Baden: Nomos).

Reyntjens, Filip 1990. Le gacaca ou la justice du gazon au Rwanda. *Politique Africaine (40):* 31–41.

Richards, Paul 1996a. War & youth in Sierra Leone. Insurgency in the context of globalisation. In *Staat und Gesellschaft in Afrika. Erosions— und Reformprozesse*, edited by P Meyns. (Hamburg: Lit).

Richards, Paul 1996b. *Fighting for the rain forest: youth, war and resources in Sierra Leone.* (Oxford, Portsmouth NH: James Currey, Heinemann).

Ropers, Norbert 1997. Prävention und Friedenkonsolidierung als Aufgabe für gesellschaftliche Akteure. In *Frieden machen*, edited by D Senghaas. (Frankfurt aM: Suhrkamp).

Ropers, Norbert and Tobias Debiel, eds 1995. *Friedliche Konfliktbearbeitung in der Staaten- und Gesellschaftswelt.* (Bonn: Stiftung Entwicklung und Frieden).

Rupesinghe, Kumar. 1995. Transformation innerstaatlicher Konflikte. Von den 'Problemlösungs-Workshops' zu Friedensallianzen. In *Friedliche Konfliktbearbeitung in der Staaten- und Gesellschaftswelt*, edited by N Ropers and T Debiel. (Bonn: Stiftung Entwicklung und Frieden).

Scherrer, Christian P 1996. *Justice in Rwanda after the genocide. A national and international response.* (Tegelen: Institute for Research on Ethnicity and Conflict Resolution (ECOR)).

Schmieg, Evita 1997. Krisenvorbeugung durch Entwicklungszusammenarbeit? *E+Z Entwicklung und Zusammenarbeit 38:* 10.

Schmieg, Evita 1998. Krisenprävention durch Entwicklungszusammenarbeit? Instrumente der deutschen Entwicklungspolitik und die Bedeutung einer strengen Rüstungsexportpolitik. In *Gewaltsame Konflikte und ihre Prävention in Afrika,* edited by U Engel and A Mehler. (Hamburg: Institut für Afrika-Kunde).

Senghaas, Dieter 1994. *Wohin triftet die Dritte Welt?* (Frankfurt aM: Suhrkamp).

Strecker, Ivo 1999. The temptations of war and the struggle for peace among the Hamar. In *Dynamics of violence. Processes of escalation and de-escalation of violent group conflicts. Sociologus supplement 1,* edited by G Elwert, S Feuchtwang, and D Neubert. (Berlin: Duncker & Humblot).

Trotha, Trutz von 2000. *Introduction.* Paper presented at the conference 'Cicatriser les violences'. Oñati 3–4.4.2000.

United Nations 2000. *Report of the panel on United Nations peace operations.* (New York: United Nations).

Vogt, Wolfgang R 1999. *Friedenskultur statt Kulturkampf. Strategien kultureller Zivilisierung und nachhaltiger Friedensstiftung.* (Baden Baden: Nomos).

Volmer, Ludger 1999. Für einen integrativen Ansatz von Krisenprävention und ziviler Konfliktbearbeitung. *E+Z Entwicklung und Zusammenarbeit 40 (4):* 100–2.

Waldmann, Peter 1998a. Bürgerkrieg - Annäherung an einen schwer fassbaren Begriff. In *Bürgerkriege: Folgen und Regulierungsmöglichkeiten,* edited by H-W Krumwiede and P Waldmann. (Baden Baden: Nomos).

Waldmann, Peter 1998b. Eigendynamik und Folgen von Bürgerkriegen. In *Bürgerkriege: Folgen und Regulierungsmöglichkeiten,* edited by H-W Krumwiede and P Waldmann. (Baden Baden: Nomos).

Waldmann, Peter 1999. Societies in civil war. In *Dynamics of violence. Processes of escalation and de-escalation in violent group conflicts. Sociologus supplement 1,* edited by G Elwert, S Feuchtwang, and D Neubert. (Berlin: Duncker & Humblot).

Weilenmann, M not dated. *Le gacaca ou la justice du gazon au Rwanda. Einige kritische Anmerkungen zu einem Artikel von Filip Reyntjens.* Eschborn: Unpublished position paper for the GTZ (Gesellschaft für technische Zusammenarbeit).

Weimer, Bernhard 1998. Frieden in Mosambik: Bedingungen seines Zustandekommens und seiner Nachhaltigkeit. In *Bürgerkriege: Folgen und Regulierungsmöglichkeiten,* edited by H-W Krumwiede and P Waldmann. (Baden Baden: Nomos).

Weiß, Anja 1997. Insider NGOs as a key to developing peace constituencies in new Eastern democracies. *Peace and Security 29:* 37–45.

Weiß, Anja 1999. Friedenallianzen schaffen — Konzepte und Dilemmata einer Unterstützung von außen. In *Friedenskultur statt Kulturkampf. Strategien kultureller Zivilisierung und nachhaltiger Friedensstiftung,* edited by W R Vogt. (Baden Baden: Nomos).

Whitman, Jim and David Pocock, eds 1996. *After Rwanda: The coordination of United Nations humanitarian assistance.* (New York, London: St Martin's Press, Macmillan Press).

Wieczorek-Zeul, Heidemarie 1999. Entwicklungspolitik als Friedenspolitik (Interview). *E+Z Entwicklung und Zusammenarbeit 40 (1):* 8–10.

Wilhelm, Jürgen 1999. Ziviler Friedensdienst. Eine neue Aufgabe für den DED. *E+Z Entwicklung und Zusammenarbeit 40 (2):* 32–3.

Zartman, I William. 1985. *Ripe for resolution. Conflict and intervention in Africa.* (New York, Oxford: Oxford University Press).

Zartman, I William, ed 2000. *Traditional cures for modern conflicts. African conflict 'medicine'.* (Boulder, London: Lynne Rienner Publications).

I

Appendix

Table 1: Types of violent group conflicts (all combinations possible)

| | International | National ('civil wars') / crossing of borders possible | | | International | (Not linked to a type of conflict) |
| | Centralised bi-polar | | Decentralised multi-polar | | | |
	International war	'Classical' civil war	Local inter-community conflicts (eg feuds, raiding, urban communal conflicts)	Warlordism	International terrorism	
Typical actors (warring parties)	Nation states	Political factions, usually one governmental and one oppositional	Local warrior and defence communities, urban communalistic groups (eg ethnic, religious)	Political and economic entrepreneurs who draw their power from violence of armed forces (warlords)	Ideologically based clandestine networks vs 'systems' (capitalism, the West) represented by nation states and/or companies	Mercenary and security companies
Example	Ethiopian-Eritrean war	US civil war, Biafra war	Turkana-Pokot conflict, Christian–Muslim conflict (Northern Nigeria)	Liberia, Sierra Leone	El Quaida, red cells	Cabinda
(Political) objectives	Control over state and territory	Control over state and territory	Enrichment, honour, fame, identity, control over limited local territory, self-defence	Enrichment, political influence, sometimes control of limited local or regional territory	Destabilizaton of hegemonic economic, cultural and political power, foundation of a new system	Profit, as representatives of their clients control over small defined sites
Main types of fighting and violence, weaponry	Battle, high-tech weaponry	Battle, guerrilla warfare, raids, terrorism, varied types of weaponry	Raids and defence against raids and attacks, simple weaponry	Raids, guerrilla warfare, terrorism, kidnapping, simple weaponry	Terrorism, usually low-tech bombs, hijacking, may be supplemented by high-tech logistics	Varied, focus on high-tech activities and security of sites, industrial or mining plants, high-tech weaponry

Table 1 Continued…

Table 1 Continued...

	International	National ('civil wars') / crossing of borders possible			International	(Not linked to a type of conflict)
	Centralised bi-polar		Decentralised multi-polar			
	International war	'Classical' civil war	Local inter-community conflicts (eg feuds, raiding, urban communal conflicts)	Warlordism	International terrorism	
Resources for fighting	Taxes and all sources of government income, sometimes donations	Donations, 'taxes' from followers, booty	Booty, sometimes also smuggling, drug trafficking, tax from followers	Booty, protection money, smuggling, drug traffic, ransom, natural resources (diamonds, gold, oil)	Donations, robbery, smuggling, ransom	Contractual payments
Professionalisation of fighters	Full-time, military service, professionals, volunteers	Full-time, professionals, volunteers, military service possible	Part-time, volunteers	Full- and part-time, (semi-) professionals, volunteers, recruitment by coercion	Full- and part-time, (semi-) professionals, volunteers	Full-time, professionals
Authority and command structure co-ordination of strategy	Centralised military hierarchy, co-ordinated strategy	Centralised military hierarchy, co-ordinated strategy, sometimes decentralised fighting units	Local fighting units no co-ordination, (hierarchy depends on local political organisation)	Fighting units with strong hierarchy, tendency to split up, no co-ordination between units	Variable from hierarchy, co-ordinated strategy, to autonomy of units (cells)	Fighting units with strong hierarchy
Links: fighters–population	Strong, fighting for and defending defined population	Strong, fighting for and defending defined population	Strong, fighting for and defending defined population	Weak, fighters fighting for themselves	Direct links weak, but committed constituency of radical supporters possible	Weak, military specialists fight and act for paying customers
'Ethics of war'	Formally yes, can be suspended	Yes, can be suspended, anomie likely	Yes, varying locally defined, enemies may be excluded	No, anomie likely	Claiming ethics linked to ideological bias, external view: no ethics of war	Varying, depending on company
Extreme war crimes	Likely	Frequent	Infrequent	Frequent	Frequent	Likely

Table 2: Peace-building in different types of violent group conflicts

| | International | | National ('civil wars') / crossing of borders possible | | International | (Not linked to a type of conflict) |
| | Centralised bi-polar | | | Decentralised multi-polar | | |
	International war	'Classical' civil war	Local inter-community conflicts (eg feuds, urban raiding, communal conflicts)	Warlordism	International terrorism	Mercenary and Security companies
Recognisable conflicting parties	Yes	Yes, sometimes weak organisation	Changing frequently, weakly organised	Changing frequently, weakly organised	Clandestine terror networks hard to identify	Yes
Leaders for negotiation available	Yes, political and military leaders	Mostly, political and military leaders, sometimes disputed	Mostly, local notables (depending on local political organisation)	Yes, warlords, followers not clearly defined	In principle yes, but negotiation unlikely	Yes, company executives, but clients in the background
Control over military action / end of fighting, demobilization and acceptance of monopoly of violence by order	Strong / likely	Strong or medium / some consent from fighters required	Varying / varying (depending on local political organisation)	Weak / no reliable order, consent from fighters required	Medium, consent of fighters needed, risk of fission / unlikely	Medium (hidden clients' interest) / depending on payment and attitude of the company
Links: fighters–population	Strong, fighting for and defending defined population	Strong, fighting for and defending defined population	Strong, fighting for and defending defined population	Weak, fighters fighting for themselves	Direct links weak, but committed constituency of radical supporters possible,	Weak, military specialists fight and act for paying customers
Influence of population over leaders	Yes, some popular support needed	Yes, popular support needed	Yes, popular support needed	No, popular support not needed	No, popular support claimed but not needed	No, popular support needed

Table 2 Continued…

Table 2 Continued...

	International	National ('civil wars') / crossing of borders possible				International	(Not linked to a type of conflict)
	Centralised bi-polar			Decentralised multi-polar			
	International war	'Classical' civil war	Local inter-community conflicts (eg feuds, raiding, urban communal conflicts)	Warlordism	International terrorism	Mercenary and Security companies
Security interests	Territorial sovereignty, security for own population and for ex-fighters	Territorial sovereignty, security for own population and for ex-fighters	Local autonomy, security for own population, security for ex-fighters	Political or economic position for leaders, security for ex-fighters	Security for leaders and ex-fighters	Keeping contracts, securing payments, security for ex-fighters
Political and economic incentives for peace (leaders)	Political and economic power	Political and economic power, sometimes political/economic advancement for the population	Honour, political and economic reward, sometimes political/economic advancement for the population	Political and economic power	Probably political or economic positions for leaders	Payment, professional recognition
Political and economic incentives for peace (fighters)	Honour, integration in security forces, social status, economic reward	Honour, integration in security forces, social status economic reward, sometimes political/economic advancement for the population	Honour, social status, economic reward, sometimes political/economic advancement for the population	Honour, social status (hardly given), economic reward, (integration in security forces)	Return to ordinary life	Payment, professional recognition

Part II

Power, Structures, Processes, and History in the Reconstruction of Peace

The Reconstruction of Peace I: African Experiences

5

Peace and Aid: The 'Programme Mali Nord' and the Search for Peace in Northern Mali

HENNER PAPENDIECK AND
BARBARA ROCKSLOH-PAPENDIECK

1   BACKGROUND

1 1   Introduction

THE NORTH OF Mali consists of three regions: Tombouctou (6th), Gao (7th) and Kidal (8th). One and a half million people live there, most of them as nomadic cattle herders, farmers or fishermen, besides traders and craftsmen in the small country towns. Droughts in the 1970s and 1980s and population growth have increased competition for useful natural resources. Demands for autonomy set the Tuareg rebellion of 1990 in motion. This rebellion led to a civil war. The *pacte national* of 1992 put a preliminary end to this war. Implementation of the *pacte* met with resistance and it came to a grinding halt. The armed conflict started again and ended only at the beginning of 1995. Representatives of the conflicting groups managed to negotiate how to contain the conflict. They conceived a new beginning of civil life in the North. To the west of Tombouctou, the region most affected by the conflict, this happened with the assistance of the 'Programme Mali-Nord'.

The infrastructure was destroyed: wells, water installations, administrative buildings, schools, health posts and roads. They had to be (re)constructed. The administration had ceased to operate. It needed help to start functioning again and to prepare for planned start of local government: the date of the first communal elections in the North was repeatedly delayed; they finally took place in June 1999.

The population had to create a new basis for its survival. The surrounding ecological zone offers only marginal chances of success even in peaceful times. The parts of the Niger valley regularly flooded by the river are decreasing. Water levels are declining. The traditional methods of semi-wetland agriculture no longer provide food security. The population has to switch to modern forms of irrigation (by motor pumps) and production of cash crops (rice, wheat). The nomadic part of the population has to fundamentally change its life style and settle down.

The Malian-German bilateral 'Programme Mali-Nord' was created in 1993 to accompany this process. The two authors manage this program since its beginning. For a period of ten years (1994 to 2004) fifty million Euro are being invested into reconstructing the public infrastructure and creating an economic basis for peaceful cohabitation.

1 2   Our Role and Perceptions

For a number of years there has been growing interest by policy makers in conflict resolution or — even better — prevention. We are often asked: How do you have to go about it? What conclusions do you draw from your experience? The generally applicable policy conclusions are simple and self-evident, truly 'Binsenweisheiten': Listen to the people, let people participate, let all parties concerned benefit equally etc. There is hardly any point in writing them down. The secret lies in the particularities. This chapter is designed to describe some of them.

We want to describe our thoughts and strategies since the summer of 1993. We do not argue on an objective, national or a regional level. We argue from a strictly personal perspective: What were the options? At which point in time did we propose or choose which option and for what reasons? What were the results?

Neither of us speaks any of the vernacular languages. We have no preference for any ethnic group concerned. Neither of us had ever done any research on or read much about conflict resolution. We therefore had to adopt a policy of common sense based on our personal experience in working and negotiating (in our professional, public and private life, within our own society and family) and we had to listen and follow people who knew or seemed to know what to do.

Neither of us had any previous knowledge of the zone of intervention. We had to accept the narrow limits of our knowledge and, therefore, had to adopt an indirect approach, a kind of 'fuzzy logic'. You have to act (by enabling others to act) without knowing exactly and down to the last detail what happens and you check the results by relatively vague indicators.

We came with a rather romantic idea of 'peace' being equal to social harmony, a society where people want to live with one another. We were surprised by the common notion that people felt *condamné à vivre ensemble*. But this is what it is. Peace is the absence of war, violence and abuse.

People continue to have prejudices towards each other, first and foremost against their neighbours. Knowledge of the other does not necessarily create love and friendship but often animosity and hostility. This is not only true along ethnic borders but also class and cast boundaries.

1 3   The Zone of Intervention and the Aims of the Program

The first German mission concerning the North Mali Program arrived in September 1993. They met with the *Commissaire au Nord*, an institution attached to the President's Office created to contain the conflict of the North (Tuareg rebellion) and to manage pacification. In talks with the various institutions of the Malian government, the representatives of some of the *mouvements*, the Non-Governmental Organisations (NGOs) and the donors it became evident, that there was one big unattended problem to the West of Tombouctou. Here the rebellion had created a no-man's land stretching from Tombouctou to the Mauritanian border.

Around forty thousand Tuareg and Arabs had fled to refugee camps in the East of Mauritania, the rest had fled to inaccessible parts of the bush or the desert within Malian territory. The black population, mainly Bellah (around sixty thousand) had left the zone to take refuge near the army camps in the larger cities (mainly Goundam). The zone was deserted not only by the people but by the administration too. Why not use the German contribution to help reconstruct this zone, which presented the biggest problem?

The Malian government found this proposal difficult to swallow. Mali proposed distributing the funds either by sectors: health, education etc, or by regions — one third of the funds for each. Neither proposal seemed good or just. The Germans insisted and suggested that others had already chosen their focus of attention elsewhere (eg the French in Gao, the Norwegians in the Gourma, FIDA in Kidal) or could do the same in other parts of the North.

The intention was to avoid watering down the intervention, to conduct a multisectoral (multidisciplinary) program and finally to anchor the program locally and to make its impact more durable. It paid to be stubborn: activities were finally concentrated on the region between Tombouctou and Mauritania.

The zone of intervention represents a number of traditional economic and social spaces. It is a zone largely flooded by the river Niger, almost inaccessible for many months of the year. Only local populations know which means of transport to utilise at which time of the season (during the rains, during the drought, during the floods). All activities were therefore — and for many other reasons — based on local knowledge.

The aims of the program were defined mutually:

— to help to bring about peace through dialogue,
— to assist in repatriating refugees (from the camps in Mauritania)
— to repatriate internally displaced persons (refugees within Mali without any official refugee status),
— to provide emergency aid,
— to combine short term measures with investments to develop the economic potential of the zone,
— to help reconstruct public infrastructure in the zone and (later),
— to bring about economic conditions enhancing peace instead of conflict.

1 4   First Orientation

In June 1994 the slow and hesitant process of integrating former combatants into the Malian army came to an abrupt halt. Niafunké and other small country towns were attacked on the 6 June. This started the most violent part of the rebellion and the most systematic repression (and ethnic cleansing campaign) against Tuareg and Arabs.

One month later, in July 1994, when we arrived in Mali, the region was inaccessible; we could only stay in Bamako. War was engaged. The number of refugees in the camps in Mauritania doubled from the middle to the end of 1994. It was hard to find out what was happening. Attitudes towards the Tuareg were extremely hostile. We could only try to establish what went on through contacts within the *Commissariat au Nord*.

All news from the North was censured. This was when we established contact with the man who later became and still is our national co-ordinator. He was a Tuareg from the zone.

Our depression grew until November 1994. On 4 October soldiers had killed the director of the Swiss Cooperation during his project visit to Niafunké. From then the region was off limits to foreigners. Our stay in Mali seemed futile and our role ambivalent. Hysteria swept Bamako. We were made to understand: our contacts with Tuareg were being registered and we should cut them out.

It was our counterpart at the *Commissariat au Nord* who encouraged us to stay.

> The fact that you take an interest is being perceived as an act of solidarity. Stay here, this conflict will not last forever and you will be much needed as soon as it is over.

The German authorities felt the same and also encouraged us to stay.

1 5   In the Refugee Camps

As we could not visit the North of Mali we decided to get an authentic picture of the situation in the Mauritanian refugee camps. This is what we did at the end of 1994. We went to Bassikounou, four hundred km north of Bamako, where the largest of the three camps was situated. Our arrival there coincided with the arrival of totally exhausted refugees who had narrowly escaped the massacre of Amoskor (near Niafunké) in November.

We talked with individuals and groups in all of the three camps. We were confronted with a refugee population who had thoroughly adopted their refugee status: no income, no responsibility. They were thinking and talking only of their rights and awaited the next food distribution while drinking their tea. We found it difficult to talk to them and assured them: Nobody in the world cared much about their fate out here and in Bamako people were more concerned about where to go dancing on a Saturday evening then about Tuareg or Arab refugees in Mauritania. Many would hope they would stay there for good.

The message of the Tuareg refugees was loud and clear. They were glad to have found refuge in Mauritania. But this was not their country. They did not speak the language. They did not wish to stay here and would like to return to Mali but they needed a guarantee of safety from the Malian government. If Germany had given funds to help them return we should invest them in Mali to facilitate their return.

We tried to formulate our own message with similar clarity: If they did nothing about changing their status, nobody else would. If they were willing to change their attitude, willing to invest themselves and develop plans how to return to their individual sites, we would be there to help them. This happened much sooner than all of us expected then.

1 6   Where to Begin

We had been discussing at length how to bring about peace in the zone concerned. Throughout the conflict there had remained pockets, where Tuareg stayed next to their black neighbours. Douékiré (in the East) and Léré (in the West) were the main points, from where one could start.

Léré was much easier to reach and had two main advantages: first it was nearby and accessible for the refugees in the camps, secondly it had a special status. The first group of integrated former combatants of the *Mouvement Populaire de l'Azawad* (MPA) was stationed there under the command of an integrated commander from Kidal. They guaranteed security for everybody, against the other movements, against the bandits and against army repression. They were not entirely integrated into the army; they were denied access to vehicles (especially the tanks) and ammunition.

But they were on site, they were armed, they knew the territory and they effectively controlled the area.

This is why the weekly market in Léré (every Friday) remained open throughout the conflict. Courageous leaders of the Tuareg population in the Mauritanian camps used this opportunity to continually check the social and political temperature.

From January 1995 to April 1995 we used the convoys from the military camp in Diabally to go to Léré. In Léré we camped on the terrace of the empty and destroyed house of the *chef d'arrondissement*. On this terrace, guarded by integrated former combatants we received representatives of those technical services (education, health, veterinary service) still present and representatives of the population (village chiefs and elders).

We encouraged them to visit their places of origin, to talk to their former neighbours and to see how they could prepare their return home. A number of leaders took us up on this. Mineni, a Tuareg chef from the southern Mema (around hundred km south of Léré) went on a number of *tours de sensibilisation* in the Fulani areas in the East and in the South. The reports of these meetings talked of crowds of people around the houses where discussions were going on, all trying to listen to what was going on inside.

These tours were possible in selected areas only. Léré was surrounded by something we called a 'cordon of hate'. The regular army created and controlled this cordon along the main routes. It was the *gendarmerie* that maintained it on the routes that had been completely cut off for years.

By using them, first with military escorts, later without them, we reopened these routes. The principal means of eroding the cordon of hate was to carefully enlarge the zone of peaceful exchange by peaceful means: dialogue. Many descriptions of these first encounters talked of great emotional scenes and people embracing each other spontaneously.

Further North the situation presented itself differently. This zone was depopulated and insecure. Groups of rebels and bandits circulated there. The army did not patrol this zone. Most of the villages were deserted. The small remaining population had fled deep into the bush. How could one open this space?

2   WORKING FOR RECONCILIATION

2 1   Creating a Socio-Political Network

In discussing strategies it was the second deputy *Commissaire au Nord*, who suggested creating a network comprising the leaders of our zone of intervention. Three of them, he said, were essential to overcome the divide in the district of Goundam. These three key people had not seen and spoken to each other for more than four years (since the outbreak of the rebellion).

The former *chef de tribu* of the Kel Antesar, the most important Tuareg clan, had been in local and regional politics since colonial time. For many years he was one of the two deputies for the district of Goundam and administrator. He represented the Tuareg population. His opposite number, the second former deputy for Goundam, a teacher by profession and member of the US–RDA, represented the Songhoi population. The national planning director in Mali, son of the former *chef de terres* (within the system of the Kel Antesar) represented the Bellah population in this region.

It was on our premises in Bamako that they met with and spoke to each other again for the first time in the early summer of 1995. They have remained members of our *Comité Consultatif* since then. The creation of this network was essential before undertaking the next steps. They were formulated in the presence of all partners. Songhoi and Bellah could easily have interpreted entry into the deserted zone as an act of aggression.

The Program's consultative committee meets without a formal voting system, the members do not receive any remuneration or privileges; there are no minutes of our meetings, there is just an agenda and everybody remembers what was discussed and recommended. There is no quorum; those present say what they think. There has never been a misunderstanding on any procedural issue since the beginning. The members of the committee are co-opted and remain members even during long absences. Since 1995 only one member of the committee ceased to be invited to meetings. The other members were the former deputy for Diré and chief of the dominant Tuareg fraction in Diré, and the founder of the only ethnic party, the RAMAT (Bellah).

The committee served to define strategies and share power among the communities. Everybody had the right to propose his candidate for the basic studies (field visits, proposal of strategy), for the site of the appropriate outlet of our program and for personnel. We did not know the area and simply followed (and participated in) the discussions. We accepted almost all of the suggestions. We never had to change any major decision, neither for a site, nor for our personnel.

The same principal of sharing power was applied when establishing our local outlets. Each town or village has its own social and communications structure. The district towns were the most difficult. It took a long time to settle disputes about the access of the competing political parties, social pressure groups and/or families of influence. Generally we pursued an open-door policy and allowed access to more or less everybody. In some cases this led to complete chaos. In Goundam, we had to seek order by officially and systematically asking the village chief, the *Imam* (religious chief) and the nobles to settle the issue and to suggest an informal group who would represent the interests of the town, village or district vis-à-vis our program.

Only parts of the administration ever accepted the rather marginal role reserved for them. The fact that we had preceded them in many cases helped. We had started to implement a policy of local government long before the rural communes were created. Many of today's *conseillers communaux* are the same people who acted as our intermediaries before. The official introduction of decentralisation and the creation of the new rural communes have not changed our way of operating.

2 2   Creating the Physical Network

Under cover of this consultative committee our program expanded its network in the field to the North of Léré. Aratène, a place in the middle of the bush was chosen by the Kel Antesar as their point of re-entry into Mali. We established our second 'antenna' there. All the others followed from the end of 1995 to 1997: Gargando, Goundam, Diré, Farach, M'Bouna, Raz El Mâ, Tin Aicha, Attara and Karal. In this way the empty space was repopulated and the physical network finally covered our zone of intervention relatively evenly.

Any such antenna consists of a house plus courtyard(s) with office, safe, solar energy, water, *chambre de passage*, storing facilities for food and other items, tools etc but also transport (vehicle, motorcycles and/or boat) and radio communication. This meant the end of isolation and increased security.

Tense moments occurred at the opening of the outlet of Aratène in the summer of 1995. Our presence there cut the bandits off. Our *chef d'antenne* received death threats and for weeks troops of the MPA guarded this establishment. Tense moments occurred again before the opening of our antenna in M'Bouna, because the last active remnants of *Ganda Koy*, the counter-rebellion movement of the Songhoi, created in 1994, operated on Lake Faguibine and prevented us from settling there.

The most important point in creating the physical network was when the bridge was made from the nomadic zone in the West to the sedentary zone in the East. Once this bridge was formed, confidence started to grow rapidly. People from both sides had continuous contact. They were part of the same network of information, services and funds and had equal access to it.

2 3   Intercommunity Meetings

It would not have been possible to bridge the two zones without a series of meetings preparing the ground. These meetings were not conceived or proposed by us. We simply funded them and discussed their contours, mainly with the parties taking part in them.

The first and probably most decisive of these meetings was a small one. It took place while conflict was still intense in the Tombouctou region.

The meeting of Aghlal (near Tombouctou) in May 1995 brought together Tuareg and representatives of Ganda Koy in the valley of the Niger. Circumstances were difficult. The Tuareg delegation had to take river transport from Mopti onwards; they had to hide during the trip and had to stay outside the towns and villages along the riverbank during the night.

The *round table* of Tombouctou in early July 1995 tried to reassure the donor community that things were on track and funds should be forthcoming now. It was financed by UNDP. Our own contribution was to rent a number of lorries from Mauritania. They permitted refugees from the camps to take part in the deliberations of the various sections (security, development etc), to raise their voice and to take the social temperature. The leaders of two communities decided to take the risk and return to Mali immediately with their families: Dofana (forty km east of Niafunké) and Tin Telout (twenty km west of Tombouctou). They were in a hurry. They wanted to catch the ongoing irrigation season starting in August.

It was shortly after this *round table* that a committee of nobles from Goundam suggested preparing an intercommunity meeting in M'Bouna. They had been seeking funds from the government. Their request had been set aside. They were determined and prepared.

What was our role? We financed it; that was the most important point — it finally cost roughly twenty-five thousand Euro. But we also wanted to know who was going to be invited. It had been designed — it soon turned out — as a meeting between Songhoi and Tuareg. We suggested inviting the Fulani population of the Tyoki and Lac Télé; this was accepted. We suggested inviting refugees from Mauritania; accepted too. We suggested inviting the Bellah population exiled around Goundam and Lac Horo; that was harder to swallow, but finally was accepted too. The point that seemed most difficult even to understand was why we insisted on the participation of women. They were already foreseen for preparing the meals in the kitchens. Women's groups too participated in the end.

The meeting surpassed all expectations. A few hundred people had been invited. More than two thousand came. There was an acute shortage of water; people had to sleep on the dunes. But they came: by foot, on donkey back, on camels or by car. And they organised one big feast. The meetings of the two working groups (security and development) produced the usual lists of needs. It was the atmosphere that mattered. There was music, dancing and singing. Theatre performances at night gave parodies of the warring parties and the audience laughingly released the tensions of the past. This meeting signalled the end of the conflict around Lac Faguibine and evened the way for the return of forty thousand people around its shores.

A series of meetings of a similar kind and smaller scale followed in the Gourma of the Tombouctou region, in Gao, Menaka and Kidal. They became a characteristic of the peace process in Mali. We continued to finance them (on a much smaller, local level) for almost two years.

3   ECONOMICS OF PEACE

3 1   The Dynamics of the Economic Emergency

Engaging in an economic emergency program turned out to be an experience like passing the straits of a river. Once you have embarked on it, there is no turning back, you can only look forward and manage problems as they come along.

When we started, we had very limited funds indeed. Funds we did not have we simply had to find. The institutional environment turned out to be friendly. The international community was highly aware of the risks involved and there was a political will to resolve the situation.

We soon started to act as a kind of clearing house between those who sought aid and those who could offer it. Contacts with the UNHCR, with ECHO and WFP were taken up in Mali, not in Europe. Programs were formulated in the field or at least in Bamako. It was the flexibility of the partners that made this possible. The fastest action by far was the emergency food aid granted by the BMZ in 1997/98. It took only weeks to have the funds available in Mali.

We rarely had the privilege of quiet reflection before taking decisions. We normally had to act before having the whole picture. We had to manage risks and had to seek the most plausible solutions. Decisions had to be taken relatively fast (although there was always the time for thorough reflection) and absolutely clearly. The parties concerned had to be fully aware of the exact content, limits and mutual engagements of the decision. That was the most time consuming part during the years 1995 until 1997. Leaders of refugee groups often had unrealistic ideas of the kind, form and extent of assistance to be granted by us. Negotiations always ended in contracts, wherever possible in written contracts that were read out and thoroughly translated (plus interpreted) before signature. The intention was to create something mutually binding, which we of course could not enforce, but we could tie our continued support to the other party's honouring the engagements. This created, we think, an important element of transparency and reliability.

In all emergencies we tried to establish needs in the immediate, short, medium and long term and aimed for the greatest compatibility. Quite often this did not cause much delay, only a decentralised form of organisation with a strong emphasis on the local level. An example: during a threatening famine around Lac Faguibine in 1997/98 eight hundred tons of cereals were delivered to the villages and hamlets not by truck but on donkey back. The villagers were paid a small sum for collecting them. It might have taken a few days longer for the cereals to arrive at the village level, but it mobilised the population and injected the price of transport into the local economy.

Preference for allocation was local before regional solutions and national before international solutions. In situations of food crisis we preferred to buy millet or sorghum at the next reasonably available source (the regions of Segou or Mopti) and asked local transporters and merchants to submit tenders. They often provided the best value for money, because they knew the local routes and conditions best.

We followed an entrepreneurial approach. The main aim of the project was to repatriate the people, to settle them at their sites of origin and to get the economy working again to allow the population to find gainful employment and cut down the refugee assistance programs. The program was prepared to help get any natural, political, social or economic obstacle out of the way. If things came to a grinding halt, because of the drought, because of invasions of rats, birds, locusts, because of hot winds, political strife, social unrest or economic crisis, any means to clear the way were contemplated and a broad range of measures financed.

An economy does not progress in big leaps but in incremental steps. It was important to inject the funds not only where it most mattered and where the push was most needed but in the right quantities and at the most even rate possible.

3 2   The Economic Cycle

The traditional local economy follows the annual cycle of rainy and dry seasons and every local item has its right moment of production within this cycle. One can't build houses during the rains, one can't produce bricks during the dry season, and cereals are bought immediately after the harvest, and so on. The outlets of the program tried to breathe with their locality and to adopt their individual rhythm. All along the valley of the Niger River bulk deliveries are only possible during the high floods (by boat) or during the low floods (by lorry). They are either impossible or extremely difficult and expensive during all other parts of the year. It took some years to understand the rhythm, to become part of the various local societies and economies and to be able to move the population towards respecting the agricultural calendar diligently.

Provisions often had to be made months in advance. Almost all construction in the region depends on the timely delivery of *moellon*, stones from the bed of the river Niger, found in two places only. These stones have to be lifted from the bed of the river when the water level is down and to be delivered to the places of construction when the level rises.

We tried to apply the same principles to food aid, an important part of the project in its early phase: buy locally, store locally, provide and store in time and use food aid to produce food. From the end of 1995 until the beginning of 2000 we experienced at last three major local food crises.

By applying these simple strategies they were mastered by delivering relatively small quantities of food aid (altogether circa five thousand tons of cereals) at the reasonable average cost of less than three hundred Euro per ton delivered where the aid was needed. Most of the food aid served directly to maintain the population during the planting season.

3 3   Local Knowledge

The geography of the project region is extremely varied. Nothing can be planned without the people who are concerned and who know the area. Little can be planned by the calendar in advance. The local people have to watch water levels and can start working in flooded areas only once the water has receded.

We soon learned not to do what we thought was right, but always to listen to the population and try to regard things their way. Nothing we started was new to the region. People have a vivid memory of local developments over two or three generations. They know what works, for what reasons and what doesn't work.

We learned to keep aims clear and simple. The multicultural and lingual composition of the region's population turned out to be helpful in this respect. Communication is cut down to essential factual information. Nuance and finesse of language gets lost in local meetings (mostly held in Songhoi) when everything has to be translated in Tamasheck, Arab or French. We came to opt for simple local solutions and simple formulas.

This strategy allowed for the regular injection of relatively large sums of money into the local economy and in the medium term it created the dynamics of sustained local economic growth. But this strategy had its obvious handicaps too. Local knowledge did not allow for much innovation. Over the years we locally bought tens of thousands of hoes around Lac Faguibine, but we never introduced any technical innovation in their local production, which might well have been possible, if that had been the aim.

3 4   Reviving Local Economic Circuits

The rebellion and its repercussions had interrupted or partly destroyed the network of local exchanges. Their destruction had already begun during the two disastrous droughts in the 1970s and the 1980s. Any economic revival in one locality depended on the revival of the other exchange centres within the region. Generally speaking, the local economy in the project region functions by weekly local markets. Here, the exchange takes place between the nomadic and the sedentary population, between the towns and the villages, between the North and the South, the East and the West and finally between the neighbouring countries, in our case between the North of Mali, Mauritania and Algeria.

The weekly markets are connected with each other in overlapping triangles. Any group of traders can cover three weekly markets on average and carries it merchandise in groups of lorries or, in the river valley, groups of *pinasses* (wooden boats with outboard motors). The size and composition of the fleet determines the possible volume of exchange. Any transport entrepreneur will only invest into an additional unit, if the further vehicle or boat can earn its money in the medium term.

Early in the development of the project we decided to avoid building up a fleet of lorries owned by the project, which would have provided a number of technical advantages (faster and reliable transport), but to rely on the use of local transport and of local markets. When we started in Léré in 1995 the market was attended by less than a dozen vehicles. The volume increased year after year and multiplied tenfold by the beginning of the year 2000.

We avoided recruiting a large number of project employees directly. We rather used local entrepreneurs (and helped them to settle in the project region) who locally recruited and employed technical staff who will remain in the region after the eventual closure of the project.

3 5 Stimulating Economic Growth

The refugees were relatively well looked after in the camps. By 1994, in the refugee camp of Bassikounou (Mauritania), they had become used to an infrastructure they could only have dreamed of at home. Wells with solar installations freely provided good drinking water. The stores of the UNHCR freely delivered the basic necessities. In the particular case of the Tuareg and Arab refugees they included a good ration of milk powder, sugar and tea. Schools and kindergartens catered for the needs of the children and the women had the choice between literacy courses, the crafts (leatherwork, knitting, crocheting, soap manufacturing and the like) or gardening.

None of this had much relevance for their re-integration in Mali. People had to pick up their particular strategies of survival and their quality of enduring hardship under the harsh conditions of Northern Mali. Nobody would build their wells, camps, villages or land if they did not do it themselves. Nobody would continue to provide free rations. From now on the formula would no longer be 'food for leisure' but 'food for work'.

Work was the key word. How to employ the largest possible number of people in the process of repatriation, re-integration and reconstruction? The program chose the obvious option: Everything had to be based on local knowledge and every measure had to be directly geared to recreate and boost local economic circuits.

One of the large vehicles for the promotion of local economic growth was the building program. Fifty public buildings were to be newly constructed, mainly primary schools with six classes. This construction program at a value of three and a half million Euro, was placed with small local entrepreneurs who took it upon themselves to employ a large number of hands at the site of the construction. This investment program, over a period of three years, created a lot of direct and secondary employment. On one large building site alone one would find up to sixty construction workers.

The construction program opted for the use of improved local materials. A heated debate engaged in the early phase. School directors and administrators insisted on construction in cement, in spite of an initial analysis, carried out by the architect in charge (from Tombouctou), which had shown temperatures of more than forty degree centigrade in classrooms of this type. He proposed a method of construction using mechanically compressed mud bricks for the inner walls and burned bricks or natural stones for the outer walls. The bulk of the construction material was therefore found in quarries near the building site. The bulk of the cost went into local wages for collecting sand, gravel or stones and manufacturing the bricks.

The income earned by the construction workers, by suppliers of construction material and the local transport companies fuelled the local economy and produced visible effects within a relatively short period of time. In Léré or Gargando the first private houses were rehabilitated some months after the public construction program started, in other cases the labour force stayed on after the completion of the construction sites and was engaged in private building schemes. In places with a good economic potential (important weekly markets etc) the induced effects soon overtook the direct effects of the program's investments.

The strategy of funnelling the funds directly through the local economy had its inconveniences. There is not a single bank in the whole area apart from Tombouctou itself. All funds had to be carried there in cash. This needed an infrastructure of safes, and constant security concern within our antennas and during the transport, but it worked without any serious incident.

3 5 1   Animal Husbandry

Within the largely nomadic social environment animal husbandry is the key sector. *La reconstitution du cheptel* was the key word. Everybody strongly suggested we should get involved in it. But what did it mean? It meant buying cattle from owners of large herds and handing the cattle over to people who did not any longer possess animals; in other words: redistributing the existing herds. This could not possibly create economic growth. The natural rate of procreation could not significantly increase by redistributing the animals. Besides, herds need a certain size to be economically viable. That means, the animals would have a natural tendency to find themselves back in the same herds they had come from.

We, therefore, concentrated on animal health and feeding only. We paid (slowly decreasing) subsidies to the veterinary service for vaccination campaigns and we supported the veterinary service by rehabilitating some of their installations and by re-equipping them (refrigerators, small motorcycles, instruments etc).

To finance the sale of animal feed during the dry seasons, we established one of the rare true credit systems within our program. There are two cotton seed presses in Mali. Their residue, small cakes of seed shells, is sold and used as animal feed, mainly for milk cows. This is a bulk operation. Ex factory you have to take a minimum of forty tons (one large truck). As this operation has a highly speculative character — large operators can buy the lot and impose monopoly prices in their regions — licences are distributed through the agricultural chambers (and a network of personal clientele relations). Small operators had no chance to obtain any. By grouping demands and by placing bulk orders running into hundreds of tons we were able to help provide the feed. The feed was sold at a fixed price, including a reasonable margin for transport and handling. This scheme has been running for four years without subsidies.

The main investment in animal husbandry was the rehabilitation, consolidation and construction of wells. All the population in the *zone exondée* (dry lands) needed wells. The majority of them had been either abandoned, neglected or deliberately destroyed (to prevent rebel forces from finding refuge). The returning population needed them for their herds. Relief organisations in the 1970s and the 1980s had introduced new techniques of well building necessitating capital investment in technical equipment and into lorries (all-wheel drive). The cost was exorbitant (about five hundred Euro per linear meter) and the teams were limited. We followed the same lines when we started, but were not able to complete six wells in one year, when many dozens were needed.

We had to change the approach and apply the same principles as in other fields. We asked the cattle herders how to go about it. Who had built their wells? Who would they like to hire now? Which part of the operation could they take charge of? Which part of the operation was ours to look after? A reasonable division of labour soon became apparent. From international funds (provided by ECHO) we paid for the steel and the cement and for specialised labour. We delivered the material to our outlets or to points further up field but still accessible for lorries. It was up to the population to collect cement and steel there and to transport it to the building site.

In most cases this was done by camel caravans. The population had to provide the building site with water (very tedious), sand and gravel.

This arrangement put a tremendous strain on the herders. There were some delays, because the caravans were too small to transport everything on time (one camel does not carry more than two hundred kg), so it takes at least fifty camels to transport what one ten ton lorry can take into the bush. But it worked. The cost was thus cut to one sixth of previous estimates.

3 5 2   Agriculture

Agriculture was the obvious sector for investment. The project region had the largest food deficit in Mali, and since the Sahel droughts had become quite used to free distribution of food aid. This project region has a vast agricultural potential.

The mass of the project region's agriculture is based on the *cultures de décrue* (after flood crops), mainly sorghum, beans, sweet potatoes and local vegetables. The largest zone for these crops are the lakes: Horo, Fati, Télé and Faguibine (altogether around hundred thousand hectares of flooded area). All depends on the extent of the flood. Our focal point was Lac Faguibine, the largest of the lakes with fertile land stretching over fifty-five thousand hectares. A large Bellah population (of about forty thousand) had resettled on the Northern and Eastern shores of the Faguibine. They returned without any reserves in kind or money. The surrounding terrain (huge dunes) is so difficult, there is no way to provide food aid in any adequate quantity from outside the lake, even from Tombouctou. The only chance of survival was producing enough food there.

Here again we relied on local knowledge and techniques only. We concentrated on providing seeds (bought and distributed locally), providing tools (axes and hoes, produced locally), mobilising the population to free the water passages from sand and debris when the water approached from Lac Télé, and on preventing pests from eating the harvests. This policy allowed the population to remain there.

Living conditions are still extremely harsh in this area. But living standards have improved considerably and people are starting to build up reserves. We had declined to give subsidies for small livestock (mainly goats in this area). People started to build up their herds from the proceeds of their harvests. To enable them to keep their cereals until the prices have stabilised on the market, we give incentives to build stores. The same stores are used for food security reserves.

3 5 3   Village Irrigation Schemes

When the level of the Niger River started to decline drastically in the 1970s and the 1980s emergency aid programs introduced motor pumps for small village irrigation schemes. They were in rapid increase when the rebellion started, and fell into a shambles during the five years that followed. The biggest scheme had been the delivery of two hundred fifty motor pumps powered by Deutz engines and financed by funds from Saudi Arabia in the middle of the 1980s. These investment programs were prepared in haste and there was not much follow up. However, through the activities of Iles de Paix (a Belgian NGO), UNICEF, UNEF and various international NGOs, small scale irrigation and its technical, economic and social components had entered the realm of local knowledge. When we started entering this field in 1995, there were many people around who had already ten or more years of experience in this area.

The first activities consisted of emergency aid: replacing motor pumps that had been stolen during the war years, rehabilitating irrigation installations that had been neglected or destroyed, and the like. With each season we broadened our scope and gathered more local entrepreneurs around us, who took over the technical work (topography, planning and carrying out the construction work). Today the teams of four local enterprises are working for the program throughout the year.

We systematised socio-economic planning by a series of local conferences where the representatives of the population negotiate who should benefit from the program in the years to come. The approach is labour intensive. The village irrigation schemes typically concern irrigation fields varying between twenty and sixty hectares that can be levelled and surrounded by small dams without the help of machinery. All work is done by hand with the help of simple tools (donkey carts, wheelbarrows, shovels, spades, buckets and the like). The beneficiaries provide all the labour.

Typically the preparation of the terrain necessitates three months' labour and four people per hectare. The labour force, poor people without the means to survive the required period without external income, is assisted by 'food for work' provided by WFP. The motor pumps have to be paid in three instalments. The price charged is equivalent to thirty-five percent of the world market price. It aims to avoid endebting the population. The development (including inputs for the first season) costs around one thousand five hundred Euro per hectare. The labour intensive approach makes it affordable.

The scheme started in 1995. Throughout 1996 to 1999 ECHO financed the scheme. From 2000 to 2002 this program is being financed by funds granted by the German Government through the Kreditanstalt für Wiederaufbau (KfW). In the course of four years (1996–99) about three thousand hectares of village irrigation fields were rehabilitated or newly constructed. Their rice production averages five tons per hectare. Roughly half of this overall production of fifteen thousand tons of paddy has to be sold to be able to pay for the next season's inputs (diesel, lubricants, repairs, fertiliser and seed); half serves to feed the population. The value of the annual production is almost equivalent to the overall investment. The current program comprises twenty-five irrigation fields totalling seven hundred hectares per annum from 2000 to 2002. Each of these investment packages will add three thousand five hundred tons of paddy to the annual production of the region.

3 5 4   Other Sectors

There was no need to finance private buildings — they are constructed in banco (mud), but people found it hard to finance the parts needing hard cash and not available: the doors, the windows — both generally made of (often corrugated) iron sheets — and the beams for the ceilings. In 1996 we, therefore, started to provide free of charge doors and windows for those who had already constructed their houses to the height of the ceiling. The value of one set (door plus window) is equivalent to fifty Euro. Since then thousands and thousands of doors and windows were provided and the entire region has been generally reconstructed.

In Léré this measure alone would not do. Here, like in other small country towns, people did not only build in *banco*, but used burned bricks. Houses of this kind need heavier doors and windows, made of full iron sheets. Their production in a decent quality needs a modern workshop, where these sheets can be cut, formed and welded. The prices of low quality iron doors and windows from Segou (the next large town in the south, three hundred fifty km away from Léré) was prohibitive, the quality of production was bad and most of them were seriously damaged during transport on the rough road leading to Léré. We, therefore, decided to help create a private workshop *Atelier du Nord* in Léré by financing the building, the initial stock and the equipment. The workshop in return had to deliver to the public a given quantity of more than ten thousand doors and windows at a fixed subsidised price, which made up for Léré's comparative local disadvantage. The price for a comparatively decent quality was now equivalent to the price in Segou.

The economic tools in this (and all other schemes) had to be simple, transparent and easy to apply and control. We concentrated on mostly marginal subsidies and avoided credit schemes. Credit could not have worked because of the immense risks and uncertainties. There would not have been any way to control credits either and social control did not exist.

3 6   The Issue of Compensation

Compensation had been one of the big issues of the *pacte national*. Everybody wanted to be compensated, for the destruction and pilfering of their houses or business, for the theft of their motor pumps and other machinery, for the damage incurred due to all interruption of business transactions. There was no way to get any compensation through German or International funds. This message was difficult to get across. We doubted that the Malian government itself would make any serious effort to compensate anyone for damage incurred during the rebellion and its aftermath. It took some time, but we succeeded in the end. After two years the issue was finally laid to rest.

In the course of six years the *Programme Mali-Nord* financed only three cases of personal compensation: the rehabilitation of the house of a Tuareg leader in Goundam, whose house and premises had been pilfered and destroyed by an agitated crowd in 1991. For equal measure the rehabilitation of the houses of his Songhoi and Bellah counterparts were financed at the same time. They had not been destroyed or pilfered but had rotted during the years of the rebellion. This was an extraordinary and symbolic measure and was meant (and understood) as a gesture not only towards the individuals concerned but also towards their communities.

An element of compensation could only lie in local economic growth. Anybody participating in this growth could find his or her part in it, either as a producer of goods or services, as a trader or shipper, or as the beneficiary of a productive investment or an investment into public infrastructure. Productive investments were of the highest interest. All productive investments naturally benefit someone, an individual or a group. This is why we paid and still pay much attention to the justice and the transparency of the allocation process. We simply refused to accept the shortcut which influential members of society often prefer.

4   CONCLUSIONS

Can development aid substantially help to create peace in the aftermath of rebellion and ethnic cleansing? The answer of the population concerned, and we heard it many times, is unanimous: 'Yes, without you, without the help of the German Government peace would not have come easily.'

The minutes of a meeting between the donors and the President of the Malian Republic (October 1999) contain the following statement:

> Trilateral mobilisation (government, civil society and donors) has worked well in the Tombouctou region. Civil society seems to be better associated with the projects (than in the regions of Gao and Kidal). The beginnings of durable stabilisation are manifest.

We think, this is a fair assessment.

What lessons can we draw from our experience?
* Peace did not come from outside, but from inside Mali.
* Peace did not come from above, but the government provided the framework and did not stop the process.
* Leaders of civil society negotiated the pace and they knew how to settle the issues.
* The program assisted them materially, financially and mentally.
* Peace did not come in one spectacular spurt. It had to conquer the terrain slowly. The warmongers subsided when they found themselves in a minority.

And finally it seems right not to have bet on the warring parties (government, army, and movements of the rebellion) when trying to enforce peace but on civil society, which did not have access to armed violence and was therefore bound to negotiate. The leaders of minorities were always the best advisors, because they had no wish (or no chance) to dominate the others.

Before the beginning of the project we were told any (permanent) investment in land would only create conflict. In practise, the contrary is the case. Serious conflicts need serious investment to be solved at a higher level of production and mutual benefit.

Once you embark on an economic emergency program there is no turning back. You need a decentralised, just, fast, transparent and reliable decision making process. People are willing to contribute seriously when they recognise their own interest.

And finally your means have to match the size of the task.

References

Lode, Kåre 1996. *Synthèse du Processus des Rencontres Intercommunautaires du Nord du Mali (d'Août 1995 à Mars 1996).* (Stavanger: Misjonshøgskolens Forlag).

Lode, Kåre 1997. *Civil Society Takes Responsibility. Popular Involvement in the Peace Process in Mali.* (Oslo: International Peace Research Institute).

Maiga, Mohamed Tiessa-Farma 1997. *Le Mali: De la Secheresse à la Rebellion Nomade. Chronique et analyse d'un double phénomène du contre-développement en Afrique sahélienne.* (Paris: L'Harmattan).

Papendieck, Henner and Barbara Rocksloh-Papendieck 1998. Vom Südrand des Azawad. Konfliktbewältigung im Norden Malis. In *Gewaltsame Konflikte und ihre Prävention in Afrika,* edited by U Engels and A Mehler. (Hamburg: Institut für Afrikakunde).

Papendieck, Henner and Barbara Rocksloh-Papendieck 1998. Attacking the Causes of Conflict. The North Mali Programme to Ending the Tuareg Rebellion. In *Development and Cooperation (D+C) 2/98:* 23–26.

Poulton, Robin-Edward and Ag Youssouf, Ibrahim 1999. *La paix de Tombouctou. Gestion démocratique, développement et construction africaine de la paix.* (New York, Geneva: United Nations).

République du Mali. 1994. *Livre Blanc sur le 'Problème du Nord' du Mali.* Bamako.

Rocksloh-Papendieck, Barbara 1999. *Flucht und Rückkehr im Mema. Geschichte einer Tuareg Familie im Sahel/Mali.* (Bamako: Coopération Allemande (GTZ/KFW) Programm Mali-Nord).

Sperl, Stefan 2000. *International Refugee Aid and Social Change in Northern Mali., Working Paper No. 22.* (Geneva: UHHCR): 1–13.

Appendix

ABBREVIATIONS:

BMZ	Bundesminister für Wirtschaftliche Zusammenarbeit und Entwicklung (Federal Ministry for Economic Co-operation and Development)
ECHO	European Community Humanitarian Office
FAO	Food and Agricultural Organisation
FIDA	Fonds International de Développement Agricole (FAO)
GTZ	Deutsche Gesellschaft für Technische Zusammenarbeit (German Agency for Technical Co-operation)
KfW	Kreditanstalt für Wiederaufbau (Bank for Reconstruction)
NGO	Non Governmental Organisation
RAMAT	Rassemblement Malien des Travailleurs
UNDP	United Nations Development Program
UNEF	United Nations Equipment Fund
UNHCR	United Nations High Commissioner for Refugees
UNICEF	United Nations International Children Fund
US-RDA	Union Soudanais — Rassemblement Démocratique Africain
WFP	World Food Program

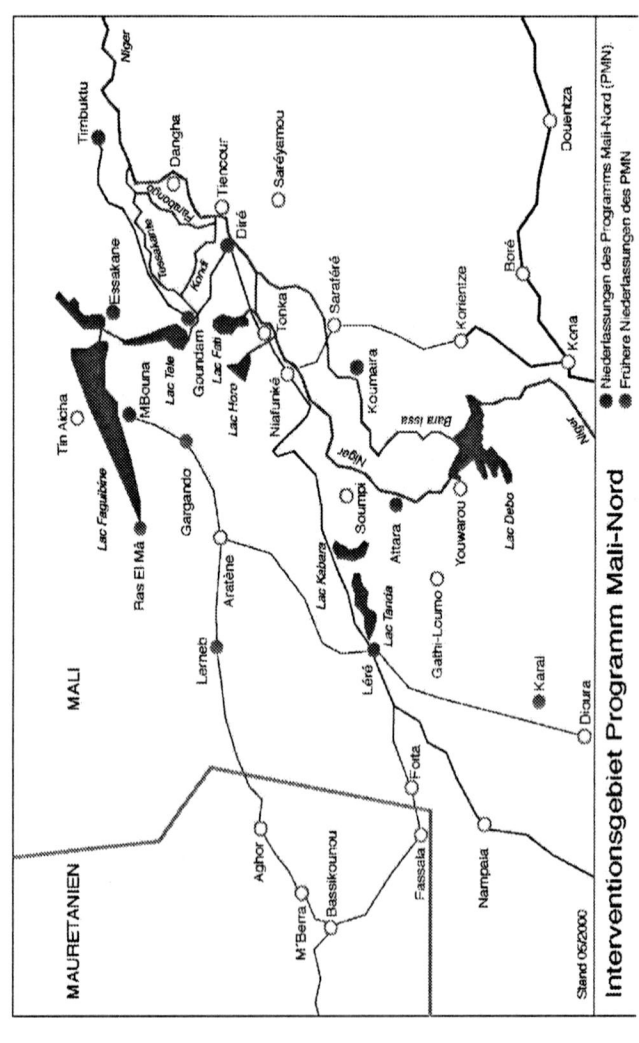

The Area of Program Mali Nord

The black points are present branches, the grey points are former branches of Program Mali Nord.

6

Roads to Peace: From Small War to Parasovereign Peace in the North of Mali*

GEORG KLUTE AND TRUTZ VON TROTHA

W E SHALL REPORT on two wars and the processes which smoothed the roads to peace. One of the two wars did not quite belong to the *Forgotten Wars in Africa,* the title of a book by the political scientists Rolf Hofmeier and Volker Mathies.[1] It was the war of the Tuareg of Mali and Niger who were fighting against the central governments in Bamako (Mali) and Niamey (Niger).[2] To a greater or lesser degree this war was at least acknowledged by the francophone media in Europe. However, in our discussion of this war we shall limit ourselves to Mali.

The second of the two wars was a war within the war of the Mali Tuareg against the government of Mali. It took place in 1994 between two rebel movements of the Malian Tuareg; it remained not only ignored by the world, but also by Mali itself. Even for those involved, this war will soon

---

* Our observations and considerations are based on many months of field research, which was carried out almost exclusively by Georg Klute between 1991 and 1998 in Mali and Niger — especially in the north of Mali. From March 1995 to October 1998 the research took place within the framework of our joint project 'Ethnicity, State and Violence' which was funded by the German Research Community (DFG). We would like to thank the DFG for its support. Any views expressed for which we do not provide a source are taken from interviews and observations which were carried out within the framework of the field work. Translation into English by Heather Kempson; all citations (whether from books or interviews) are *in italics.*

[1] Hofmeier, Matthies (1992).

[2] Strictly speaking this war of 'the' Tuareg consisted of two wars, one of the Tuareg of Mali against the Mali government, the other of the Tuareg of Niger against the Government in Niamey. At this point we will not go into the national reference system of the Tuareg rebels, which has deeply influenced the behaviour of the parties involved in this war. This national reference system, be it Mali or Niger, exists in spite of the ideology of the *temust* — a unit of descent, language and above all dignity and morals, where all differences and quarrels of the Tuareg amongst one another belong to the past — and in spite of the Utopia of a cultural and political autonomy, which goes beyond the postcolonial state boundaries, even a Utopia of a Tuareg state (see Klute 1995a, 146f; Klute 1995b, 55ff).

belong to the *forgotten wars in Africa* as even today no one likes to speak about this civil war. As the saying goes: *Wa okayan, okayan. What is over is done with.* This war will be the focus of our analysis.[3]

We shall divide our observations and considerations into three parts. Following a rough historical outline of the Second Tuareg Rebellion, we begin by investigating how peace was achieved in the fratricidal war between the rebel movements of the Second Tuareg Rebellion in Mali (Part I). Our theoretical aim in this first part is threefold. First, we consider the road to peace as a process of establishing power. The road to peace is a road to rule. The theory of peace is part of the theory of domination. Secondly, we wish to emphasise that under the present conditions of the postcolonial West African state and the decreasing appeal of the occidental state model,[4] those processes of power-building which occur at the local level become central. Thus, the theory of peace is also a theory of the forms and development of local rule. Thirdly, the analysis of local rule must free itself from traditional concepts of power. Instead we must look out for new forms of power, taking an interest above all in those forms of political domination which we call 'parastate rule'.[5]

---

[3] Both wars are closely linked. The seeds of war among the Malian Tuareg can even be found on the road which led to peace in the war against the Malian government — which complements the idea of Wilhelm Mühlmann (1940), that war and peace belong together in such a way as to suggest that on the road to peace, war and peace are not necessarily irreconcilable.

[4] See van Creveld (1999), von Trotha (1999a).

[5] Here we cannot go into detail concerning the concepts of parastate and parasovereignty (see Klute 2000, 1998; Klute, v Trotha 1999; v Trotha 2000a and b, 1999a). Only the following should be noted. By 'parastate' and 'parasovereignty' we understand, firstly, the institutional and, secondly, the legal side of this kind of rule. In this type of rule social and political centres of power and relevant nongovernmental groups have taken over a part of the rights of sovereignty of the central authority or of the recognised, ie formal, and therefore mostly legally sanctioned duties in the core area of state administration. This transfer of power and duties is not provided for by the constitution. The process of handing over of sovereign rights and basic state administrative duties is a kind of expropriation procedure of state sovereignty and occurs by means of processes of 'informal decentralisation' and 'privatisation'. Expropriation is typically carried out by groups and organisations which are in direct competition with the state and its administration. At the heart of this procedure we find the power groups of the colonial and postcolonial intermediary. They include the responsible groups of the administrative chieftaincy and development aid organisations, in particular the so-called non-governmental organisations (NGO).

Accordingly we understand in the following by parasovereign chiefdom (PCH) a chiefdom that typically was an administrative chiefdom under in colonial and postcolonial rule. Just like the precolonial chiefdom and the administrative chieftaincy in colonial and postcolonial times the political rule of the PCH is usually not exercised by a single chief but by a group, whose members are often related to one another by consanguinity and tribal membership. In many cases the chiefdom consists of leading families, clans and tribes. The members might take on quite different duties in the chiefdom, and the fulfilment of these duties frequently entails serious conflicts between the members of the chief group (see Klute 1998).

The PCH is marked by an 'intermediary concept of domination'. All actions must serve to ensure co-operation with the central government, to protect 'one's own' population from the demands of the central government and to ensure the role of the chiefdom as intermediary between the 'outside' (central government, international donors etc) and the 'inside'. In its

By following these theoretical aims we challenge basic arguments within the discourse of peace and development politics,[6] which we call the 'planning' or 'centrist fallacy' and the 'exotic fallacy'. The 'planning fallacy' goes right through most peace initiatives and development aid in war and crisis zones, and is the result of a mental prison. It presumes a degree of statehood which never existed in postcolonial societies of West Africa. It blusters about the reintroduction of the state monopoly of violence or a national policy of *power sharing*,[7] and is doubly blind. It overlooks the power processes at the local level which can simultaneously promote peace and yet contradict the aims of the national peace program. It fails to see the connection between peace-promoting measures and the processes of local power-building. It conceptualises these connections as pathologies which are commonly attributed to the 'traditionalism' of local communities. It is blind to the dynamics between peace-promoting measures and the creation of new forms of rule.

The 'exotic fallacy' turns the antitraditional argument of the planning fallacy on its head and turns a supposed pathology into a source of strength. It builds on the conflict resolution competency of 'traditional authorities' and resumes responsibility for strengthening them.[8] It is blind to the conflicts of communities described as 'traditional' and shares with the planning fallacy the inability to discover new actors and new structures. Typically, it accepts at face value the traditionalising rhetoric and its legitimations. Above all, it reflects the one-sidedness of the planning fallacy. What in the planning fallacy is blindness towards the local is in the exotic

intermediary role the PCH has to appear indispensable to both the members on the inside and the representatives of the outside, and to provide the chiefdom with as much autonomy as possible.

The PCH tries to establish a regional monopoly of violence and thus forces the central government and administration to drop their monopolistic claim to the means and the practice of violence. With the means of violence, which the PCH has at its disposal, it is a relatively effective threat to the central government and to the internal competitors for power. It expropriates from the central state the right to occupy leading positions and all other offices lying within the field of chiefdom — a right that the colonial and postcolonial state always reserved for itself and more or less maintained (see Trotha 1994a, 262 ff). In place of the precolonial principle of a 'rule over people' the PCH puts in place a territorial principle of rule and can do this far more successfully than the colonial and postcolonial state.

Because there are severe problems of translating the German adjective 'parastaatlich' into English, we use the adjective 'parasovereign' bearing in mind that for an English reader we thus cannot always stick to our differentiation between the institutional ('parastate') and the legal side ('parasovreignty') of parastate rule. We also cannot avoid to use from time to time the awkward neologism 'parastatelisation' which emphasises the process of becoming a parastate.

[6] See Feltes (1996), Gleichmann (1997), Zimprich, Gleichmann (1997).
[7] See Gleichmann (1997, especially pp 6 and 18).
[8] One of the United Nations publications on the peace process in Mali, which otherwise is above all a representation of the special role the UN representatives (the authors) played in the peace process in Mali, romances an independent Mali tradition in politics by which peace in Mali might be achieved. This *kuma* or policy known as *palaver tree-tradition* is said to have enabled the peaceful resolution of conflict between the parties and to have laid the foundations for the type of democracy particular to Mali (see Poulton, Ag Youssouf 1998, 104 ff).

fallacy the underestimation of the role of the state and of international crisis intervention.

The analysis of the war between the rebel movements throws a sharper light on the role of power-building in peace processes at the local level. It enables us in Part II to determine the links which exist between the local peace processes and the programs and peace processes, which are initiated and dealt with at the national level. We shall investigate these links by using two exemplary phenomena. On the one hand we shall take a look at *the Programme d'Appui à la Réinsertion socio-économiqe des Ex-Combatants dans le Nord du Mali* (PAREM) which was conceived as a demobilisation and reintegration program for ex-rebels and, according to the Malian government and the international donor countries, became one of the most important measures in the process of establishing and maintaining peace in Mali. On the other hand, we will continue the discussion of the *Programme Mali Nord* (PMN),[9] which Henner Papendieck and Barbara Rocksloh-Papendieck present so clearly and vividly in the preceding chapter of this book. PMN is not only one of the most important reconstruction programs in North Mali but has also become a *Deutsche Gesellschaft für Technische Zusammenarbeit* (GTZ) program par excellence. Taking PMN as an example, we shall ask how development programs can complement the processes towards parasovereign forms of peace and peace maintenance. A conclusion will provide a summary of the general findings and hypotheses.

One further methodological remark should be added. In order to achieve our theoretical aims, especially to highlight the role of local politics in peace processes, and following the demands of 'thick description',[10] we do not spare the reader many local details. Political power and peace processes and local ones in particular are very fragile[11] and cannot be understood if one does not get a basic idea of the tightly woven web of actors, their social relationships, their culture, and history.[12]

A SHORT HISTORY OF THE SECOND
TUAREG REBELLION IN MALI[13]

The north Mali Tuareg rebellion was one of those *small wars* or *low intensity conflicts (LIC),* which according to many observers are the wars

---

[9] Program North Mali.
[10] See Geertz (1994).
[11] See Trotha (1994a).
[12] To make it easier for the reader not so familiar with the case we present here, many details are mentioned in the footnotes. By this procedure we accept that the number of footnotes increases pretty much and might look a bit Teutonic for an English or American reader.
[13] Only a brief overview can be given here. For further details see Abrous (1993, 1990); Acord, Novib, Oxfam (1995); Ag Ahar (1990); Baqué (1993); Bellil (1990); Bellil, Badi Dida (1993);

of the future.[14] It was the revenge for many defeats.[15] The most important were the bloody defeats in the uprising of 1963/64 against the postcolonial regime of *Modibo Keita*. This First Tuareg Rebellion[16] completed the reversal of the precolonial power relationship between the *white* Tuareg nobility and the *black* rulers of the postcolony.[17] It reflected above all defeat by contempt, indifference and shameful neglect. For the greater part of twenty-four years, from 1963 to the end of 1986, the military authorities declared the Tuareg region a restricted area and cut it off from all normal relations with the rest of the world.[18]

The rebels were recruited principally from the ranks of migrant workers and refugees from the momentous drought of 1972/73 and the great drought of 1984/85. In the beginning of 1990 the Algerian authorities sent around two thousand people back to Mali. Other migrants and refugees came from Libya. Among the latter were a few hundred who had been fighting in Libya's Islamic Legion for a number of years and had set up

Bernus (1990); Bourgeot (1994a and b, 1992, 1990a and b); Claudot-Hawad (1994, 1993, 1992, 1990); Dayak (1992); Dröge (1992; 22 ff); Hawad (1990); Klute (2000, 1995a and b, 1991a and b, 1990); Krings (1995).

[14] For the concept of 'small war' see Callwell (1994); for the concept of 'low intensity conflict' see van Creveld (1998); see also Trotha (2002, 1999b).

[15] See Klute (1996). If one considers this important side of the rebellion, the murdering and the cruelty of the rebels towards the representatives and soldiers of the Malian government and the opposing militia was remarkably mild. For the total number of victims this relative control of violence had doubtlessly far-reaching consequences. According to our assessment of the sources available at the moment then we have at least 1,333 dead; if we add to these the number of those killed about whom we have uncertain facts then we have a maximum number of 2,720 dead.

Whether maximum or minimum, in both instances the number of dead underlines the fact that the Second Tuareg Rebellion was a comparatively 'small' warlike dispute — even more so if we think of the hundreds of thousands and even millions who were murdered at the time in wars in Africa. From a theoretical and comparative point of view this quantitative side of the rebellion is highly significant. However, we should not leave any doubt that this war also unleashed brutal mass violence — and consequently had burdened the road to peace with a bloody mortgage. In each year of the war there massacres by the Malian army and their militia against the Tuareg population and by the rebel groups against the black population, above all the Songhai.

[16] The background to and the events that took place in the First Tuareg Rebellion, the Kel-Adagh revolt, are hardly known even to the academic community. Apart from short notes and comments on individual aspects (see Anonyme 1964; Ag Bay, Belli 1986; Ag Sidiyene, Klute 1989) there is only one detailed description in the literature (Boilley 1999).

[17] The African population of Mali which does not belong to the Tuareg people labels the Tuareg as *blanc* referring to the light colour of the skin of many Tuareg, especially of those of noble descent.

[18] Except for soldiers and prisoners, who were sent to the penal colony which the region of Kidal was transformed into, all access to the north of Mali was strictly controlled, at least on paper. It meant, for example, that historical, cultural and sociological field research about the Tuareg of Northern Mali was as good as non existent. Only the British ethnologist, Jeremy Swift, thanks to a special permit and under the watchful eye of the Malian army, was able to carry out research for a short time in 1971 before he was again expelled (Swift 1979, 15 f). Until 1987 Swift remained the only (foreign) academic in the Adagh.

secret associations of Tuareg in exile. In addition, there were those refugees or their offspring who had sought asylum from the henchmen of the government of Modibo Keita in various countries in West Africa after the uprising of 1963/64.

The rebellion in Mali had three phases. The first phase consisted of the successful struggle against the Malian army. It ended with the *Treaties of Tamanrasset* in January 1991.

The first phase began when the Malian army bundled into camps the migrants and refugees who came back to the country at the beginning of 1990. Since the Malian secret service knew of the existence of secret Tuareg organisations in exile, it took advantage of the situation in the camps to arrest a large number of their inhabitants. At the end of June 1990 a group of armed rebels attacked the town of Menaka in North East Mali and freed those who had been arrested. This successful military operation was the signal for further military attacks against the Malian government or *Mali*, as the Tuareg of Northern Mali say. In the second half of 1990, the rebels, who had organised themselves as the *Mouvement Populaire pour la Libération de l'Azawad* (MPLA), achieved surprising military success against the Malian army.[19] Though in the first phase of the struggle no more than about two hundred experienced guerrillas executed all the military operations, the rebel army forced Mali to deploy in the north at least two thirds of the active Malian army, ie four of six thousand men. The rebels countered with a typical guerrilla campaign. The civilian population were the main victims of the army's search and destroy missions which they employed to capture the extremely mobile rebels. The harsh behaviour of the army in turn caused the population to take the rebels' side. Increasing numbers joined the MPLA.

In this situation the Tuareg rebels benefited from the changed global political situation at the beginning of the 1990s and the serious crisis of the 'neopatrimonial predatory regime' of Moussa Traoré, which was due to fall in March 1991. In order to rid itself of at least one of the conflicts which was shaking the foundations of the Traoré regime, Moussa Traoré's government signed a peace treaty with the MPLA under the mediation of Algeria in January 1991. In the *Treaties of Tamanrasset*, as the peace agreement was known from then on, the signatories agreed to a *special status* for the north of Mali, which was practically equivalent to autonomy for the Tuareg. Moreover, the north was granted unheard-of economic concessions which would mean a heavy mortgage on the future of the peace process — and which can only be seen as an expression of the irresponsibility of a regime in ruins.[20]

---

[19] *Azawad* is the name given to the region to the north of Timbuktu. It has become synonymous with the whole region of northern Mali which is inhabited by the Tuareg and which they consider to be *their* territory.

[20] In one of its most irresponsible acts, the Malian government declared itself ready to give 47.3% of the Fourth Investment Programme of the State of Mali to the Tuareg while

Implementing the Tamanrasset Treaties proved almost hopeless. Furthermore, the successful fight against Mali had unleashed neotribal, social and political dynamics among the northern Tuareg. These dynamics would become the driving forces for the rebellion's second phase. The rebel movement splintered and continued the struggle against Mali.

In spite of the agreement of Tamanrasset, some rebel groups went on with their attacks in spring 1991. The leaders of the MPLA, who had changed their name to the *Mouvement Populaire de l'Azawad* (MPA) after the conclusion of peace, tried to play down these actions. The dissidents, organised shortly afterwards as the *Front Populaire pour la Libération de l'Azawad* (FPLA), came above all from the groups who had suffered most severely from the hands of the Malian army. In addition, a few months later the *Armée Révolutionaire pour la Libération de l'Azawad* (ARLA), another splinter group of the MPA, was founded. The Arab nomadic groups of Mali had already created their own organisation in 1990, the *Front Islamique Arabe de l'Azawad* (FIAA).

One reason for the splintering of the rebel movement was that among the various Tuareg groups the Ifoghas from the Adagh in Northern Mali had succeeded in making the MPA a tool for their political ambitions and military confrontations. They took over leading positions in the MPA, whereas other groups were hardly represented. This domination by the Ifoghas set up a process of splitting along 'tribal' lines. The splits did not reflect 'traditional' but rather neotribal identities.

The splits went back to alliances and hostilities which had formed during French colonial conquest. As the only Tuareg group in Mali the Ifoghas had offered no resistance to the advancing colonial troops at the beginning of the last century. On the contrary, as allies and militia for the French they had supported the colonial 'pacification'. The new colonial masters rewarded them for their efforts by creating an independent tribal confederation. The tribal groups who had organised themselves in the FPLA and ARLA had followed a clearly different policy towards the French colonial power. Even if they had not offered open resistance to the advancing colonial power, they had at least adopted a waiting stance. The ARLA in particular became a rallying point for all the groups of the Adagh who opposed the supremacy of the Ifoghas. Ideologically the ARLA expressed their disapproval of the Ifoghas by means of a radically egalitarian discourse.[21]

There was not only an internal differentiation within the rebel movement, but also a differentiation among the African population of Northern

---

simultaneously agreeing that all the Tuareg would be exempt from all taxes and tolls for the next three years. Upon learning of this, a storm of indignation erupted among Malians who live in the south, and who constitute almost 90% of the population.

[21] See on this and further background to the conflict Klute (1995b).

Mali opposing the rebels. In reaction to the raids of the Tuareg against settlements along the Niger river, the *Songhai* militia mobilised against the *white* Malians in a *Chasse aux Blancs*. With the support of some parts of the Malian army, it carried out pogroms against the Tuareg and Moors. These pogroms resulted in mass flight of the Tuareg and Moors to Mauritania, Burkina Faso, Niger and Algeria. The number of war refugees reached one hundred thousand.

However, the political situation in Mali changed radically after Moussa Traoré's regime fell. The new transitional government made another offer to negotiate at the end of the National Conference in the summer of 1991.[22] After many months of talk, mediators from France and Mauritania, *Edgar Pisani* and *Ahmad Baba Miské*, helped the warring parties conclude the *Pacte National* in April 1992, which ended the second phase of the rebellion.[23] In this treaty the Malian government was able to get its way in many respects: the idea of federalism was dropped, together with the idea of an Azawad region, which was again replaced by the term 'the North of Mali'. In one of the pact's most important agreements, the Malian government agreed to incorporate a greater number of rebels into its armed forces and public service. The Malian government, however, got around to commit itself to a definite number of people thus to be integrated.

The FPLA, in the meantime the strongest rebel movement, refused to sign the pact whose most prominent architects were once again, albeit in a newly organised form, the MPA.[24] Accordingly, the situation in Mali showed little change. The supporters of the FPLA continued their attacks. Additionally, armed bands of former rebels operating beyond the control of the larger rebel movements increased their actions. The young men acted on their own initiative and preferred to rob travellers and transports of any kind, especially those of the international aid organisations.[25] The few overland roads and important tracks were only passable under military escort.

---

[22] In all West African states which at the beginning of the 1990s were trying to establish democratic governments the so-called *conférence nationale* became a constituent assembly and a forum at which, often at great risk to its members, accounts could be settled with the preceding government.

[23] Pisani, a former Minister of Agriculture and EU-Commissioner, was a director of the *Institut du Monde Arabe*, an influential member of the French Socialists and personal adviser to the then French President, François Mitterand. *Miské* was an influential 'eminence grise' in the political life of Mauritania.

[24] In order to facilitate the negotiations between the Malian Government and the rebels, Algeria promoted a coalition of the various rebel movements so that they could speak with one voice. Consequently in December 1991 there was a meeting in El Goléa, Algeria, where the various rebel movements organised themselves into a common alliance called *Mouvements et Fronts Unifiés de l'Awazad* (MFUA).

[25] The international aid organisations were (and still are today) favoured targets because their four-wheel drive vehicles are highly valued equipment under desert conditions. To carry out military or other armed actions they are trump cards which cannot be overestimated. With mounted machine guns they provide a highly effective combination of mobility and fire power.

Nevertheless, there was still hope of peace. The slogan 'Peace for economic development' which guided Pisani's attempts at mediation, seemed to be gradually bearing fruit. In the second half of 1992 the French helped the Malian government to form the first military units from army and former rebel personnel which they called *mixed patrols*. The mixed patrols deployed in the north were to guarantee public safety. By the beginning of 1993, the regular Malian army had absorbed more than six hundred rebels. Official plans provided for a further three thousand fighters. State administration was slowly gaining ground in the northern regions once again. International donor organisations made significant financial means available for the promotion of peace.[26] The newly elected president *Alpha Oumar Konaré* convinced the northern population of his peaceful intentions. Within the FPLA support for the hard-liners dwindled during the course of 1993. In summer 1993 the FPLA signed the National Pact.

The FPLA's joining of the National Pact did not bring about peace. Instead, the war entered its third and bloodiest phase. We call this phase the 'ethnicisation' of the conflict. Its major characteristics were a renewed and ongoing dissolution of administrative structures of the central Malian government in the northern region and ethnic strife between *white* and *black* Malians, particularly in 1994.

In May 1994 the foundation of *Le Mouvement Patriotique Ganda Koy* (MPGK), commonly abbreviated to *Ganda Koy*, was announced. They were a militia, in which former Songhai members of the army came together to fight the Tuareg and openly propagated the murder and expulsion of Arab and Tuareg nomads. After a unit of the regular army, consisting of integrated former rebels, was ambushed by the *Ganda Koy*, three of the four rebel movements (ARLA, FPLA, FIAA) left the National Pact and started their attacks again. The MPA maintained its political course and refrained from renewed battles with *Mali*. Once again tens of thousands fled as the rebel attacks started a new cycle of reprisals and pogroms against the *white* Malians.

---

[26] From a report and proposal of the GTZ for a planned Immediate Help for Mali North (which later became PMN) from September 1993, it was apparent that at this time a number of donor countries, international organisations or non-governmental organisations were planning to invest in northern Mali: the UNHCR to the tune of $3.5 million (of which, however, only $200,000 were actually available), the UNDP (UN Development Program) 2 x $100,000, the FED (Development Fund of the European Community) $5 million ECU, France (not counting the transfers to the various EU programmes) FFR 30 million, Germany DM 30 million, the USAID (US Agency for International Deleopment) $10 million, which would be administered almost completely by US nongovernmental organisations, Switzerland SFR 2.2 million, Italy Lira 3.8 billion, and the Netherlands G 4.5 million which would all go to CARE. These funds, mostly designated as emergency aid programmes, reconstruction or promotion of the peace process, totalled some 40 millions EURO. Even if only the planned (and not the actual) investments are given here, all the donor countries had set aside considerable sums for the peace process.

Almost at the same time, at the beginning of 1994, the second war, which we will here consider to be the 'war within a war', broke out. The two movements of the northern Mali Adagh, the ARLA and the MPA, stood in opposition to one another. The ARLA justified starting this war by saying that they had to eliminate the traitors of the MPA in order to be free to take up the fight with the Malian army. The MPA argued that their signatures on the National Pact obliged them to remain loyal to the Malian Government.

The conflict reached its first peak at the end of February 1994 when Colonel *Bilal Saloum* was killed in pursuit of *bandits*. The colonel was one of those officers who had been highly decorated by the Libyans for their service in the Islamic Legion in Libya and Chad. Before the beginning of the Tuareg rebellion he had commanded the Legion when they won back the Aouzou strip in the north of Chad. He was 'second in command' of the MPA, in accordance with the agreement of the National Pact he was a colonel in the Malian army and was a member of the *Supervisory Commission of the Agreements of the National Pact*.[27] In the beginning of 1994 in the so-called *mixed brigades* he hunted down bandits who included ARLA fighters who saw these supposed 'bandit hunts' only as an attempt by the MPA to crush all other movements in order make themselves the only militia in the north of Mali.

His death gave rise to great indignation in the MPA. An MPA commando set out to pursue the supposed murderer, traced him and believed that they had killed him in battle. In fact the culprit survived the attack with serious injuries. In return the ARLA rebels did something which at the time seemed to be a bold and sophisticated move but which meant the beginning of the end of the ARLA's claim for rule. They kidnapped *Intallah ag Attaher*, the head of the Ifoghas, who called the tune in the MPA. But the price the ARLA had to pay for its move was high. Two days after Intallah's kidnapping an MPA unit under the command of *Iyad ag Rhali*[28] attacked an ARLA group near Kidal, the main town of the region, and demanded the release of Intallah in return for the release of captured ARLA members. The MPA's offer was so designed that it sent out two signals at the same time. The first was: 'We will do everything in our power for our chief'. The second was: 'We are so powerful that we can go to the extremes without risking our dignity and military dominance.' The MPA 'paid' sixty prisoners for the release of their leader. This move by the MPA

---

[27] *Commission du suivi du Pacte Nationale*; this institution also followed the pattern of the commissions which were set up in all West African countries during the transition to democratic representation — in particular to carry out democratic elections.

[28] *Iyad ag Rhali* was the military leader of the MPA, a fearless daredevil and the highly gifted military 'brains' behind most of the decisive operations in the war against Mali. He also served as a link between the MPA and the Malian Government — Iyad was appointed personal adviser to president Konaré after the signing of the National Pact.

inflicted three wounds on the ARLA from which it never recovered. One was military, the other was moral and social, and the third was political. The ARLA revealed their military inferiority when their victory turned into a humiliating defeat. Their boldness turned out to be an ill considered piece of impudence which, instead of challenging the claim for leadership of the Ifoghas and Intallah in particular, simply confirmed it. By mundering Bilal Saloum the ARLA alienated all the black Tuareg in the group of former slaves, to which Bilal Saloum belonged.[29] It lost the support of all the other groups who were not vassals. Apart from the *Imghad*, the former vassals, all groups turned away from the ARLA and towards the MPA. Unlike the ARLA, the MPA had proved that they were not only ready but also capable of giving their members what is at the heart of 'good leadership': protection of the weak, law and order. The ARLA became an exclusive and therefore isolated movement of the Imghad.

In the following weeks and months there was no longer any doubt that the MPA were the stronger force. Concerning the ARLA, the MPA complied with Iyad's order: *That's enough now. Attack them!* The ARLA were driven from their bases in *Tigharghar* and Kidal and could no longer win back the upper hand, even if the fighting between the MPA and the ARLA continued throughout the year and losses were comparatively high. With the logistical support of the Malian army the MPA defeated the ARLA by the end of 1994 and won the fratricidal war.

The defeat of the ARLA showed that the Malian army and their MPA allies could only be defeated with great difficulty by military means. At the same time the civilian population of Northern Mali were becoming so war weary that 'traditional' leaders and speakers of the rebel movements initiated reconciliatory meetings between the ethnic groups of North Mali. These culminated in a solemn peace ceremony in March 1996 in Timbuktu, *La Flamme de la Paix*, which sealed a peace that however fragile, has lasted to this day. The peace agreements of the National Pact of 1992 were taken up again and made allowance for Ganda Koy, the Songhai militia, which then joined the pact. The Second Tuareg Rebellion in postcolonial Mali had ended.

PART I   ON THE ROAD TO PARASOVEREIGN PEACE: FROM
SOCIAL REBELLION TO PARASOVEREIGN CHIEFDOM

The fratricidal war was a bloody fight. There were attacks, kidnappings, and killings. The fight was part of a political and social struggle driven by

[29] While the press in Mali paid hardly any attention to the war among the Tuareg, there were extensive reports about the murder of Bilal. Most commentators attributed racist motives to the *white* murderers of Bilal.

the hope for a new order of Tuareg society after the rebellion. If revenge played a role, then it was the revenge of vassals who rebelled against the arrogance and infringements of the powerful. Even the victory of the MPA failed to bring back established relationships. They were gone for good since the rebellion and the democratisation of Mali had destroyed the foundation of the administrative chiefdom, which since colonial days had confirmed the power of the Ifoghas in northern Mali.[30] But with the victory of the MPA, the Ifoghas and their chiefdom pointed the way for an order which could be capable of bearing the future of a parasovereign chiefdom that would restore a lasting peace between the warring parties. The relevance of the victory lay in the ability of the chiefdom to create peace. How was this peace achieved? The answer lies in a consideration of two basic elements of intermediary rule, which are just as essential for the new parasovereign chiefdom: domination over people who feel that they are part of the chiefdom, and their protection from violence.

1 1   Peace Strategies I: Aid, Posts, and the Restoration of Affiliation

'Whoever does what he does not believe in will eat what he does not like.' With this saying an informant summarised the result of the fratricidal war. It was the year 1995, just one year after the end of the war between the two rebel movements, between MPA and ARLA. The defeated Imghad of the ARLA had to eat what they did not like. They had to bear the consequences of their defeat. They did what they themselves did not believe in: by their war-like challenge of the MPA they questioned violently the supremacy of the noble and free groups.[31]

It would be rash to dismiss our informant as an early, isolated 'turncoat'. A year later at the end of 1996, no-one in the Adagh openly questioned the rule of the Ifoghas. The process of the renewed recognition of their rightful rule was completed. Even observations which everyone regarded as correct before the fratricidal war were being played down if they put the Ifoghas in a bad light. Rumours over rustling for which the Ifoghas were responsible

---

[30] On the theory of administrative chiefdoms, see Beck (1989), Klute (2000, 1999, 1998), Trotha (1994a).

[31] Two things should be mentioned here. First, our informant was one of the noble *Idnan* who had taken part in the establishment of the defeated ARLA until in 1993 they formed their own militia, called *Base autonome pour l'unité de l'Azawad* (BAUA), locally known as *Base autonome de Timetrine*. BAUA, however, was never recognised by the Malian government, and did not take part in the war between the ARLA and the MPA. Secondly, except for the Ifoghas all groups in the Adagh — not only the defeated vassals but also the free and the other nobles and vassals — believed that the supremacy of the Ifoghas should be broken by violent means. All groups in the Adagh had come together in the ARLA to oppose the domination of the Ifoghas. Now, by hindsight, the violent efforts of the vassals were deemed wrong, and the vassals were considered to have justly suffered defeat.

were dismissed as propaganda and poor attempts by the vassals to justify their uprising. Former opponents considered necessary and legitimate even the violence carried out by the Ifoghas.[32] At the end of both wars (against Mali and between the MPA and the ARLA), the only militia left in the region was the MPA, the militia of the Ifoghas. The Ifoghas had weapons, even if not officially. The MPA and the chiefs of the Ifoghas had forbidden the vassals who fought on the side of the ARLA against the Ifoghas to enter the region for five years. The Ifoghas threatened to immediately shoot any armed person they came across in the region. Moreover, former ARLA members had to return stolen goods. In both senses of the word the Ifoghas were firmly and unshakeably in the saddle.[33] The return of uncontested power and the legitimacy of the Ifoghas was not the result of mere opportunism on the part of the defeated. Instead, the Ifoghas won their position by clever moves of reconciliation.

One move was based on the agreements of the National Pact regarding the integration of former rebels into the army and the Malian civil service. Considering the material-economic side of affiliation, the Ifoghas ensured that those groups, which had distanced themselves from the ARLA and had gone over to the MPA, got material and financial aid and posts.

For the Ifoghas it was equally important that the former opponents once more saw and felt themselves part of the postwar order. The Ifoghas had to overcome themselves, because in their eyes the Imghad had proved themselves to be what the ruling Ifoghas had always pictured the vassals to be: untamed and eager for spoils, people who could hardly belong to the law-abiding community of the Adagh.

1 1 1   Social Reintegration: A Marriage and a Visit of Reconciliation

Two events marked the beginning of the reintegration of the vassals into the order of the Adagh. The first event is a marriage, the second a visit.

News of the marriage caused quite a stir in the region. It was no less than the marriage of Iyad ag Rhali, General Secretary and military leader of the

---

[32] In a conversation a Malian Arab said: *Order must be maintained here by someone. The Ifoghas did not do it [ie they did not restore order — GK/TT], because they enjoy violence but because they are the strongest. Such things can and must be done by the strongest. In addition, thieves or criminals are arrested, beaten and handed over to the authorities not because the Ifoghas enjoy it, but because they are thieves and criminals. They deserve it. That's only normal.*
The statement must be considered against the background that the Malian Arabs were organised in the *Front islamique arabe de l'Azawad* (FIAA) and had been opponents of the MPA in 1994. There had even been military conflicts, as the MPA had taken part in the destruction of a FIAA base by the Malian army.
[33] See *Amawal* of 27 December 1994. The peace agreements between the ARLA and the MPA are printed in Amawal. Amawal is a Mali newspaper read by the Tuareg.

MPA. The bride was an Imghad and the former wife of a man who used to be Iyad's best friend and comrade in arms,[34] but had become a bitter enemy when Iyad and his former comrade confronted each other in the war between MPA and ARLA, between Ifoghas and Imghad. Everyone in the region was sure about the political nature of the marriage. But one was unsure of the kind of marriage policy which was pursued by this union. There were those who simply declared the bride to be the spoils of war — the vassals could not even keep their women. Others, the majority, looked on the marriage as a sign of reconciliation. The union with the former wife of the vassals' best fighter meant to them that the Imghad belonged once again to the community of the Adagh.[35] The voice of the majority won through.

In May 1996 word spread in Kidal that *Abderrahmane Galla*, the military leader of the ARLA, was visiting Intallah, the chief of the Ifoghas. The visitor asked his host for peace and forgiveness. This was both a personal and a general request. Two years before, Galla had been responsible for the kidnapping of Intallah mentioned above. Now, two years later, the chief of the Ifoghas acknowledged and granted the request for forgiveness. He told his visitor that he had no problems with the past and had banished all hatred from his heart. Intallah even suggested a reconciliatory meeting the next day. During the night threatening letters were delivered to the leader of the ARLA. But the meeting took place peacefully. Intallah asked all to forgive and forget. Afterwards his guest visited relatives and friends in the region and departed unmolested.

---

[34] Iyad ag Rhali and his friend were together in Libyan exile where the two men were recruited by the *Islamic Legion*. If Iyad ag Rhali was an Ifoghas and his friend an Imghad, it did not prevent them from fighting together with the Legion in Lebanon excelling as courageous and daring fighters. They had jointly planned the rebellion in Mali and had returned secretly to Niger at the beginning of 1990. On 30 June 1990 they had fought together the Tuareg attack in Menaka, mentioned above.

[35] As proof of the reconciliatory nature of the marriage the oral history of the region offered a significant story. It goes like this:

In the First Tuareg rebellion the leaders of the revolt were arrested on Algerian soil and were handed over to Mali by the Algerian authories. When the leader of the arrested rebels, the brother of today's Ifoghas chief, was brought in chains back to Mali, the grandfather of the bride yelled publicly at the defeated leader: *See the son of Attahar* (the father of today's Ifoghas chief who had died shortly before — GK/TT). *He is bound in chains. That is good.* The following night Attahar appeared to the grandfather in a dream and asked him: *Where do you want to burn? In this world or the next?* The next morning the grandfather told publicly of his dream. In the evening he lit a lamp which he had erroneously filled with petrol instead of paraffin. The explosion set fire to his house which burnt down. With serious burns, the grandfather was taken to the hospital in the same plane as the chained leader of the rebels, and died during the flight, while the leader of the rebels was pardoned after 15 years in prison.

Thus, when today a vassal family, whom the Ifoghas have hated for at least three generations, give one of their daughters in marriage to one of the most prominent leaders of the Ifoghas, then there are indeed signs of reconciliation.

Two things are remarkable about this visit. One is that the visitor was a member of a lineage of vassals who had entered into a number of marriages with a 'free' lineage. According to local logic Galla, 'owing to his birth', could not be as untempered and greedy for spoils as the 'pure' vassals. Following the principle of differential integration, the Ifoghas thus granted priority of affiliation to these 'free' or 'semi-free' people. A short time after the meeting between Intallah and Galla a delegation from ARLA made up of exclusively 'free' or 'semi-free' vassals arrived in Kidal to negotiate the modalities of the demobilisation and reintegration program. At the end of these negotiations the Ifoghas announced on the local radio that from now on money from the program for the incorporation of former fighters would be paid out first to members of the ARLA. The MPA fighters, ie above all the Ifoghas, would have to be patient.

The second point was that Intallah validated his high standing as a mediator and initiator of peace.[36] Such mediatory and peace initiating services are part of the pattern of group strategies, which are characteristic of the intermediary chiefdom.[37] Up to now, they determine the power politics of the Ifoghas. Today, they are combined with a more or less successful claim of the Ifoghas' chiefdom for a regional monopoly of violence putting the Malian government as well as the internal competitors of the Ifoghas, especially the ARLA, in their place and improving the road to parasovereign chieftaincy.

1 1 2   Symbolic Reintegration: The Re-writing of History

As the visit of Gallo in Kidal demonstrates, the Ifoghas always accompanied the economic and social reintegration of the 'greedy' and 'treacherous' Imghad into the Adagh by gestures and signs which flow from the high awareness of the ruling Ifoghas, that symbolic links are particularly binding. Thus, they also set about to rewrite the history of the Ifoghas and Imghad. They began to reorganise the legitimatory resources of history and to make up a new tradition based on the unity of Imghad and Ifoghas due to consanguinity and on the care of the strong for the weak.

The chiefs' group put *Mohamed Lamine Mohamed Fall* in charge to re-establish genealogically the affiliation of the vassals with the community of the Adagh.[38] Mohamed Lamine could be described as a propaganda

---

[36] When during the first uprising in the 1960s his elder brother had led the revolt from Algerian territory, he offered himself as mediator between the two opposing parties. While his brother was arrested and handed over to Mali in chains (see above, note 35), the younger brother, Intallah, became chief. Intallah performed similar mediatory roles during the rebellion of 1990 and again in the war between the MPA and the ARLA.

[37] See above, notes 5 and 30.

[38] Here, like in the ideolgy of *temust* (see above, note 2), the tendency of ethnic ideas is demonstrated to reconstruct ethnicity as a genealogical, 'natural' order.

minister and is just the right man for the job. He is a fluent, multilingual speaker and has learned the art to persuade his audience during his exile in Libya.[39] In the tradition of an Arab scholar he reconstructs now the genealogy of each group and each family in the region and records it in school notebooks. He believes to be able to trace all families back to five forefathers who were related to one another. In his new vision of the history of the relations between the Ifoghas and Imghad the existence of the Imghad, the vassals, is a myth. There are no Imghad in the region. According to Lamine, the Tuareg within the rule of the Ifoghas are all interrelated. The label Imghad is not a primordial, but a secondary, less significant social distinction. It was established for those groups who over the years had become weak, both politically and militarily, and had to submit to the supremacy of strong families. Therefore, it would be more appropriate to call the Imghad groups *tilaqqawen*, the poor. But being related to the Ifoghas, the poor should not stand up violently against the ruling Ifoghas. People are just not violent towards members of their own family.[40]

It is still too early to say whether the old ideology of a basic community between ruler and ruled, here expressed in the concept of consanguinity, will convince the vassals, the ruled. Above all, the question remains open, whether the Imghad can accept their fate as 'poor relatives' and patiently submit to the rule of the Ifoghas. In any event, it seems that the Ifoghas are satisfied with the new relationship between the Imghad and themselves. As the poor, the vassals are once again an essential part of the Adagh.[41]

1 2   Peace Strategies II: Protection from Violence

Oral history is heterogeneous history. According to the position and status of the storyteller or the time and conditions under which the story is told, the versions of the local history of the Adagh show considerable variation. Two versions are of interest here. The first is a 'vassals' story', as we call it, and was recorded shortly before the rebellion in 1988. The second is the 'nobles' story' and dates back to 1996, just after the rebellion.

---

[39] There he was an aide to *Ahmed al-Gashati*, a member of the Libyan Revolutionary Committee which was responsible for *Saharan Affairs*. His job as aide was to persuade the Tuareg in Libyan exile to join the Islamic Legion. Even today, he is still engaged in persuading and convincing his fellows of the Tuareg and, especially, the Ifoghas' cause.

[40] Mohamed Lamine made a tour of the region in order to convince the vassals of their true origins and to urge them to honour the kind of conduct you expect between relatives.

[41] At least, the Ifoghas have no doubts as to the reality and legitimacy of their rule confirming Max Weber's (1964, 157 f) concept of the belief of legitimacy which stresses the feature that the rulers themselves have to believe in the legitimacy of their rule.

In the 'vassals' story the beginning of the Ifoghas' rule in the Adagh is placed at the end of the 19th century, shortly before the arrival of the French. At this time *Illi*, the grandfather of today's chief, was elected chief by a gathering of regional nobles. However, when Illi took office, the Tuareg from the neighbouring Menaka in the south were still ruling the region. *They* (ie the Menaka Tuareg — GK/TT) *are the strongest and they protect the land.* For this protection the Menaka Tuareg levied a tribute signifying that all the Tuareg of the Adagh are vassals of the Menaka Tuareg. Under Illi's leadership a group of fighters started to improve on sword fighting in which the Menaka Tuareg had been far superior to the Ifoghas. The Ifoghas practised so successfully that thanks to their newly acquired military capabilities they chased away the Menaka Tuareg. They 'offered' their 'protection' to 'the poor', for which they demanded tribute. Thus, in the vassals' story the rise of the Ifoghas is due to the Ifoghas' striving for power, profit and status: *It was the wild lust of power, the desire for butter* (ie tribute — GK/TT) *and the love of leather tents.*[42]

The 'noble story' clearly differs from the vassals' one. Laying the ruler's claim for time and the noble claim for genealogical time in particular, the beginning of the Ifoghas' rule dates back to one or two generations earlier, to Illi's father or even his grandfather *Diffa*. According to the noble story, it was the great-great-grandfather of Intallah who had already opposed the rule of Menaka. In addition, the noble story paints a rather different picture of the circumstances that gave rise to the Ifoghas' rule: *Originally the Menaka Tuareg ruled this land. Then there was war with the Ifoghas; at the time the Menaka Tuareg knew no organisation or law. It was thus: No one could inherit from their relatives when they died* (because the nobles took away the inheritance — GK/TT). *No one could wear beautiful clothes when they got married* (because the nobles took the wedding gift for themselves — GK/TT). *The rule was purely arbitrary!*[43] *Diffa thus said to the Menaka Tuareg: 'There are no laws here.' And so there was fighting. That is why people rebelled against the Menaka Tuareg. That is why the Menaka Tuareg fought with the Ifoghas. [...] Diffa moved away. He said he could not live with them. Only his relatives remained here. People said to the Menaka Tuareg: 'You cannot rule alone'* (ie without laws — GK/TT)! *It continued until they had driven them completely from the Adagh and into the Menaka region. Now the Ifoghas remained and ruled and protected the land. Khammadan who had raised Illi ruled here [...]. When the infidels* (ie the French colonial invaders — GK/TT) *came, they lived with them together. But the infidels set up their laws and the Ifoghas set up their laws.*

---

[42] Nobles distinguish themselves socially by their leather tents.
[43] Interestingly Georg Klute's informant used the concept of *istighmar*, which comes from the Arabic *isti'mar* meaning exploitation as well as colonial rule.

There was tribute to be paid, there were all these things, but they were easy to bear.

Although the stories shed very different light on the history of the Ifoghas, both stories share the view that protection and tribute play a key role. But here again, the vassals' story deviates strongly from the story of the Ifoghas. In fact, it seems to be taken from Charles Tilly's writings about state-building as organised crime.[44] In the vassals' story, the rulers are like bands of racketeers. They impose their 'protection' on the vassals and collect tribute from the blackmailed until they are chased away by a stronger band. By distinguishing between good and bad rulers, the nobles' story opposes this Tillyan view of the vassals. It emphasises that only bad rulers take from the ruled without any law or order and whenever and whatever they like. Instead, good rulers want an ordered relationship. Above all, they want a unified law to which all are subject. Significantly, in the nobles' story the Arabic word *shari'a* is used to denote the law of the Ifoghas. That is, good rulers follow divine law and are consequently subject to it just as much as their vassals.[45] The Ifoghas thus assert the rule of even divine law and the protection of the weak. Violence on their part is a duty and works for upholding the law and the protection of the weak. This duty is even more binding upon the Ifoghas because they claim to be of Sharif origins. Direct descendants of the Prophet can hardly do otherwise.

In the eyes of *Zayd ag Attaher*, the leader of the 1963/64 rebellion, the legitimation constructed in the noble story was at the roots of the First Tuareg Rebellion.[46] It would also be taken up in the war between MPA and ARLA.

The beginnings of the war in 1994 did not resemble at all the noble claims. The Ifoghas could hardly protect themselves, let alone the 'poor'. The majority of the MPA fighters were integrated into so-called *mixed brigades* made up of units of the Malian army and former rebels.[47] The brigades were responsible for safety and order in the northern parts of the country. The members of the other rebel movements integrated into these brigades provided only three quarters of the total number of MPA fighters in these brigades.[48] Thus, the behaviour of many members of the rebel movements who had been left without provisions resembled that of robber gangs. In addition, there were also a number of officious though not formally

---

[44] Tilly (1986); see also Trotha (1994a, 28, 35 f).

[45] For the law of the French, the infidels, the profane concept *alqanun* is used for law.

[46] *Zayd ag Attaher* justified the 1963/63 revolt by saying that the socialist government of Mali had wanted to establish neither an Islamic constitution nor a Ministry for Islamic Affairs. So he had risen up in order to protect the land from lawlessness, from the lack of divine law.

[47] At this point the number amounted to 358 persons.

[48] At this point in time their number amounted to 282 fighters.

recognised militias who made themselves known by their raids. Indeed, whoever had a chance, armed himself. The members of the Songhai militia were among them. As mentioned above, hundreds of civilians were killed on both sides. Almost half the Tuareg and Moorish population of Mali fled the country. Contrary to the claims of the noble story, the armed conflict between the rebels and Mali had reached the phase of 'generalised violence', as we call it. The phase matched rather well the state of nature depicted by Hobbes: the state monopoly of violence had broken down, and no party could offer protection from violence. People's lives were *poor, nasty, brutish,* and for many *short.*[49] But in this situation, the Ifoghas chose a strategy of war and power which is very close to Hobbes' ideas. It was based on the assumption that the party which succeeds in justifying its violence against others and wins the 'basic legitimacy' of protection from violence[50] attracts followers, accumulates opportunities for power, and will finally establish its own rule. This is precisely what happens at the beginning of the war between the MPA and the ARLA.

The first operation of the war did not initially look like a powerful opportunity for the Ifoghas. In fact, it ended with the death of colonel Bilal who had been ambushed by ARLA fighters. At first glance, the whole operation seemed a heavy blow at the MPA. But the Ifoghas saw their chance, because they saw the social side of the death. *Black* Bilal was a descendant of former slaves who up until this point had frequently been the victims of all sorts of disputes. If Bilal's murderer was punished and the law was enforced, then the members from the rank of former slaves would turn to the MPA and to the Ifoghas in general.

Immediately after the news of Bilal's death, high-ranking MPA officers, who had refused to be integrated into the Malian army, set out to punish the murderer by pulling out all the stops of intermediary rule, on which the Ifoghas chiefdom was based. They requested the delivery of the murderer to Malian authorities and justice, the return of Bilal's body, his weapons, his vehicle, and finally the support of Bilal's family by the ARLA. The ARLA refused, and the war took the turn we have already described. The Ifoghas' policy worked out. The former slaves joined the ranks of the MPA for the war with the vassals making up for numerical inferiority of the MPA. Until the new recruits had finished their training, the MPA did not openly confront the ARLA, but remained in the protection of the garrisons of the Malian army which the ARLA did not dare to attack.

The last twist of fate to the disadvantage of the ARLA was the kidnapping of the Ifoghas' chief, again a serious defeat for the Ifoghas which they were able to turn once more into a victory, since they trusted the logic of legitimacy which is based on the protection of the poor and weak. After the

---

[49] Hobbes (1965, 65).
[50] For the concept of 'basic legitimacy', see Popitz (1999, 221 ff), Trotha (1994 b).

successful rescue of the kidnapped chief, the war was decided. All groups turned away from the ARLA. The vassals were isolated. Even if the battles lasted until almost the end of 1994, the Ifoghas had shown that they were willing and able to protect the defenceless 'poor' from the violence of others. They had won the political and social struggle against the ARLA. The rest was only a question of not making any military mistakes. The Ifoghas did not.

In retrospect, it seems that the Ifoghas took for granted the desertion of the 'poor' from the ARLA and the Imghad's cause and the return to a rule which seems to be even stronger than at the beginning of the rebellion: '*They always take the side of the strongest. That is the way the poor are!*'

PART II   PAREM AND PMN: FROM PEACE MANAGEMENT TO PARASOVEREIGN PEACE

The peace strategies of the Ifoghas in the war against ARLA and other competitors cannot be separated from the mechanisms of peace making, that were set up in the more general war of the Tuareg against Mali during the Second Tuareg Rebellion. Today, the *local arena*[51] is always related to national and frequently to international politics. In particular, that applies to the powerless and poorly organised states of postcolonial West Africa. Taking PAREM as an example, we highlight some aspects of these relationships between the local, the national, and the international. In addition, a brief look at PMN (Program Mali North) draws attention to the fact that the road to peace by parastatalisation of intermediary local power centres is not limited to former administrative chiefdoms. It is also found in development programs like PMN which appear to be firmly anchored in the national centre of the postcolonial state and its relations to the international world of donor countries. Consequently, we argue, that the parastatalisation of local power and its ruling centres is the result of very different roads to peace which converge.

2 1   PAREM or the Parastatalisation Dividends of Demobilisation and Reintegration Programs for Ex-combatants[52]

Peace making in the Second Tuareg Rebellion followed the advise of Edgar Pisani, one of the leading negotiators in the peace process, as we already

---

[51] On the concept of the 'local arena' see Bierschenk, Olivier de Sardan (1999, 1998). However, the central government and its administration and the international dimension of the local arena are underestimated in the work of the Bierschenk group (see Klute 1999, 163).
[52] In this part, we shall neither investigate the whole programmes nor contribute to project evaluation. Here we focus exclusively on problems of parastatalisation which are involved in the kind of programmes PAREM and PMN stand for.

pointed out. The advise is summed up in the slogan: 'peace in exchange for economic development'. On the one hand, it meant that procedures were implemented which have become basics in the world of peace making after armed conflict.[53] The re-incorporation of ex-soldiers and ex-rebels into civilian or ordinary military life is among them, and at the end of the Second Tuareg Rebellion it was the task of PAREM to make it work.

Many rebels in the Tuareg Rebellion and elsewhere ask themselves: What are we going to do after war? What do we get out of peace — we who have risked our lives and put up with hardship and misery? At every meeting between rebel movements, militias, and the Malian government the question was raised. Already in the Tamanrasset agreements of January 1991 and especially during the subsequent negotiations entered into by *the Commission de suivi de l'application de l'accord de Tamanrasset* in Gao,[54] the MPA and the FIAA had committed themselves to supply the government with lists of fighters who would then be integrated into the Malian armed forces. Although no figures are given in either of these documents, the texts can be read in the sense that all fighters listed by the MPA and the FIAA should be incorporated into the armed forces of Mali.[55] About one year later it was agreed explicitly that on a voluntary and individual basis all members of the MFUA would be integrated into the uniformed units of the Malian state.[56] The first group of 640 ex-rebels entered the Malian army in spring 1993.

2 1 1   The 'Policy of Figures' or How Many People should get Assistance from PAREM?

A year later, in April and May 1994, the negotiations between the MFUA and the Malian government continued in Algeria. For the first time the question was raised, what would happen to ex-rebels who could not be

---

[53] See Feltes (1996), Gleichmann (1997), Zimprich, Gleichmann (1997).

[54] These negotiations took place between 5–7 March 1991.

[55] See Accord sur la cessation des hostilités. Le gouvernement de la République du Mali d'une part, et le mouvement Populaire de l'Azaouad et le Front Islamique d'autre part (signé par le Colonel Ousmane Coulibaly pour le governement de la République du Mali et par Iyad ag Ghali pour le Mouvement Populaire de l'Azaouad et le Front Islamique Arabe) Tamanrasset 6 janvier 1991, as well as the attached protocols of the various negotiating rounds of Tamanrasset documented in Procès verbal de la première réunion de la commission de suivi de l'application de l'accord de Tamanrasset du 6 janvier 1991, Gao, 7 mars 1991 (signé par le Colonel Ousmane Coulibaly pour le gouvernement de la République du Mali et par Iyad ag Ghali pour la délégation du Front Populaire de l'Azaouad et du Front Islamique Arabe de l'Azaouad).

[56] The procedure of incorporation included a set of criteria to be met by the ex-rebels according to the positions chosen for them. See République du Mali: Pacte national conclu entre le gouvernement de la République du Mali et les Mouvements et Fronts Unifiés de l'Awazad consacrant le statut particulier du Nord du Mali. In *Journal Officiel de la République du Mali*, 34ème année, No 3 (special), 11 avril 1992, Bamako.

taken into the armed forces or the civil service. The MFUA confronted the Malian government with a figure of 7,000 armed members of the rebel movements it represented.[57] However, the Malian government only conceded to take charge of a further 1,500 ex-rebels, thus altogether 2,140.[58] There remained some 4,860 rebels who were not taken care of. This number became the basis for all further negotiations over the incorporation of former rebels or militia men into civilian life. The story of this number is remarkable. We will mention only three major topics.

First, all figures given for the number of rebels or ex-rebels were hardly coherent because they were based on different, frequently complicated criteria.[59] Secondly, the number had hardly anything to do with the number of rebels or militia men who were armed at some point during the rebellion. The number reflected nearly exclusively the power relations between the various rebel groups and the state of Mali at the time of the negotiations. Finally, the development of this figure shows that PAREM was partly at odds with its original aims of demobilisation and re-incorporation of ex-rebels into civilian life. Instead of breaking up armed organisations by offering possibilities for reintegration into civilian life, PAREM simply strengthened de facto the rebel movements and militias. After peace was finally declared in 1996, the armed movements and militias disbanded de jure but by no means de facto, and welcomed numerous new members because of PAREM.

For the first time a program for the re-incorporation of ex-rebels was suggested in July/August 1995 at a meeting between representatives of donor countries, development agencies and the Malian government. A trust fund was set up to cover the expected costs, and the United Nations Development Program (UNDP) was charged with implementing the program.[60] In May 1996, the UNDP submitted a *Program for the Support of Ex-Combatants in Northern Mali* (PAREM) which was to run for eighteen months.[61] In the draft of the program the number of ex-fighters who were

[57] In these negotiations the MFUA represented four rebel movements represented: MPA, FLA, ARLA, FIAA. The number of 7,000 was first mentioned at a meeting that the MFUA held in Gao for preparing the negotiation with the Malian government in Algeria (see MFUA: Résolutions de la rencontre du bureau de coordination des MFUA tenue à Gao du 31 mars au 09 avril 1994 (7 p).

[58] See Le Républicain of 1 June 1994: Le texte intégral des accords d'Alger/Document: gouvernent — MFUA procès verbal de la réunion d'Alger entre le gouvernement de la Républiqe du Mali et les Mouvements et Fronts Unifiés de l'Azawad (10–15 may 1994).

[59] Sometimes the figures refer to those who are or are to be incorporated into the Armed forces of Mali, sometimes to those in the civil service, and on other occasions to those in civilian life.

[60] See Présidence de la République/Commissariat au Nord: Note de présentation du plan d'actions issues des résolutions et recommandations de la rencontre Gouvernement du Mali — Partenaires au développement sur les régions du Nord Mali, 31 juillet 1995 (29 p); Présidence de la République /Commissariat au Nord: Commission paritaire. Gouvernement-Partenaires au développement sur les régions du Nord Mali. Compte rendu de réunion,17 août 1995 (2 p).

[61] See PNUD, Mali; Programme d'appui à la réinsertion des ex-combattants dans le Nord du Mali (PAREM), 16 mai 1996 (27 p). PAREM was due to end on 31 October 1997.

to be incorporated into civilian life was estimated to be around 8,000. The draft claimed that 6,610 rebels, who could not be integrated into the armed forces, had already been *counted and identified*. In fact this number — like all numbers before and since — was based neither on a count nor on an identification of ex-rebels. It was not even a reasoned estimate. It was based on a simple addition and, in fact, purely and simply the result of negotiations between rebel movements, militias, the Malian government and the participating experts.[62]

With these *around eight thousand* men the amazing increase in ex-rebels was by no means over. In summer 1996, the Ganda Koy got the Malian government to concede another 150 places in PAREM, and thus started a new round of haggling over quotas. Every movement, including Ganda Koy, got the right to a further 150 places, altogether, 750 places. Following their victory against the ARLA and having become the strongest rebel movement of all, the MPA was even able to push through an increase of 400 further places in its quota. The final result was that the 4,860 fictive ex-rebels without provision of January 1994 became 9,500 armed rebels and militia men in 1996 for whom PAREM should provide assistance.[63] No longer, the number of 9,500 men with legal claims to assistance by PAREM had anything to do with the number of rebels and militia men who at some point in the rebellion had actually carried arms or who had been active in the logistics of the war.

The 'policy of figures' had tangible result. The sums of money which were allocated to the various movements in Mali were considerable. All in all EURO 4.2 millions (DM 8.5 millions) were handed out, the MPA and Ganda Koy getting the lions' share.[64] The MPA received 31.3 per cent of all

---

[62] The base, from which the count started, were the 4,860 members of the MFUA who were not taken care of during the negotiations in Algier in 1994. To these 4,860 'ex-rebels' were added another 1,750 members of the Ganda Koy. As all figures, this figure too had been politically negotiated. In the meantime, the Malian government had recognised the Ganda Koy as a rebel movement though until spring 1995 only those movements had been legally recognised which had signed the National Pact in 1992. It granted Ganda Koy 2,000 *armed fighters*. 250 were to be integrated into the armed forces of Mali, the remaining 1,750 into civilian life. Thus, the simple figure of 6,610 *counted and identified* ex-rebels was made of 4,860 MFUA members and 1,750 members of Ganda Koy.

How could the 6,610 ex-rebels become *the around eight thousand persons* for whom PAREM should be responsible? The answer is to be found in the rational magic of counting twice a group of 1,630 ex-rebels who from autumn 1995 on had been confined to reception camps by the Malian army, could not or did not want to be taken into the armed forces or Mali's civil service, but who had already been included in the maximum figure of 7,000 the MFUA had confronted with the Malian government during its negotiations in Algiers in 1994.

[63] In a provisional, internal report of the situation the total number of those affected by PAREM was put at 9,504 on 31 July 1997 [see PNUD: Situation du fonds d'affectation spéciale (Trust Fund) du PNUD pour le Nord de Mali au 31.07.1997].

[64] As a matter of fact the total costs of PAREM were much higher, almost $12 million or about EURO 10 millions (DM 20 millions). The additional costs resulted from project and administration costs as well as experts' salaries.

posts and money. The MPA did especially well in comparison with their regional competitor ARLA, which received only 13.4 per cent of all posts and money. There was a similar imbalance between the MPA and ARLA regarding the quota for the integration of ex-rebels into the armed forces of Mali. The MPA received almost double the quota of the ARLA.[65]

However, the sums that ended up in the hands of most of the movements' members were modest and generally not materially beneficial.[66] All the more, PAREM was a great chance for the rebel movements' and militias' claims for money and power. In accordance with the patterns of colonial and postcolonial intermediary power, it enabled the armed movements to distribute money and jobs, to strengthen old and new ties, and to create new dependencies. At least in the case of MPA, PAREM even yielded dividends for the parastatalisation of the Ifoghas' chieftaincy.

2 1 2   The Parasovereign use of PAREM by the Ifoghas

The MPA used the opportunities PAREM offered in two ways. It took PAREM to boost its efforts for the integration of former opponents into the social life of the Adagh and to strengthen its claim for devolution, that is, for the right to decide on the filling of public offices in the region. In the strategy of 'differential integration', the leaders of the MPA and the chiefs of the Ifoghas combined both efforts.

The first measure undertaken by the MPA and the Ifoghas was to offer their old regional opponents, the noble tribe of the Idnan, 400 places in PAREM. As has been mentioned above, the Idnan militia, BAUA, was not recognised by the Malian government and was consequently not accepted into any of the integration programs. Acting on behalf of the Ifoghas, the MPA rewarded the loyalty of the Idnan after the kidnapping of the chief Intallah when all the Idnan broke off with the ARLA and went over to the MPA. The Idnan did not hesitate to accept the offer of the MPA. By the MPA's offer to the Idnan, the Ifoghas underlined their claim for regional leadership and the confirmation of their policy towards Mali during the past years as well as their claim to distribute jobs and to fill public offices. In addition, they refuted the image that the 'vassal's story' of the rise of the Ifoghas mentioned above depicts, and seemed to validate their own 'noble story'.

---

[65] The share of the Ganda Koy in the posts and money of PAREM was around 27.8%. In absolute numbers, the distribution of posts and money between the different movements was as follows: MPA=2,988 posts, equivalent to about DM 2,689,200; Ganda Koy=2,650 posts, equivalent to about DM 2,385,000; FPLA=1,367 posts, equivalent to about DM 1,230,000; ARLA=1,274 posts, equivalent to about DM 1,146,600; FIAA=1,264 posts, equivalent to about DM 1,137,600.

[66] The aid which was distributed to individuals was comparatively small. In terms of figures, some EURO 450 (DM 900) per head went to individuals, a sum which in the north of Mali is just sufficient for the purchase of two (average) camels. They cannot really qualify as *assistance to reintegrate into civilian life*.

The case of the Idnan was not the only one, in which the leaders of the MPA and the Ifoghas put the interests of their 'own people' last. With the distribution of money from the budget of the regional PAREM offices in Kidal,[67] the groups which had deserted from the ARLA and had sought MPA protection were favoured over Ifoghas fighters. Over and above, the Ifoghas rewarded loyalty, even when it occurred at a rather late date and could not be financed by the international demobilisation and integration programs. They hired people as night watchmen, bricklayers, drivers etc or arranged jobs for them outside PAREM. With their distributive politics the MPA leaders and the heads of the Ifoghas made clear to everyone in the region that those who put someone in a public office, create posts in the civil service, arrange jobs, and distribute aid are the ones who are in power. They used PAREM to consolidate and strengthen their position of power as winners of the internal war in the Adagh.

Of particular significance for the parasovereign ambition of the Ifoghas are the facts that the financial resources and even the means of power which fell to the MPA through PAREM are not decided and controlled by the government in Bamako but by foreign donors. After the rebellion had destroyed the state monopoly of violence, PAREM allowed the financial resources of the chiefdom to be put on an independent footing and made it possible for the Ifoghas to appropriate the distributive function, which belongs to the basics of any system of power and particularly to state rule. PAREM demonstrated the continuing weakness of the postcolonial government as well as the sovereignty of the Ifoghas in its dealings with donors. It kept alive and underlined the claim of the Ifoghas chieftaincy for dealing directly with foreign countries, governments, and NGOs. It even gave rise to dream again about the reversal of the colonial and postcolonial power relationship in Mali by putting the Ifoghas chiefdom in direct contrast to the marauding 'prey policy' and 'spoils culture' of colonial, but above all, postcolonial rule.

2 2 PMN or from Decentralised Peace to the Parasovereign Effects of Development Agents

PAREM dealt with the urgencies represented by a few thousand ex-rebels who had to be turned away from the path of war, had got to invest in peace, and whose hopes and especially interests had to be met. But Pisani's principle for peace in Mali went beyond the immediate task to answer questions put up by more or less demanding ex-rebels and concerning their proper future. What was required were the reconstruction

---

[67] The office was run by an MPA officer.

and the economic development of the northern region, which would bring about economic and social stability, would enable the rapprochement and finally at least the coexistence of the hostile groups, and would open up perspectives for a peaceful future for the people in North Mali. For the achievement of these aims the *Program Mali North* (PMN) played a key role.

PMN was to be funded by two organisations, the German *Kreditanstalt für Wiederaufbau* (KfW) and the *Gesellschaft für Technische Zusammenarbeit* (GTZ). After the early withdrawal of the KfW it was mainly the GTZ which managed the program. As the preceding chapter of this book has already presented, the GTZ relied on the economist Dr. Henner Papendieck and the sociologist Dr. Barbara Rocksloh-Papendieck. It entrusted them with the task of drafting and implementing a construction and development program for the north. Today, PMN is one of the most successful development programs of the GTZ.[68]

PMN began its work in 1994. Its general goals were sober and refreshingly free of the professional jargon which is an integral part of the bureaucratic world of development agencies and its 'discourse'. It abandoned the jargon of *promotion of responsibility, participation* and *sustainability* and aimed at the more obvious but no less ambitious. PMN made it his business to halt the social and economic decline of the northern region, to stabilise the social and economic development and — what could hardly be hoped for in 1994/95 — to arrange for the reconstruction of the destroyed northern regions. PMN tried to achieve these goals by means of a program consisting of three elements: The Moors and Tuareg refugees who had returned from neighbouring states and especially from the camps of Mauritania, should be provided with humanitarian aid to help them over their immediate needs.[69] The reintegration of the returnees should be supported by measures which promised to create short and medium term incomes for the returnees as well as for those who had stayed in Mali and

---

[68] PMN grew to nine offices and three branches in the region concerned — apart from the head office in Bamako managed by the Papendiecks and a Malian colleague of them. Between August 1993 and August 1999 alone they had been raising around DM 44 millions from various sources , above all from Germany, but also from multilateral development organisations (see Akzente 1998, p 15).

[69] In all its basic activities PMN follows what might be called the 'responsibility principle'. As we understand, this principle goes beyond the principle 'help for self-help' ('Hilfe zur Selbsthilfe') which as become small change in the discourse of aid. The definition of what aid has to consist of as well as the granting of aid are tied to specific, tangible and actual steps on the part of those who are to be supported by PMN. Already in the phase, when the refugees in Mauretania were expected to return to Mali, PMN, for example, emphasised that the refugees and people who had been expelled should be responsible for the organisation of their return to Mali. A PMN report from 1998 reads as follows: *The important message was always: 'Your return is your problem, not ours. Take care of it!' Those who are affected should inspect the area they are going to return to and plan a strategy of how to take hold of it and build it up.*

were to be put in the position to cope with the burden of returning refugees and to incorporate the latter in the local conditions. The support for those who had stayed in Mali during all the years of political turmoil and war should minimise the relatively high conflict potential which always exists between those who return and those who had stayed.

In our view, the success of PMN is closely connected with the fact that in the beginning PMN resisted to convert these lofty aims into some catalogue of measures — which is a convenient measuring rod of legitimation and usually fits for the evaluation systems of donors but might soon become a bureaucratic Procrustean bed. Instead, PMN developed from continuous talks with all those in the region who shared the aims of PMN and became actively involved in the program, on whom the work of PMN was concentrated, and to whom it was also more or less strictly limited. In fact, in its beginnings PMN was less a program than a process of remarkably high organisational — and risky — flexibility. This flexibility enabled immediate responses to up-coming conflicts and to peace initiatives emerging in the course of the program, to the immediate needs of the people in the region, to the visible or reasonable requirements of reconstruction, and to the successful as well as questionable results of the measures initiated by PMN.[70] Accordingly, the result of PMN was a composite mixture of measures. PMN helped to construct transit camps and purchased tools, mats for tents, doors and windows for mud huts. It bought grain to bridge the time before the first harvest and to feed the needy left empty-handed after their return to Mali. It financed the *Rencontres intercommunautaires* and provided organisational assistance for these peace meetings between groups, which many times had clashed

---

[70] PMN tried to check the potential pitfalls of continuous communication and flexibility by one structural arrangement which was decisive for its development. It set up a strongly personalised decision-making process — which, one should add, picks up the principles of personalisation and orality so deeply embedded in African social and political life as well as it starts from the practical insight that in order to construct an order worth living you need men and women who are intelligent, sensible, and reliable as well as experienced, well respected and even more or less powerful in their communities, and above all who show public spirit and are able to look beyond their selfish interests. At the centre of this decision-making process were and still are the founders and organisers of PMN, Dr. Rocksloh-Papendieck and Dr. Papendieck, and an advisory committee, *Comité consultatif*. The latter plays a key role for assuring the approval of the Malian government and consists of persons representing the relevant groups and interests of the region on which PMN focuses. In addition, the Papendiecks have committed themselves to the principle of consensus meaning that only those decisions will become effective about which unanimity between the Papendiecks and the Comité consultatif and within the latter is reached — somehow a practical version of Habermas' communicative action. But very much unlike the Habermasian model of discourse, this decision-making process is comparatively exclusive and highly asymmetrical in its relationship to the outside. It is a kind of council of elders — again having some affinity with the African political tradition, and especially with the structure of a chiefdom. PMN as 'development chiefdom'? We shall not pursue this question here. But the question should be kept in mind, when one enquires about the parastatality of PMN (see also Trotha 2004).

violently in the time of war. In particular, it helped to finance schools or to renovate , in one way or another existing ones which were often badly hit by the war. It lent a hand to equip administrative departments with furniture and to reconstruct the medical and veterinary infrastructure. It got involved a great deal for the construction of irrigation perimeters. It spent money to train engineers and to build and run radio stations. Nothing seems to have been left out as far as the successful stabilisation and the reconstruction and future of the region was concerned. In this composite mixture of measures, PMN did not admit of any limits of responsibility. It did not accept the restrictions which belong to principles of province or portfolio. It became involved where it seemed to be mean-ingful. It acted where it seemed likely that the three aims of PMN would be met successfully.

Accordingly, during its existence PMN frequently changed its place within the administration of Mali — from the *Commissariat of the North*[71] to a newly created *Ministry for the arid and semi-arid zones*, then to the *Ministry for the Environment*, and finally to the *Ministry for Public Works, Resource Management, Environment, and Urban Planning* where PMN is based today. The Malian government was limited to a protective role. This role guaranteed a certain flow of information between PMN and the Malian government. But above all, it secured the necessary political protection from any encroachment upon one struc-tural element of PMN which supports the whole construction: PMN's far-reaching autonomy from the Malian government and from its admin-istration in particular. PMN did not assist the Malian administration in the region for which PMN was responsible. It *was* the administration. It administered the region wherever the future was being planned, hostile groups were being brought together, and the region was renovated, reconstructed, and developed.

PMN's political and organisational autonomy realised a claim NGOs had been pressing for years, and which to exercise openly was only possible after the collapse of the postcolonial dictatorships at the beginning of the 1990s. In conjunction with the 'restructuration' and 'decentralisation' of West African states, a greater 'autonomy' of NGOs became a development strategy. PMN profited from the new discourse and was to set a good exam-ple in Africa for the emancipation of development aid from governments which had lost almost any credibility. According to a report, PMN *points the way to the future; it shows how development co-operation can be par-ticipatory, transparent, organisationally independent and without any great*

---

[71] The *Commisssariat du Nord* was provided for in the National Pact and encompasses a mediatory and advisory role for northern questions. Above all it is a sinecure for high-ranking and difficult representatives of the rebel movements.

administrative intervention, and can be planned and put into practice on the spot. Consequently, PMN became largely independent from the Malian government by mobilising powerful resources.

In Mali, PMN has become the most important program of the GTZ and Germany, one of Mali's leading donor countries. Thus, PMN has a powerful backing through its relationship with the GTZ and Germany. In view of its budget, PMN was and is financially powerful and at the same time financially independent of the Malian government. In addition, PMN has powerful local resources. It deals directly with the local population and their representatives and is their immediate contact and partner.[72] In connection with the then still precarious peace between the former war zones and the Malian government, the organisational arrangements of PMN, mentioned above, thus made PMN an agent of power *in* the region, an advocate *of* the region and a speaker *for* the region.

In view of the autonomy of PMN backed up by powerful resources, the notions of 'participation' and 'decentralisation' in the present discourse about development acquire a new meaning. They are metaphors for the parasovereignty of development aid. They favour to circumvent national governments and to establish direct relationships between development organisations, especially international ones, and local institutions and their representatives. They give preference to decision-making mechanisms and organisational structures, which are independent from the central governments and their administrations, programmatically as well as de facto. They are conceptual tools to promote parasovereignty in the centre of state rule. With PMN 'decentralised peace' becomes 'parasovereign peace'.

SUMMARY

The routes to peace are the roads of power-building. Among the latter are the roads of local power-building. The roads are taken by 'traditional authorities' as well as by new actors. They are walked along by ethnic groups, members of colonial and postcolonial administrative chiefdoms, and the ex-warriors of the post-clausewitzian war. Above all, they are used by experts and members of international organisations of conflict management and development aid. Being thus a kind of *corso* of extremely different actors, the routes to peace become roads to new forms of political domination.

---

[72] When, for example, representatives of a region which is not part of the areas of PMN, ask a German visitor who is on a *mission* in Mali for some help for their region, they demand from him to approach neither the German embassy nor the German government, and certainly not the Malian government. Instead, they request the visitor of addressing the responsible members of PMN and of getting PMN interested in the region.

One of these new types of political domination, which we call 'parastate rule', arises in peace processes of the kind of wars which the Malian Tuareg waged against each other and *Mali*. The Ifoghas and their chieftaincy needed peace in order to reconstruct, consolidate, and enlarge their rule. They made peace by transforming military victory over their internal opponents into parasovereign rule. This rule appropriates the monopoly of violence of the Malian state within the regional limits of a territorialised chiefdom. It retains the right to occupy regionally or nationally important posts, and finally tries to establish direct relations with international organisations of conflict management and development aid thus ensuring control over the financial resources of power.

On their way to parastate rule, the Ifoghas had to solve two problems. They had to re-integrate their internal opponents and enemies during the fratricidal war of 1994 and to secure the function, according to Hobbes any kind of sovereign rule has to fulfil: they had to offer protection from violence. Since colonial and postcolonial times both problems have been familiar to the Ifoghas chieftaincy as an administrative chiefdom. In their efforts to solve the problem of integration, the Ifoghas strongly restrained the politics of spoils on the part of their 'own people' and made powerful use of resources which have been made available to them from national and international peace and reconstruction programs thus emphasising that the 'local arena' includes systematic earnings both from the 'national' and the 'international arena'. In addition, the Ifoghas were highly aware of the power of symbols. Following a politics of restrain they validated the self-legitimations of their rule captured in an historiography which we call the 'noble story'. Also, they ingeniously set out to re-write the history of the Adagh. The aim of the 'new history' was to ease the social division into 'upper' and 'lower' estates by constructing historical kinship ties between the rulers and the ruled, between the Ifoghas and the Imghad.

The Hobbesian task was no less complicated than to manage the re-integration of the former enemies into the post-war order of the Adagh. But, certainly, it was bloodier, less refined, and less subtle. It meant military victory over the armed internal opponents, especially the ARLA, the rebel movement of the Imghad, and to make the most of the stalemate in the war between *Mali* and the armed movements of the Malian Tuareg. The Ifoghas succeeded in both cases. Their armed movement, the MPA, defeated the ARLA and gained the 'basic legitimacy' of protection from violence which was even more appreciated in the Adagh, because it meant the way out of the frightening condition of generalised violence. At the same time and having the MPA at their disposal, the Ifoghas were able to threaten credibly the Malian army and to effectively deny the Malian state its monopoly of violence. Therefore, the Ifoghas offered armed protection from their local and regional competitors as well as from *Mali*. Their protection had an 'inner' and 'outer' dimension.

But the course to parasovereign peace the Ifoghas adopted was not a purely local phenomenon. It was and is deeply affected by processes of political reconstruction, which might change the very character of the post-colonial African state based on the western model which was never achieved. On the one hand, The Ifoghas' path to parastate rule was smoothed and shortened by international programs like PAREM aimed at the demobilisation of ex-rebels. The Ifoghas directly transformed PAREM into a major asset of their parasovereign strategies of peace making. Convincingly they pursued the 'policy of figures' and profited from the economic, social, and legitimising qualities of PAREM. On the other hand, the course to parasovereign peace was also followed by PMN. Completely funded from outside and having an the exceptional autonomy from the Malian government and administration, PMN reduced the role of the Malian state and its administration in the reconstruction of peace and order in North Mali to a status short of mere symbolic character. While following another road to parasovereign peace, backed-up by the current development rhetoric of 'decentralisation' and 'participation', PMN thus joined the Ifoghas' route to peace in a political order which is rapidly distancing itself from the usual pattern of the nation state.

REFERENCES

Abrous, Dahbia 1990. Le prix de la survie ou le deuil d'un passé. *Revue du Monde Musulmane et de la Méditerrannée 57, Nr 3*: 163–81.

Abrous, Dahbia 1993. 'Peuple de l'Azaouad', tamurt ou comment négocier une définition de soi. In *Le politique dans l'histoire touarègue*, edited by Hélène Claudot-Hawad. (Aix-en-Provence: Les Cahiers de l'IREMAM).

Acord, Novib, Oxfam 1995. *L'étude sur le Nord du Mali*. De la Tragédie à l'espoir. (Bamako: AMAP).

Ag Ahar, E 1990. L'initiation d'un ashamur. *Revue du Monde Musulmane et de la Méditérannée 57, Nr 3*: 141–52.

Ag Bay, Cheikh, Rachid Bellil 1986. Une société touareg en crise: Les Kel Adrar du Mali. In *Awal 2*: 49–86.

Ag Sidiyene, Ehya, Georg Klute 1989. La chronologie des années 1913/14 à 1987/88 chez les Touaregs Kel-Adagh du Mali. *Journal des Africanistes 59 (1–2)*: 203–27.

Akzente focus *Réalisations de la gtz. 1998. Special issue about 'Mali'*. (Eschborn: Deutsche Gesellschaft für Technische Zusammenarbeit (GTZ)).

Anonyme 1964. Les opérations militaires contre les rebelles du désert. Communiqué du Secrétariat à la Défense et à la Sécurité du Mali (Source: L'Essor du 15-8-1964). *Afrique Contemporaine, Sept–Oct 1964*: 14.

Baqué, Philippe 1993. Camps de réfugiés touaregs en Mauritanie. Les rapports nord-sud et l'aide au développement. In *Le politique dans l'histoire touarègue*, edited by Hélène Claudot-Hawad. (Aix-en-Provence: Les Cahiers de l'IREMAM).

Beck, Kurt 1989. Stämme im Schatten des Staats: Zur Entstehung administrativer Häuptlingstümer im nördlichen Sudan. *Sociologus 39:* 19–35.

Bellil, Rachid, Badi Dida 1993. Evolution de la relation entre Kel Ahaggar et Kel Adagh. In *Le politique dans l'histoire touarègue*, edited by Hélène Claudot-Hawad. (Aix-en-Provence: Les Cahiers de l'IREMAM).

Bellil, Rachid 1990. Une nouvelle forme d'action. Le mouvement associatif à Tamanrasset. *Revue du Monde Musulmane et de la Méditerannée 57, Nr 3:* 153–62.

Bernus, Edmond 1990. Continuité et ruptures chez les Illabakan du Niger. *Revue du Monde Musulmane et de la Méditerannée 57, Nr 3:* 183–8.

Bierschenk, Thomas, Jean-Pierre Olivier de Sardan 1998. *Les pouvoirs au village. Le Bénin rural entre démocratisation et décentralisation.* (Paris: Karthala).

Bierschenk, Thomas, Jean-Pierre Olivier de Sardan. 1999. Dezentralisierung und lokale Demokratie. Macht und Politik im ländlichen Benin in den 1980er Jahren. In *Dezentralisierung, Demok-ratisierung und die lokale Repräsentation des Staates. Theoretische Kontroversen und empirische Forschungen / Décentralisation, démocratisation, et les représentations locales de la force publique. Débats théoriques et recherches empiriques*, edited by Jakob Rösel, Trutz von Trotha. (Köln: Rüdiger Köppe).

Boilley, Pierre 1999. *Les Touareg Kel Adagh.* (Paris: Karthala).

Bourgeot, André 1990a. Quadrillages et pâturages: des Touaregs sacrifiés. *Journal des Anthropologues 40–41:* 135–46.

Bourgeot, André 1990b. Identité: parcours nomades. Faits et représentations. *Etudes Rurales 120, Oct–Déc 1990:* 9–15.

Bourgeot, André 1992. L'enjeu politique de l'histoire: vision idéologique des événements touaregs. 1990–1992. *Politique Africaine, Nr 48:* 129–34.

Bourgeot, André 1994a. Révoltes et rébellions en pays touareg. *Afrique contemporaine, No 170:* 3–18.

Bourgeot, André 1994b. Le corps touareg désarticulé ou l'impensé politique. *Cahiers d'Études Africaines 136, 34, Nr 4:* 659–71.

Callwell, Charles E Col 1994. Small Wars. In *War*, edited by Lawrence Freedom (London, New York: Oxford University Press) (England first 1906).

Claudot-Hawad, Hélène, ed 1990. *Touaregs. Exil et résistance, Revue du Monde Musulmane et de la Méditerannée 57, Nr 3.* (Aix-en-Provence: Édisud).

Claudot-Hawad, Hélène 1992. Bandits, rebelles et partisans: vision plurielle des événements touaregs, 1990–1992. *Politique Africaine, Nr 46:* 143–49.

Claudot-Hawad, Hélène 1993. La coutume absente ou les métamorphoses contemporaines du politique chez les Touaregs. In *Le politique dans l'histoire touarègue*, edited by Hélène Claudot-Hawad. (Aix-en-Provence: Les Cahiers de l'IREMAM).

Claudot-Hawad, Hélène 1994. L'évolutionnisme bien-pensant ou l'ethnologie à sens unique. *Cahiers d'Études Africaines 136, 34–34;* 673–85.

Creveld, Martin van 1998. *Die Zukunft des Krieges.* (München: Gerling Akademie) (American first 1991).

Creveld, Martin van 1999. *Aufstieg und Untergang des Staates.* (München: Gerling Akademie) (Engl first 1999).

Dayak, Mano 1992. *Touareg, La Tragédie.* (Paris: Jean-Claude Lattès).

Dröge, Kai 1999. *Die Tuaregrebellion in der malischen Presse. Eine empirische Untersuchung.* Unpublished Master thesis. (Siegen: Soziologie, Fachbereich 1, Universität Siegen).

Feltes, Silke-Katinka. 1996 *Demobilisierung und Reintegration von Ex-Kombattanten. GTZ-Erfahrungen und Aktivitäten in sieben afrikanischen Ländern.* GTZ-Dokumentation. (Eschborn: Deutsche Gesellschaft für Technische Zusammenarbeit, Abteilungen) 403 and 426.

Geertz, Clifford 1994. Dichte Beschreibung. Bemerkungen zu einer deutenden Theorie von Kultur. In *idem, Dichte Beschreibung. Beiträge zum Verstehen kultureller Systeme,* pp 7–43. (Frankfurt a M: Suhrkamp) (American first 1973).

Gleichmann, Colin 1997. *Concepts and Experiences of Demobilisation and Reintregration of Ex-Combatants. Guidelines and Instruments for Future Programmes.* Eschborn: Gesellschaft für Technische Zusammenarbeit (gtz), Division 426 Emergency and Refugee Aid, Division 403 Organisation, Communication, Management, Programme Team Demobilisation and Reintegration.

Hawad 1990. La Teshumara antidote de l'état. *Revue du Monde Musulmane et de la Méditerannée 57, No 3:* 123–38.

Hobbes, Thomas 1965. *Leviathan, or the Matter, Form, and Power of a Commonwealth, Ecclesiastical and Civil.* (Dent ua: Everyman's Library) (first 1914/1651).

Hofmeier, Rolf, Volker Matthies, ed 1992. *Vergessene Kriege in Afrika.* Göttingen: Lamuv.

Klute, Georg 1990. Die Revolte der Gastarbeiter. Die Auseinandersetzung zwischen Tuareg und Regierung in Mali und Niger. *Blätter des IZ3W, No 169:* 3–6.

Klute, Georg 1991a. Die Iforas-Tuareg im Bergland des Adrar. Eine ganz andere Herrschaft. *Der Fremde, 2/91:* 134–38.

Klute, Georg 1991b. Die Revolte der *ishumagh.* In *Ethnizität und Gewalt,* edited by Thomas Scheffler. (Hamburg: Deutsches Orient-Institut).

Klute, Georg 1995a. Der Tuaregkonflikt in Mali und Niger. In *Jahrbuch Dritte Welt 1996. Daten, Übersichten, Analysen,* edited by Joachim Betz, Stefan Brüne, (Deutsches Übersee-Institut Hamburg. München: Beck).

Klute, Georg 1995b. Hostilités et alliances. Archéologie de la dissidence dans le mouvement rebelle des Touareg au Mali. In *La démocratie déclinée, Cahiers d'É-tudes africaines, No 137, vol 35:* 55–71.

Klute, Georg 1996. *Die Poesie der Revolte. Kassettenmusik bei den Tuareg.* Manuskript. (Siegen: Soziologie, Fachbereich 1, Universität-Gesamthochschule Siegen).

Klute, Georg 1998. Vom administrativen Häuptlingtum zur regionalen Parasouveränität. In *Working Papers on African Societies, Nr 26,* edited by Thomas Bierschenk ua (Berlin: Das Arabische Buch).

Klute, Georg 1999. Lokale Akteure des Dezentralisierungsprozesses im Norden von Mali. In *Dezentralisierung, Demokratisierung und die lokale Repräsentation des Staates. Theoretische Kontroversen und empirische Forschungen / Décentralisation, démocratisation, et les représentations locales de la force publique. Débats théoriques et recherches empiriques,* edited by Jakob Rösel, Trutz von Trotha. (Köln: Rüdiger Köppe).

Klute, Georg 2000. Vom Krieg zum Frieden im Norden von Mali. In *Afrika und die Globalisierung*, edited by Peter Hahn, Gerd Spittler, 455–72. (Münster: LIT).

Klute, Georg Trutz von Trotha 1999. *Parasouveränität. Gedanken über einen Typus intermediärer Herrschaft*. Vortrag, gehalten auf der Tagung 'Macht und Herrschaft' der Sektion Entwicklungssoziologie und Sozialanthropologie der Deutschen Gesellschaft für Soziologie in Marburg vom 10–12 Juni 1999.

Krings, Thomas 1995. Marginalisation and Revolt among the Tuareg in Mali and Niger. *GeoJournal 36, Nr 1*: 57–63.

Mühlmann, Wilhelm E 1940. *Krieg und Frieden. Ein Leitfaden der politischen Ethnologie. Mit Berücksichtigung völkerkundlichen und geschichtlichen Stoffes*. (Heidelberg: C. Winter's Universitätsbuchhan-dlung).

Popitz, Heinrich 1999. *Phänomene der Macht*. (Tübingen: Mohr) (first 1986/1968).

Poulton, Robin-Edward, Ibrahim Ag Youssouf 1998. *A Peace of Timbuktu. Democratic Governance, Development and African Peacemaking*. (New York, Genf: United Nations Publications).

Rösel, Jakob 1999. Decentralization: Some critical remarks on an ideal and a strategy. In *Dezentralisierung, Demokratisierung und die lokale Repräsentation des Staates Theoretische Kontroversen und empirische Forschungen / Décentralisation, démocratisation, et les représentations locales de la force publique. Débats théoriques et recherches empiriques*, edited by Jakob Rösel, Trutz von Trotha. (Köln: Rüdiger Köppe).

Swift, Jeremy 1979. *The Economics of Traditional Nomadic Pastoralism. The Tuareg of the Adrar n Iforas (Mali)*. Unpublished Ph.D Dissertation. Sussex.

Tilly, Charles 1986. War Making and State Making as Organized Crime. In *Bringing the State Back In*, edited by Peter B Evans, Dietrich. Rueschemeyer, Theda Skocpol, 169–91. (Cambridge: Cambridge University Press) (first 1985).

Treiber, Hubert 1984. 'Wahlverwandtschaften' zwischen Webers Religions- und Rechtssoziologie. In *Zur Rechtssoziologie Max Webers. Interpretation, Kritik, Weiterentwicklung*, edited by Stefan Breuer, Hubert Treiber. (Opladen: Westdeutscher Verlag).

Trotha, Trutz von 1994a. *Koloniale Herrschaft. Zur soziologischen Theorie der Staatsentstehung am Beispiel des 'Schutzgebietes Togo'*. (Tübingen: Mohr).

Trotha, Trutz von 1994b. 'Streng, aber gerecht' — 'hart, aber tüchtig'. Über Formen von Basislegitimität und ihre Ausprägungen am Beginn staatlicher Herrschaft. In *Legitimation von Herrschaft und Recht / La légitimation du pouvoir et du droit. 3. Kolloquium deutsch-französischer Rechtsanthropologen / 3e Colloque franco-allemand des anthropologues du droit*. Sankt Augustin, 20–25 November 1992, edited by Wilhelm JG Möhlig, Trutz von Trotha, 69–90. (Köln: Rüdiger Köppe).

Trotha, Trutz von 1999a. Über den Erfolg und die Brüchigkeit der Utopie staatlicher Herrschaft. Herrschaftssoziologische Beobachtungen über den kolonialen und nachkolonialen Staat in Westafrika. In *Verstaatlichung der Welt? Europäische Staatsmodelle und außereuropäische Machtprozesse*, edited by Wolfgang Reinhard, 223–51. (München: Oldenbourg).

Trotha, Trutz von 1999b. Das Ende der Clausewitzschen Welt oder vom Selbstzweck des Krieges und der Vorherrschaft des 'Krieges geringer Intensität'. *Soziologische Revue 22*: 131–41.

Trotha, Trutz von. 2000a. Rêves, doutes, courage, avenir. La décentralisation entre les rêves de dérmocratie de base, le scepticisme libéral démocratique, l'Etat central impuissant et l'avenir para-étatique. In *Atelier 'Décentralisation en Afrique occidentale et centrale', Bamako, 9 au 12 novembre 1999, Documentation, Tome I: Résultats de l'atelier,* edited by Deutsche Gesellschaft für Technische Zusammenarbeit (GTZ), Département 42, Réformes politiques, économiques et sociales, 17–28. (Eschborn: Deutsche Gesellschaft für Technische Zusammenarbeit).

Trotha, Trutz von 2000b. Die Zukunft liegt in Afrika oder vom Zerfall des Staates, von der Vorherrschaft der konzentrischen Ordnung und vom Aufstieg der Parastaatlichkeit. *Leviathan 28:* 253–79.

Trotha, Trutz von 2002. Über die Zukunft der Gewalt. *Monatsschrift für Kriminologie und Strafrechtsreform 85, No 5:* 349–68.

Trotha, Trutz von (2004). Stationen und Formen der Parasouveränität. Bausteine für eine Theorie parasouveräner Herrschaft oder Beobachtungen über das *Programm Mali Nord.* In: *Grenzgänge(r). Beiträge zu Politik, Kultur und Religion. Festschrift für Gerhard Hufnagel zum 65. Geburtstag,* hrsg. v. Sigrid Baringhorst, Ingo Broer, pp 188–223. Siegen: Universitätsverlag Siegen – universi.

Vallet, Michel 1990–99. La vie au Sahara et en zone saharo-sahèlienne. Chronique de Michel Vallet. In *La Rahla — Amicale des Sahriens — Le Saharien, 2/1990 (No 114) — 1/1999 (No 148).*

Weber, Max 1964. Die Typen der Herrschaft. In *Wirtschaft und Gesellschaft. Grundriss der verstehenden Soziologie,* Studienausgabe, Erster Halbband, edited by Johannes Winckelmann. (Köln, Berlin: Kiepenheuer & Witsch) (first 1922/1918–20).

Zimprich, Elke, Colin Gleichmann 1997. *When Combatants Become Civilians. GTZ programmes for demobilisation and reintegration of ex-combattants.* (Eschborn: Gesellschaft für Technische Zusammenarbeit (gtz), Division 426 Emergency and Refugee Aid).

7

Legislation and Decentralisation in Uganda: From Resistance Councils to Elected Local Councils with Guaranteed Representation

DIRK BEKE[1]

1 INTRODUCTION

THE AIM OF this chapter is to contribute to legal anthropology by analysing the legislation process, not in the sense of formal legal procedures, but by examining the process in its political and social environment and by exploring the impact of the new rules. It is thus a contribution to legal anthropology in the field of public law in Africa. It will examine the origin, the objectives, the recent evolution and the implementation of the legislation concerning decentralisation in Uganda. Although elements of traditional leadership will be examined, the focus of attention will be also on the political environment and the role of other local actors, such as non-governmental organisations (NGOs) and foreign donors. The present decentralisation in Uganda must be seen as an important element of the global policy reform that started in 1986 after more than twenty years dictatorship and civil war.

We cannot deny, notwithstanding the ongoing unrest in the northern districts and on the western borders, that today the large majority of the Ugandan population lives in a normalised environment with modest possibilities for development. It is also clear that, although opposition to the no-party regime is growing, Museveni's National Resistance Movement was able to derive its legitimacy largely from the fact it brought stabilisation

[1] This study is partly the result of a research project on decentralisation in Uganda for the Belgian department of development co-operation done in 1998–99 by Jan-Lodewijk Grootaers, Dirk Deprez and myself. The research is based on desk-study of the abundant literature and on about fifty interviews with different people involved in the decentralisation process (from cabinet-minister down to women representatives at the parishes).

and peace after the long years of atrocities committed by the former multi-party and military regimes.

The aim is to analyse a more or less normalised situation, not merely its beginnings immediately after the restoration of peace, so that its evolution during the period after the civil war may be highlighted.

The main questions are: To what extent are the new rules concerning the local governments and decentralisation created by the state as instruments in a process of legal engineering? What is the impact of legal evolutionism on the behaviour of the state? What are the unwanted effects of the new legislation for the regime of Museveni?

It is clear that the new laws and constitutional rules are presented by the government as indispensable instruments for creating political stability, restoring the functioning of local governments and guaranteeing development. At the same time it may be seen that the regime of Museveni wants to legitimate the process of decentralisation by describing it as a result of more or less spontaneous self-organisation by the people.

We will analyse the different opinions about the origin and the further development of the local councils with the following question in mind: is the legislation the result of an evolution based on grass-roots organisation or is it mainly a creation of the regime? We will also explore the extent to which the new legislation has opened further opportunities for political participation, in particular that of women. Another question is the degree to which popular participation at the local level can develop under a so-called 'no-party regime'.

2   NEW LOCAL ADMINISTRATION: PARTICIPATION WITHOUT PARTIES

Shortly after Museveni came to power in Kampala, he proclaimed the so-called no-party system. His new ruling National Resistance Movement (NRM) was declared not to be a political party but an all-inclusive organisation operating at local, district and national level. Political parties were held responsible for the political instability that had led to the political turmoil and civil war. They were considered to be divisive structures that encouraged ethnic separatism. Although political parties were not formally forbidden, a ban was declared on party political activity.

In 1999, political parties are legal organisations. They can formulate statements to newspapers but they cannot participate as parties in any election or organise rallies and demonstrations. Opposition candidates can only participate in local and in national elections as individuals; they are not allowed to refer to political parties.

As regards local administration, one of the first measures of the new regime of the NRM was the formalisation and integration of the *Resistance*

Councils (*RCs*) into a new local government system based on the five levels of local government, which already existed. In 1987, the Resistance Councils and Committees Statute was adopted.[2] Its most significant measure was the general introduction, at each of the five levels, of an elected leadership through the establishment of councils and committees that were to function parallel to the existing hierarchy of appointed chiefs and executives (Kasumba 1997, 8).

The Resistance Councils and Committees Statute elaborated on the five-tier system and conferred on the local councils and committees large powers and responsibilities for local matters. Even judicial powers were included at the *RC3* and *RC2* level. At the same time, the Statute trimmed down the former authority of the chiefs and subordinated them to the local councils. Kasumba (1997, 9) is in no doubt that this was the beginning of the process of Power Shifting.

The formalisation of the *RCs* and their integration in an overall system of elected local councils was the start of the decentralisation reform. The reform was continued with the adoption in parliament, in 1993, of the Decentralised Local Government Statute. In this legislation the appellation *Resistance Councils* (*RCs*) was replaced by the more neutral designation *Local Councils* (*LCs*).

The global reform policy of decentralisation was reinforced by the new constitution of 1995. Chapter eleven (Local Government, arts 176 to 208) formulates the basic regulations and principles concerning decentralisation, local governments and local units. Finally in 1997, a new Local Government Act was passed in parliament. This new legislation has been presented as an Act to amend, consolidate and streamline the existing law on Local Governments in line with the new Constitution.

3   THE ORIGIN AND DEVELOPMENT OF THE LOCAL RESISTANCE COUNCILS AND COMMITTEES

An important element of legal anthropology in the field of public law is to acquire an insight into the origin of new rules, structures and institutions. The main question in this chapter is whether the new legislation must be understood as a kind of a confirmation or formalisation of newly arisen local institutions, or whether these institutions are rather the result of new legislation which has been used as an instrument by the state to create a local bureaucratic framework.

---

[2] The Resistance Councils and Committees Statute No 9 of 1987 was completed with the Judicial Powers Statute of 1988 and the Resistance Councils Statute No 6 which made the subcounty (RCIII / LCIII) the most important local unit.

It is interesting to see how the process of formalisation of the *Resistance Councils* (*RCs*) has received quite diverging interpretations and comments in the literature (academic analyses, official reports and political statements).

The system of *RCs* is, of course, not an invention of the NRM of Museveni, as the official political doctrine likes to hint today. Even in Uganda, similar systems were used by the Amin-regime, in the form of village security councils, and under Obote's UNLF rule. Under these former regimes, such committees were mainly administrative and security organs of the state at the local level, superimposed on the other existing state organs. They were not a creation of the local population but were forced on it from above (Ddungo 1994, 368). The question is whether the Resistance Councils that emerged during the struggle of the National Resistance Army (NRA) of Museveni against the second Obote regime can be compared with the former local security committees or whether they were less state imposed.

The strategy of resistance councils has also been used in other places of the world. This tactic partakes of a well-known global strategy of guerrilla warfare by which village people are encouraged to create resistance councils. This kind of new, village-based, grassroots structure of local administration and participation has proven its effectiveness in several guerrilla wars. It enables the speedy creation of a basic administration to fill up the local administrative and political vacuum. Armed resistance movements see in these new grassroots structures a means to gain support for their struggle. Let it be noted that Museveni, in earlier days, underwent a trainee-ship with *Frelimo* in Mozambique.

Tidermand (1994, 201–3) describes how, in the regions conquered by Museveni, the new councils and committees were originally not so much a part of the particular military strategy of the NRA as an answer to the disappeared or collapsed structures of state-administration in the conquered areas.

The author also explains how the creation of the resistance councils underwent a long process of trial and error. Until mid 1982, the NRA's tactic was first to convince influential people of the villages of the legitimacy of its struggle, and then to give those people responsibilities in the new resistance councils. The problem was that whenever these notables failed to act in the interests of the local population, the NRA was still identified with them. To avoid this risk, therefore, the whole village was asked to elect its representatives. Out of this procedure emerged a whole hierarchical structure of gradual elected councils — parallel with the administrative structures — with at the bottom the village council (*Resistance Council 1* or *RC1*) and at the top the district council (or *RC5*). The new councils acquired the responsibility for local government and the administration of justice at the local level. For the NRA they became an indispensable structure in the war effort. For the rural people involved they were a new form of democratic local government, a popular system to ensure law and security and, even more so, a well organised structure through which the state-bureaucracy, which was seen as an enemy of the citizen, could be resisted. Howes (1997, 21) and Brett (1994) relate how a degree of stability began to return under this new system.

Oloka-Onyango and Barya (1997, 123–24) explain that the change in Uganda resulted from a curious marriage of the intelligentsia and the peasantry but not from what remained of the civil society that formed the NRM. The two authors describe the *RCs* as village grassroots structures of political organisation and participation, which, they emphasise, considerably influenced the extent to which civil society was able to impose significant pressure on the state-apparatus. They echo the observation of Jjuukoo (1996, 187) that the *RCs* possessed a manifest duality: popular at the grassroots level, but at the same time more state instruments at higher levels. This state influence even had a tendency to increase with the process of the consolidation of the NRM-regime.

Makare (2000, 8) writes that, over time, the roles of the *RCs* have enormously expanded and that their 'watchdog' functions have substantially changed from the voluntary ones of 1986 to the new ones of the 1990s and have become part of the bureaucratic structure of government.

Oloka-Onyango and Barya admit that the *RCs* played a crucial role in the expression by the ordinary people of discontent towards the former elitist and distant actors in civil and political society, who were considered responsible for the general deterioration. Many of the former forces, and particularly the political parties, had become so discredited that there was little possibility of them finding popular support.

The two authors argue that the success of the *RC* experiment lays in the fact that it not only addressed the concerns of the rural population but was also an attempt to alter the existing political structures based on the omnipotent chief (see also Mamdani 1995, 233). Makara (2000, 3) concurs with this view and writes that the RCs started to curb the powers of the local chiefs — who hitherto have held absolute administrative as well as judicial power. Oloka-Onyango and Barya conclude:

> With the marginalisation of the chief and the commencement of a vigorous process of decentralisation, the stage was set for a continual strengthening of local as opposed to central structures of governance.

The initial system of elections of the *RCs* was direct only at the village level (RC1); at the higher levels elections were indirect with elected members of one level forming the electorate, which chose representatives at the next level up. The result of this type of indirect system is, as Ddungo (1994, 373) also remarks, that the higher we go, the more the electorate shrinks in proportion to the population and that the right to recall representatives at any level only belongs to the representative body immediately below it.

Ddungo (1994, 368–69) gives a brief but interesting classification of the different attitudes towards the RCs. He states that bureaucratic views describe them as units for implementing government policy more effectively. Democratic views describe them more as organs of the people through which civil servants, the state bureaucracy and even the military can be controlled at the local levels. A third view, strongly subscribed to by organised political parties, sees them as units of one political group, the NRM of Museveni, and argues that the system is used as an alibi for the present no-partyism. Finally Ddungo mentions a fourth view, which he indicates rightly as the semi-official version, that takes *RCs* simultaneously as rgans of the people, organs of the Movement, and organs of the state.[3] He states that this last view implicitly assumes an identity of interests among the people, the Movement and the state and that this reasoning favours administration over politics. He concludes that in this way the institutions created to promote popular participation are subsequently reoriented toward the consolidation of bureaucratic rule.

Ddungo's last conclusion is questionable because a legislative framework which guarantees popular participation can generate forces, in this case at the local and district levels, that bureaucratic or authoritarian rule can hardly turn back. It is precisely the aim of this study to examine the degree to which the new generation of the *RCs*, the present *LCs*, are consolidating bureaucratic rule and, conversely, the extent to which they are able to ensure popular participation at the local levels.

However, Ddungo's description of different situations in different areas is undoubtedly correct. The author states that the legal and political structure of the *RCs* was uniform throughout the country but that *RCs* tended to mean different things in different parts of the country due to the geographically varying nature of practice. In some parts of the country the role was policy-making within the framework of the NRM. In other parts it was a struggle against the state, the army, police, courts, bureaucracy etc. up to and beyond the provisions of the legal framework of the *RCs* (Ddungo 1994, 402–3). The difference can largely be explained by geographical variation in the popularity of the NRM and the political forces and ethnic influences operating in the regions.

We must also repeat here that the *RCs* underwent a mutation due to popular pressure and that finally the legislation establishing the *LCs* introduced for the local governments direct elections, thereby giving them a much more representative character.

---

[3] This point of view was also reflected in a lot of our interviews with official and semi-official spokesmen.

4   THE LOCAL GOVERNMENTS ACT[4]

The Local Government Act of 1997, and also the former Statutes of 1987 and 1993, can be considered to be, to a large extent, the result of an evolution of the *RCs*, but an evolution within the limits imposed by the NRM-regime. Regarding the evolution towards more political democracy, the new legislation confirms the idea of participation through elections at the different levels of local government.

The Act provides a well-structured legal framework for the devolution of government functions. The Act of 1997 confirms the replacement of the pre-1986 administrative structures and the legal reforms that were achieved by the statutes of 1987 and 1993 and that led to interesting possibilities for genuine decentralisation. Various units of local government as autonomous institutions of governance have been created. The districts (*LC5*), municipalities (*LC4b*) and sub-counties (*LC3*) have been established as corporate units with larger autonomy than the other levels of local government.

The Act stipulates, in a very detailed manner, the different tasks and responsibilities of each level and lays down rules and regulations for the functioning of local administration, local planning and local development. It establishes the competencies and gives guidelines for local administration and defines the relationship between the local authorities and the central government departments. On the practical side, the Act empowers the local governments to mobilise resources locally and to decide on their use. They can hire their own staff with a separate civil servant system and the councils can supervise administrative staff (Makara 2000, 3). Finally the new legislation offers possibilities, as we will see, for decentralised international co-operation and at the same time it is clear that donor co-operation has become an important support for the implementation of decentralisation.

5   THE PRESENT LOCAL GOVERNMENT STRUCTURE

The structure of the local governments and administrations can be briefly explained by analysing the five different levels (*see Appendix, Scheme 1*).

At the grassroots level we find the village with the village council or Local Council One (*LC1*). The council comprises all of the adult residents; they elect nine members for the village executive or committee.

---

[4] The Local Governments Act, 19 March 1997. *Acts Supplement to the Uganda Gazette*, N°19 Volume XC, 24 March 1997.

From four to seven neighbouring villages form a parish or a ward (*LC2*). The members of the village committees together with the councillors from the *LC3* elected in that parish or ward constitute the council of the parish or ward. This council elects an executive committee of nine members for the *LC2* level. The average population of a parish in rural areas is about five thousand people; in urban areas it is more.

The third step is the sub-county, town, municipal or city division (*LC3*), made up of four to seven *LC2* units. The members of the council are elected directly; they elect an executive committee and a chairperson (the term 'chairman' has been banned in the legislation).

At the fourth level (*LC4*) we find two different types of local structures: the county in rural areas and the municipality in urban areas.

The county council is only an administrative unit. It comprises the members of the subcounty committees together with the councillors from the district council (*LC5*) elected in that county. The county council elects a chairperson and vice-chairperson. The average population at this level is about one hundred thousand.

The municipality, on the contrary, has full local government status. It has a council that is elected directly and also a directly elected municipal chairperson (mayor). The council elects an executive committee.

The highest level (*LC5*) is the district or the city, where council members and the District Chairperson are elected directly. The council elects the members of the executive committee.

The Act makes a distinction between local governments (decentralisation) and local administrative units. Local governments are: the district or city (*LC5*); the municipality (*LC4*), but not the county (also at the level of *LC4*); and the subcounty, town, municipal and city divisions (*LC3*). The Act provides for these local governments most of the characteristics and typical instruments for genuine decentralisation (Mawhood 1983, 9–11). They possess a separate legal existence, a directly elected council and chairperson, their own budgets and tax revenues and the power to issue bylaws and local regulations.

The county (at *LC4*), parish and ward (*LC2*) and the village (*LC1*) have the status of administrative units. They have some modest characteristics of autonomy, such as a (limited) budget and an executive committee, but their council is elected indirectly (except in the villages). They have neither a separate legal existence nor their own tax revenues. Nevertheless, it must be noted that the village fulfils an important local political electoral role because — as we have explained — every resident of eighteen or more is a member of the village council and this council forms the electorate for the members of executive committee, who are also the members of the parish and ward councils (*LC2*).

The Act contains also some very interesting elements in order to make up the balance between legal engineering and legal evolutionism. Remarkable in this regard are the system of reserved seats for women and 'minorities', the 'lining-up system' for elections and the place of traditional leaders. These elements will be examined in detail in the next chapters, but first a clarification is needed related to the terminology concerning 'minorities'.

6   LOCAL ETHNIC MINORITIES AND THE CONFUSING TERMINOLOGY CONCERNING 'MINORITIES'

An overview of the administrative structure related to the ethnic composition of Uganda today shows that almost no district is mono-ethnic. This internal multi-ethnicity is often seen as the reason for local conflicts. A frequent response to these conflicts has been to split up districts. The danger is that this process is leading towards fragmentation, resulting in areas too small to administer efficiently, in particular too small to guarantee the presence of a viable (administrative) infrastructure and of competent officials.

It is noteworthy that in the elected councils, there are reserved seats for women, for youth and for 'minorities'. The wording 'minorities' however refers to handicapped, and not to ethnic or religious minorities.

7   THE ROLE OF WOMEN AND 'MINORITIES' IN THE DECENTRALISATION PROCESS

The Ugandan legislation imposes a system of guaranteed representation for women, who must comprise at least one-third of every Ugandan local council. This guaranteed female representation reflects beyond any doubt a very important example of legal engineering to introduce a significant participation of women in politics. This legal commitment, although welcomed by women's associations and many individual women, is not the result of pressure or the actions of women's associations or large women's groups but is the result of a well-deliberated initiative coming from the top echelons of the NRM.

The legislation also stipulates that at least one of the members of the Executive Committees shall be a female (Local Governments Act, art 17 (3) and art 26 (3)). This guaranteed representation is not an isolated regulation but works in concert with other governmental actions on behalf of women. For example, under a special Ministry of Gender, at the various levels of local administration, women's councils look after the position of women in politics and in employment. However it is frequently reported that these councils, and even the Ministry of Gender, suffer from a lack of resources and staff.

Regarding the results of women's guaranteed participation in local politics, Howes (1997, 17) reports that conventional gender roles, which usually involve a rigid and unequal division of labour, create for women a lack of time for meetings. Besides, in many of the traditional communities, women are confronted with a proscription on addressing male chiefs. A study of Tamale (1998), moreover, indicates that once the legal commitment of one-third of seats for females is achieved, the majority of male politicians often consider it unnecessary to appoint more women to political and administrative organs.

The fact that at least two seats are guaranteed to youth representatives and at least two to representatives of the handicapped ('minorities'), in each case one male and one female, in every elected council is also remarkable. The complete system of representation is explained in scheme 2 (*see Appendix*). This system of guaranteed seats in the councils is for the Ugandan state and for the present regime a strong element in its legitimacy, especially in the eyes of donors. It reflects a useful image of 'political correctness'.

The guaranteed representation of women must be seen not only as an emanation of the progressive ideas of the NRM leaders but also as a tactical move to acquire the support of a large group of the population. At the same time it is a counterweight to the male-dominated traditional structures. It is clear that these measures have opened up opportunities for women and 'minorities' and that anybody attempting to close the door on these opportunities will have to face enormous opposition.

8   ELECTIONS AND THE 'LINING-UP SYSTEM'

Uganda uses two types of elections: the 'normal' secret ballot and the special 'lining-up system'. At the higher levels, the district, city (*LC5*) and the municipality (*LC4*), the elections for councillors, other than those for the reserved seats for women, are conducted by secret ballot. At the lower levels and at all levels for the one-third reserved seats for women, they are conducted according to the 'lining-up system'.

For the lining-up system, candidates and local electors gather at a central place. To guarantee minimum participation a strict quorum of one third of the persons entitled to vote is required. The votes are cast by counting the electors lined up behind their preferred candidate, candidate's agent or portrait of the candidate (Local Governments Act, art 135, 6). The system was introduced for the elections for the *RCs* and, despite criticism of its lack of secrecy, formalised in the new legislation for the lower levels and for rural areas because of its simplicity and low cost. It must be admitted that it allowed the new regime to organise elections without adjournment and it proves that the process of elections in an environment with a lack of bureaucratic infrastructure and resources can take off.

It should be noted that candidates for elections are obliged to pay a registration fee. This fee is designed to ensure the serious intentions of the candidate and a minimum support for his/her candidature. Several interviews with local councillors, however, cited the relatively high registration fee as a serious hindrance to participation, in particular for representatives of the rural population.

9   DECENTRALISATION AS A WAY OF PASSING ON PUBLIC FUNCTIONS TO NON-GOVERNMENTAL ACTORS

The government is using decentralisation as a step in a process of passing on public functions to NGOs and other actors in the civil society (*société civile*) and even to private companies. The local entities are receiving more and more responsibilities. This transfer of powers and duties corresponds with the idea — or wish — that should the entities not be able to cope with all these new tasks they will have to ask for the help of these outside agencies. The official reason is that at the local level there is a better view on the necessities and on the possibilities and dynamism but the passing on of responsibilities is also taking place because it offers the prospect of savings in the national government's budget.

Concerning the activities of the NGOs, and of other groups of the *société civile* in Uganda, it has been recorded that they play a key-role in the development of greater participation at the local level. Besides, many of these actors are active in the field of local development and are offering public services such as education, public health care, arbitrage and conflict resolution. In this context, it is important to mention that in addition to the many NGOs working on the basis of the aid of donors, there are — in Uganda — many groups, which have been functioning for a very long period without any real foreign aid (Curtis 1999, 285–86).

However, the actual almost unlimited mobilisation of non-governmental actors raises questions about co-ordination, and more importantly, the lack of democratic structures, transparency and accountability. These organisations are almost never accountable to the local population (Mandani 1996, 94). There is a real danger that the supervision and auditing of the administration as it is imposed within the official decentralised structures will be de facto neutralised, as has already become clear during interviews and in reports. In a few cases non-governmental actors use their own strong (financial) position to influence the local policy to their own advantage.

Finally, attention has been drawn by Okoka-Onyango and Barya (1997, 134–35) to the paternalistic attitudes of the (foreign) NGOs. The authors mention also that these NGOs are pursuing short-term goals and focus on activities at a micro-level rather than on long-term economy, policy and social service at the macro level.

10   THE RELATIONSHIP BETWEEN THE *SOCIETE CIVILE*, ETHNIC AND RELIGIOUS MOVEMENTS AND TRADITIONAL LEADERS

In many studies, the notion prevails that the mobilisation of the civil society guarantees greater local participation and democracy, and that, conversely, ethnic and religious movements and traditional leaders hinder such a development. Also in Uganda there is a strong tendency towards ethnicisation, mainly with regard to official duties, and towards the attempt by traditional leaders to maintain or to enlarge their influence.

Okoka-Onyango and Barya (1997, 117) argue — in their study on Uganda — that ethnic and religious movements have to be seen together with, and not as opposed to, the *société civile*. One should not underestimate the ability of these movements to make alliances with other social groups, which influence social life. In the view of these authors, traditional cultural and religious organisations should be involved in discussions about the role of the *société civile*, especially when these organisations don't oppose democratic principles. Below, the extent to which traditional leaders and clan structures play a role in present-day local politics in Uganda is examined.

11   THE ROLE OF TRADITIONAL LEADERS IN LOCAL GOVERNMENTS

After brief recognition and integration in national politics just after independence, the kingdoms and other traditional powers were abolished. In July 1993, however, new legislation was approved which provided for the restoration of most of the Ugandan traditional monarchies. However, these were limited to purely ceremonial and cultural functions. They are not integrated in the present policy of decentralisation, although the new legislation of 1997 gives the possibility for two or more districts to co-operate in the fields of culture and development and form Councils, Trust Funds or Secretariats (Local Governments Act, art 9). Some members of the Buganda elite see this form of co-operation as a step towards federalism (Nsibambi 1998, 109). On the other hand, it is stated — as we will clarify — in the constitution and in the law that cultural leaders cannot be elected as local councillors.

A first remark is that the situation of the traditional authorities varies considerably from one area to another within Uganda. There are areas with strong royal families (such as Buganda), areas where the traditional monarchy has lost much of its prestige and its social power, and areas where the population has never had any traditional monarchy, where the traditional structures are based on simple clans, usually defined as acephalous. Nevertheless, not only the traditional monarchy but also even the clan-relationship in some regions seems to have a significant effect on politics; their influence is particularly important in local elections. Recent developments show that certain clan-leaders have acquired a greater moral authority than some of the traditional monarchs.

The support among the population for a stronger political role for their traditional leaders is far from unanimous. It has to be reported that even in areas with a powerful monarchy, people do not always openly favour a restoration of the king's political power. This reluctance is one of the reasons why in the territory of the Buganda, consisting of various districts, many of the councillors refuse to transfer competencies from their district councils to a common (Buganda) council for co-operation in traditional and cultural matters, as has been envisaged in the constitution (Mukholi 1995, 51).

The policy of the regime regarding the role of traditional leaders in the process of decentralisation is ambivalent. On the one hand, we see that the official restoration of the traditional and cultural leaders since 1993[5] and the confirmation of this restoration in the Constitution of 1995 assume that those leaders can play a positive role in the promotion of democratisation and decentralisation. On the other hand, article 246 of the constitution imposes strict limits on their role. It states that:

'(a) a person shall not, while remaining a traditional or cultural leader, join or participate in partisan politics and (b) a traditional or cultural leader shall not have or exercise any administrative, legislative or executive powers of Government or local government'.

The Local Governments Act of 1997 repeats that:

'A person shall not be elected a Local Government Councillor if that person (...) (c) is a traditional leader as defined in Clause (6) of Article 246 of the Constitution.'

It is clear that the intention of the official doctrine is to restrict the competencies of the traditional leaders to so-called cultural matters. During our interviews, official spokesmen repeatedly emphasised that their role is purely ceremonial and cultural. Present politics, however, show that the regime of Museveni solicits the traditional leaders for political support and for co-operation in the processes of decentralisation and local development.

The recognition of traditional leaders is not free of danger to local and regional particularism. In a recent study, Van Acker (2000, 157–67) states:

the 'cultural' restoration of the traditional kingdoms is [in principle] at odds with the spirit of the decentralisation process and introduces the risk of manipulation of the political process on the basis of ethnic arguments.

---

[5] From 1993–94 on, the *Kabaka* of Buganda, the *Omukama* of Tooro and of Bunyoro, and the *Kyabazinga* (or *Isebantu*) of Busoga are officially recognised.

The reality in Uganda shows that the strict line between politics and cultural matters, on which the official doctrine insists, is often no more than an illusion (Mukyala 1998). Our study reports several interesting examples of clear links between state politics and traditional leaders.

In the Bunyoro kingdom, a conflict between two brothers regarding the succession to the kingship (or *Omukama*) had to be resolved by a state court (Doornbos and Mwesigye 1995, 67). The present king, whose title is still contested by some of the Nyoro, is entangled in a judicial battle with the local (elected) council and administration over former royal properties that are used by the local administration (*New Vision*, 22 January 1999). In this way, it is clear that the Bunyoro king cannot rely on important financial income and sees his influence diminished.

In Buganda, on the other hand, the monarch (or *Kabaka*) seems to have sufficient support to count on large financial incomes from voluntary contributions. In addition, the government has confirmed the return of his former royal properties. This opens, of course, large opportunities for local development. The present *Kabaka* does not hesitate to take political stances, such as when he had his (traditional) Prime Minister pose with Museveni during the presidential campaign. This support for the regime, however, does not deter the *Kabaka* from criticising governmental actions that could weaken his position, for instance the proposed amendments to the Land Bill.

Another example of the strong political relevance of traditional leaders is that of the king (or *Omgabe*) of Ankole. The Ankole kingdom was one of the formerly recognised monarchies. At this point, however, the *Omgabe* has not been officially restored, first because the heir to the throne is not accepted by a part of the population and second because the question is politically very sensitive because Museveni is himself an Ankole of royal descent.

On the one hand, it is clear that the selective recognition of certain traditional leaders is an important element in present governmental politics. On the other hand, a number of non-recognised traditional leaders, such as the paramount clan-leader of the Alur, the *Rwoth*, are trying to gain governmental sympathy and support for official recognition.

Finally, we may note the attempts of the government in co-operation with the well-known Ugandan NGO, ACORD, and with support of the Belgian department of development co-operation, to grant the Acholi clan-leaders, in the northern districts, a special role in restoring peace with the rebels of the Lord Resistance Army (Doom and Vlassenroot 1999, 30–4). Without any doubt, this is a highly political matter.

A notable feature of the discussion of the role of traditional leaders is the different interpretations of legislative terminology. Traditional leaders and their supporters don't hesitate to classify traditional land matters under cultural matters. Apolo Nsimbambi, in 1999 Prime Minister, who is also a member of the Buganda elite, emphasised that the Constitution doesn't exclude traditional leaders from politics as such but only from partisan politics.[6]

The government uses, in a strategic manner, the official doctrine, confirmed in the Constitution and the Local Governments Act, to win the political support of the traditional leaders but at the same time to keep legal instruments as a big stick to limit their power or to ensure their support.

12   THE INFLUENCE OF FOREIGN DONORS AND EXPERTS ON THE PROCESS OF DECENTRALISATION

With regard to decentralisation and donors, it must be emphasised that 'decentralisation' and women's representation in the local councils have clearly been used to gain the support of foreign donors.

Regarding NGOs, first of all we must make reference to their previously mentioned positive and negative impacts. Another problem in the process of passing on competencies is the fact that many NGOs are existing and working thanks to aid from foreign countries. This fact increases dependence and endangers self-reliance. It relieves the central government, yet at the same time it affects the freedom of choice of local administrations, and it hinders co-ordination between local governments, general macro-development and a harmonious development of the different regions of Uganda.

Recent dismissals in the administration, stimulated by the IMF, seem to have often been implemented in a way that was neither very neutral nor very rational. During interviews people explicitly advocated a check by the IMF on the implementation, and above all in the selection of the officials remaining at their posts, as opposed to a mere conditionality in the general policy.

Beside the question of a greater involvement of foreign experts in the implementation of the development policy, we should also report the concern regarding the risks of acceding to careless foreign advice and demands. Okoka-Onyango and Barya (1997, 134–35) — among others — point to the danger of the often ill-considered recommendations of foreign experts with regard to democratisation. These experts often fail to take into account specific local problems. The authors mention that *Good Governance* is far too often reduced by donors such as the World Bank to technical question, to accountabiliy, to respect for human rights and formal legal security. Too little attention is paid to the social consequences of such a policy; there are, for example, few attempts to promote indigenous control over things such as privatisation. Ellen Hauser (1999, 621–41) describes how important

---

[6] Interview with Apolo Nsibambi, Kampala, 28 August 1998.

international donor support has been considered compatible with Ugandan government's reluctance to introduce multi-partyism. The author explains this tolerant attitude mainly by the international reasons of the donors. She stresses the danger of this indulgence to long-term sustainable democracy mainly because the no-party system is neglecting the need for coalition building.

Concerning the general process of decentralisation in Uganda, we may not omit to emphasise that, as Kasumba (1997, 3) remarks, the donors' input has offered the most significant (financial) support for decentralisation. At this point we see that the success of the decentralisation process is not only important for the image of the government but also for the image of the donors. The commitment to decentralisation has clearly been donor-driven (Makara 2000, 3).

13   CONCLUSION: DECENTRALISATION FOR THE PURPOSE OF THE REGIME IS GENERATING LOCALLY 'COUNTERVAILING POWERS'

The use of decentralisation for the purpose of both the creation and the control of a local sphere of power has established new administrative structures which, intended or not, offer new possibilities for local countervailing powers.

After the coming into power of Yoweri Museveni's National Resistance Movement (NRM) in 1986, local resistance councils were incorporated in an official process of decentralisation. The NRM clearly saw the development of decentralised authorities as a means to strengthen the power of the central government at the local level, and also to legitimate the regime and so called 'no-partyism'. Internal politics in Uganda show that the attitude of the Museveni regime was very dualistic: growth and evolution of the civil society (*société civile*) was sometimes allowed and sometimes opposed. Civil society activity in Uganda has, since 1986, virtually exploded. This was partly because of the weakened power of the state but it also shows the degree of confidence among civil society actors that their activities would be tolerated (if not always welcomed) by the regime (Oloka-Onyango and Barya 1997, 121–22).

The mainly top-down process of formal decentralisation has quite soon generated its own local dynamism. The development of grassroots structures and participation by means of the NRM *Resistance Councils* and *Committees* has, to a great extent, opened up possibilities for the population to exert pressure on the state, in spite of the fact that these structures were imposed in a top-down way (Okoka-Onyango and Barya 1997, 114). These local countervailing powers clearly have found a new outlet in the regulations concerning decentralisation. During elections, for example, many candidates coming from outside the NRM participate. In spite of the frequent manipulations and abuse of administrative privileges by the NRM, and in spite of the de facto monopoly of this NRM to act — at the local level — as an organised political 'party', in many of the local authorities, representatives of the NRM have been voted out. A direct and logical consequence of this is the demand of these elected councils for greater autonomy and more financial support, as well as the demand that the legally established decentralisation principles be properly implemented.

In this context it's also important to remark that the present decentralisation is used, or is at least useful, as an alibi for the no-partyism of Museveni. Elements such as guaranteed and strong representation of women and a guaranteed minimum representation of youth and handicapped people reinforces the image of political correctness and are presented as a worthy substitute for multi-partyism. This image has been extremely successful in convincing foreign donors that help is deserved (Hauser 1999, 625–27). In Uganda, recent demands partly generating from within the decentralised councils, however, are more and more contesting this no-partyism. The evolution in the legislation shows that today concessions have been made by the regime to extend the direct election of the members of the different councils.

The official process of decentralisation has also been used by traditional chiefs and clan leaders, who according to the constitution can only have a cultural and ceremonial role, to strengthen their demands to be recognised as actors in local administration. Some traditional leaders have interpreted the explicit prohibition on traditional leaders from participating in 'party politics' as not being a prohibition from participating in politics in general. On the one hand the new regulations on the position of traditional leaders make clear that these authorities still have a lot of influence and that legislation has to take their power into account. Yet, on the other hand, the regulations are an attempt to wrap the traditional leaders up in the system and to use their influence to the advantage of the regime.

In addition, we may also note that in Uganda decentralisation is used by the central government to pass on responsibilities to local administration. Apparently the government expects that local administrations will have to pass on many of these tasks to NGOs or to have them privatised (which is more or less the same).

Regarding the present legislation on decentralisation, including the guaranteed representation for women and 'minorities', we can conclude that it contains interesting promises for more political participation. The legislation on the role of traditional leaders reflects an ambivalent but strategic approach designed to cope with the social and cultural realities, the government's interests and the claim for democracy at the local levels simultaneously.

Finally, to summarise the balance of legal instrumentalism (legal engineering) and of legal evolutionism, we can reach the following conclusions: Most of the new rules concerning the local governments and decentralisation are shaped by the NMR regime as instruments to create order and to guarantee the functioning of a workable local administration after more than twenty years of civil war. At the same time they are used as instruments by the present regime to ensure and to legitimise its power. The legislation also reflects, however, a large portion of legal evolutionism, accepted in a more or less pragmatic way by the regime, but containing unwanted effects for the regime because it grants an efficient legal framework to countervailing powers.

REFERENCES

Brett, EA 1994. Rebuilding Organisational Capacity in Uganda under the National Resistance Movement. *The Journal of Modern African Studies 32/1:* 53–80.

Curtis, Donald 1999. The Elusive Promise of NGOs in Africa: Lessons from Uganda, by Susan Dicklitch. *African Affairs 98/2:* 285–86.

Doom, Ruddy, and Koen Vlassenroot 1999. Kony's Message: A New Koine? The Lord's Resistance Army in Northern Uganda. *African Affairs 98:* 5–36.

Doornbos, Maarten, and F Mwesigye 1994. The New Politics of Kingmaking. In *From Chaos to Order: The Politics of Constitution-Making in Uganda.* (Kampala: Fountain Publishers) 61–77.

Ddungu, Expedit 1994. Popular Forms and the Question of Democracy: The Case of Resistance Councils in Uganda. In *Uganda: Studies in Living Conditions, Popular Movements, and Constitutionalism,* edited by Mamdami, Mahmoud, and Joe Oloka-Onyango. (Vienna: JEP Book Series) 385–404.

Hansen, Holger Bernt, and Michael Twaddle (eds) 1998. *Developing Uganda.* (Oxford: James Currey).

Hansen, Holger Bernt, and Michael Twaddle (eds) 1995. *From Chaos to Order: The Politics of Constitution-Making in Uganda* (Kampala: Fountain Publishers).

Hansen, Holger Bernt, and Michael Twaddle (eds) 1991. *Changing Uganda.* (London: James Currey).

Hansen, Holger Bernt, and Michael Twaddle (eds) 1988. *Uganda now: between decay and development.* (London: James Currey).

Hauser, Ellen 1999. Ugandan Relations with Western Donors in the 1990s: What Impact on Democratisation. *The Journal of Modern African Studies, 37, 4:* 621–41.

Howes, Mick 1997. NGOs and the Development of Local Institutions: A Ugandan Case Study. *The Journal of Modern African Studies, 35/ 1:* 17–35.

Jjuuko, FW 1996. Political Parties, NGOs and Civil Society in Uganda. In *Law and the Struggle for Democracy in East Africa,* edited by Joe Oloka-Onyango. (Nairobi: Claripress) 180–98.

Kasumba, George 1997. Decentralising Aid and its Management in Uganda: Lessons for Capacity-Building at the Local Level. *Working Paper No 20, European Centre for Development Policy Management (EPDPM).*

Makara, Sabiti 1998. Institutional Relationships Between Political and Administrative Leaders in the Decentralisation Process. In *The Quest for Good Governance: Decentralisation and Civil Society in Uganda*, edited by Apolo P Nsibambi. (Kampala: Fountain Publishers) 63–102.

Makara, Sabiti 2000. Linking Good Governance, Decentralisation Policy and Civil Society in Uganda, *www.afrst.uiuc.edu/Makerere/Vol_2/chapter_five.html*.

Mamdani, Mahmoud 1995. The politics of democratic reform in Uganda. In *Landmark in Rebuilding a Nation*, edited by Peter Langseth, James Brett et al. (Kampala: Fountain Publishers).

Mandani, Mahmoud 1996. The Politics of Democratic Reform in Uganda. *East African Journal of Peace & Human Rights 2/1*.

Mukholi, David 1995. *A complete Guide to Uganda's Fourth Constitution, History, Politics and the Law*. (Kampala: Fountain Publishers).

Mukyala-Mukiika, R 1998. The Role of Traditional Leaders in the Promotion of Good Governance in the Perspective of Decentralisation in Uganda. In *The Quest for Good Governance: Decentralisation and Civil Society in Uganda*, edited by Apolo P Nsibambi. (Kampala: Fountain Publishers) 216–64.

Nsibambi, Apolo P (ed) 1998. The Quest for Good Governance: Decentralisation and Civil Society in Uganda. (Kampala: Fountain Publishers).

Nsibambi, Apolo P 1998. The Financing of Decentralisation for Good Governance. In *The Quest for Good Governance: Decentralisation and Civil Society in Uganda*, edited by Apolo P Nsibambi. (Kampala: Fountain Publishers) 103–62.

Nsibambi, Apolo P 1996. The Role and Place of Culture and Decentralisation in Uganda's Struggle for Pluralism. In *Law and the Struggle for Democracy in East Africa*, edited by Joe Oloka-Onyango. (Nairobi: Claripress) 362–71.

Nsibambi, Apolo P 1991. Resistance Councils and Committees: A Case Study from Makerere. In *Changing Uganda*, edited by Hansen, Holger Bernt, and Michael Twaddle. (London: James Currey) 279–98.

Okola-Onyango, Joseph, and JJ Barya. 1997. Civil Society and the Political Economy of Foreign Aid in Uganda. *Democratisation 4/2* 113–38.

Tamala, Sylvia 1998. Democratisation in Uganda: a Feminist Perspective. In *Changing Uganda*, edited by Hansen, Holger Bernt, and Michael Twaddle. (London: James Currey).

Tidermand, Per 1994. Le système des conseils de résistance. In *L'Ouganda contemporain*, edited by Prunier, Gérard, and Bernard Calas. (Paris: Karthala) 193–208.

Van Acker, Frank 2000. Ethnicity and Institutional Reform: A Case of Ugandan Exceptionalism? In *Politics of Identity and Economics of Conflict in the Great Lakes Region*, edited by Doom, Ruddy, and Jan Gorus. (Brussels: VUB University Press) 149–73.

Appendix

Scheme 1: Local Government Structure of Uganda (1997)

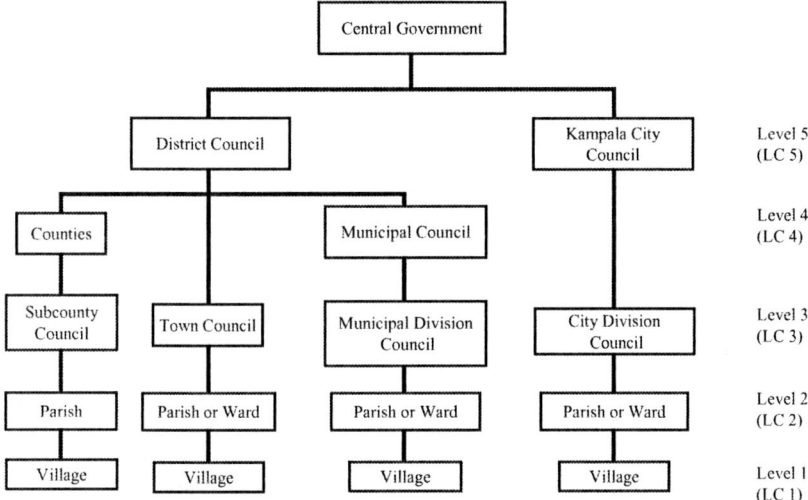

Scheme 1: Local Governments Structure of Uganda (1997)

LOCAL GOVERNMENTS	ADMINISTRATIVE UNITS
Level 5: District Council and City Council — separate legal existence — directly elected council — directly elected district chairperson — council elects executive committee — own tax revenues — own budget — power to issue bylaws and local regulations (district law or ordinance)	**Level 4a: County** — council: members of the executive committees of the sub-counties and the councillors of the District Council elected in the County — council elects from and among its members a chairperson and a vice-chairperson — own (limited) budget
Level 4b: Municipal Council — separate legal existence — directly elected council — directly elected mayor — council elects executive committee — own tax revenues — own budget — power to issue bylaws and local regulations	**Level 2: Parish and Ward** — council: members of the executive committees of the Villages and the councillors of the Level 3 council elected in the Parish — council elects executive committee — own budget — judicial powers

<u>Level 3: Subcounty Council, Town Council, Municipal and City Division Council (Local Governments)</u>
— separate legal existence
— directly elected council
— directly elected chairperson
— council elects executive committee
— own tax revenues
— own budget

— power to issue bylaws and local regulations
— judicial powers

<u>Level 1: Village</u>
— council: every resident of 18 or more years old
— elects executive committee
— own budget

Scheme 2: Composition of the District Councl

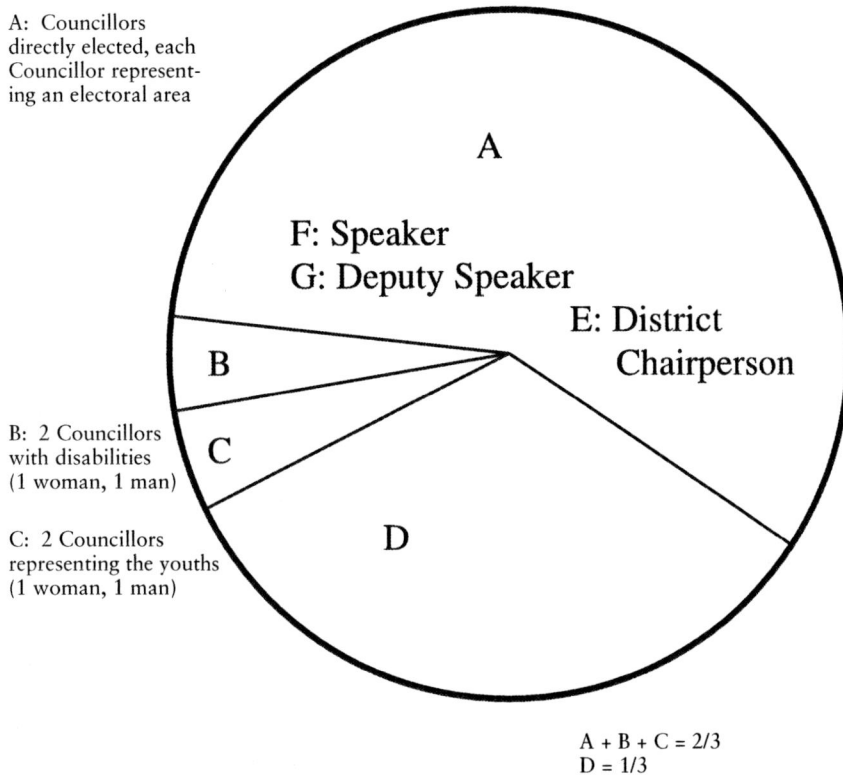

A: Councillors
directly elected, each
Councillor represent-
ing an electoral area

A

F: Speaker
G: Deputy Speaker

E: District
Chairperson

B

B: 2 Councillors
with disabilities
(1 woman, 1 man)

C

C: 2 Councillors
representing the youths
(1 woman, 1 man)

D

A + B + C = 2/3
D = 1/3

D: Women Councillors elected separately;
their number should form one-third of the council

E: The District Chairperson is separately and directly elected

F and G: The Speaker and the Deputy Speaker are elected by and in the Council

8

The South African Truth and Reconciliation Commission: 'The Truth will Set You Free'

WILLEMIEN DU PLESSIS

1   INTRODUCTION

'The truth will set you free' became a slogan of the South African Truth and Reconciliation Commission as reiterated by its chairperson Bishop Desmond Tutu.1 The preamble of the Promotion of National Unity and Reconciliation Act2 stresses

> the need for understanding but not for vengeance, a need for reparation but not retaliation, a need for *ubuntu*3 but not for victimisation.

South Africa has a long history of violence and disregard for human rights. The pre-1994 government believed they were above the law, and many gross violations of human rights were committed in the name of law and order while the real motive was the enforcement of apartheid.4

---

1 Anon (1997a, 18).
2 34 of 1995.
3 Justice Langa described ubuntu in *S v Makwanyane and Another* 1995 3 SA 391 (CC); 1995 2 SACR 1; 1995 (6) BCLR 665 as 'a culture which places some emphasis on communality and on the interdependence of the members of the community. It recognises a person's status as a human being, entitled to unconditional respect, dignity, value and acceptance from the members of the community such persons happens to be part of.' In the same decision Justice Mokgoro stated the following (par 307–8): 'Its spirit emphasises respect for human dignity, marking a shift from confrontation to conciliation.' Cf also Sindane (1997, 147–62); Truth and Reconciliation Commission (1998a, 126–27) that likens ubuntu to restorative justice.
4 Truth and Reconciliation Commission (1998a, 24–43). For an overview of the different *apartheid* laws, cf Truth and econciliation Commission (1998a, 448–96); Truth and Reconciliation Commission (1998b, 5–41). For an overview of official Commissions of enquiry from 1960–95, cf Truth and Reconciliation Commission (1998a, 498–508). Cf Truth and Reconciliation Commission (1998b, 42–162) for a discussion of the involvement of the security forces outside South African borders.

The negotiated Constitution of the Republic of South Africa 200 of 1993 provided for the possibility of a Truth and Reconciliation commission.[5] Such a Commission was instituted in terms of the Promotion of National Unity and Reconciliation Act[6]. The Act provided inter alia for a Truth and econciliation Commission under the chair of Bishop Tutu, an amnesty committee consisting of lawyers, a committee for gross violations of human rights[7] and a committee for redress and rehabilitation.[8]

In deciding how to approach the work of the Commission there were different options. To ensure a country that respects human rights, South Africans had to face their history. One of the options put forward was similar to the Nuremberg trials. This was decided against as none of the sides in the struggle defeated the other and therefore no one as victor could bring the other to trial. It would also have been too costly in a country where resources could be spent more adequately. The criminal system that requires proof beyond reasonable doubt was also not regarded as necessarily the best way to establish the truth. It was also possible that the purpose of truth and reconciliation would be defeated as the security establishment would not have participated and might have led the country to a bloodbath.[9]

To only forget the past would also defeat the purpose — the wounds would only fester, victims might be victimised and other might have got obsessed with their own hurt.[10] Therefor blanket amnesty was not introduced but individuals had to apply for amnesty. The applicant had to satisfy the amnesty Commission that he or she fell into one of the criteria as set out in the Promotion of Truth and Reconciliation Act.[11] People wanted for example to know where their family members were buried or why they were killed or disappeared, for in African culture it is very important to know where your ancestors or children are buried.[12]

The Commission investigated not only violations by the previous government but also by the different liberation and resistance movements such as the ANC,[13] PAC[14] and AWB.[15] The report of the Commission was met

[5] Cf 2 hereafter.

[6] 34 of 1995.

[7] For an overview of the workings of this Committee, cf Truth and Reconciliation Commission (1998a, 277–93).

[8] For a discussion on the setting up of the Commission cf Truth and Reconciliation Commission (1998a, 44–47). For the mandate of the Commission and their interpretation thereof cf Truth and Reconciliation Commission (1998a, 48–102). Methodology and process are discussed in Truth and Reconciliation Commission (1998a, 135–73).

[9] Truth and Reconciliation Commission (1998a, 5–6, 122–25). Cf also Goldstone (1997, 17–23).

[10] Truth and Reconciliation Commission (1998a, 7).

[11] Cf 2 hereafter. Cf also Loots (1995, 20–22); Anon (1998b, 39–40).

[12] Du Plessis (1995, 56).

[13] African Nationalist Congress.

[14] Pan-African Congress.

[15] Afrikaner Weerstand Beweging (Afrikaner Resistance Movement).

with mixed reactions. Both the ANC and the National Party tried to prevent the publication of the report. Some people complained that it contained some untruths; others were glad that the story was written.[16]

The proceedings of the Commission were open and transparent and submitted to the scrutiny and criticism of both the press and the general public.[17] Similar Commissions elsewhere in the world have met behind close doors. The extensive work of the Commission was completed in a record period of two and a half years. They had to work through numerous written and oral presentations. They received inter alia 21,000 submissions of people dealing with violations of human rights[18] — most of these people were Black and female who appeared on behalf of their dead next of kin.[19] It was impossible for the Commission to present a comprehensive presentation of the history and the truth of what happened in South Africa since 1960 — the history was too complex and extensive. The Commission therefore chose to provide a perspective on this terrible history of South Africa.[20] As Tutu (1998a) stated to engage South Africans 'to come to terms with (their) past and, in so doing, reach out to a new future.'

The Commission realised that there was no simple definition of reconciliation and therefore identified certain essential elements, namely that reconciliation is both a goal and a process, that there are different levels of reconciliation which include coming to terms with painful truth, reconciliation between victims and perpetrators, reconciliation at community level, the promotion of national unity and reconciliation as well as reconciliation and redistribution.[21]

In this chapter the Promotion of National Unity and Reconciliation Act will be discussed firstly, after which the causes and motives for the commitment of gross violations of human rights will be referred to. The Truth and Reconciliation Commission's report will then be dealt with as well as their proposals for the way forward. The criticism and shortcomings of the report will also be referred to. Then, amnesty will be discussed, followed by a discussion of the question of restorative justice and whether reconciliation is a pipe dream.

---

[16] Cf also the views of the chairperson in his book, Tutu (1999) and one of the Commissioner's Krog (1999) as well as 6 hereafter.

[17] Cf also Truth and Reconciliation Commission (1998a, 104–15).

[18] Cf the names of the people who suffered gross violation of human rights — Truth and Reconciliation Commission (1998e, 26–107).

[19] Truth and Reconciliation Commission (1998a, 165–73). Various sessions were held in the different regions of South Africa, enabling victims and the public access to the hearings of the Commission — cf Truth and Reconciliation Commission (1998a, 392–447).

[20] Truth and Reconciliation Commission (1998a, 1–2; 1998e, 5–6).

[21] Truth and Reconciliation Commission (1998a, 106–10).

2 PROMOTION OF NATIONAL UNITY
AND RECONCILIATION ACT[22]

The negotiated interim Constitution of the Republic of South Africa, 1993[23] laid the basis for the Truth and Reconciliation Commission:[24]

> This Constitution provides an historic bridge between the past of a deeply divided society characterised by strife, conflict, untold suffering and injustice, and a future founded on the recognition of human rights, democracy and peaceful co-existence and development opportunities for all South Africans, irrespective of colour, race, class, belief or sex.
>
> The pursuit of national unity, the well-being of all South African citizens and peace require reconciliation between the people of South Africa and the reconstruction of society.
>
> The adoption of this Constitution lays the secure foundation for the people of South Africa to transcend the divisions and strife of the past, which generated gross violations of human rights, the transgression of humanitarian principles in violent conflicts and a legacy of hatred, fear, guilt and revenge.
>
> These can now be addressed on the basis that there is a need for understanding but not for vengeance, a need for reparation but not for retaliation, a need for ubuntu but not for victimisation.
>
> In order to advance such reconciliation and reconstruction, amnesty shall be granted in respect of acts, omissions and offences associated with political objectives and committed in the course of the conflicts of the past.

In the light of the 1993 Constitution the Promotion of National Unity and Reconciliation Act[25] was passed through parliament.

A Commission for Truth and Reconciliation consisting of at least eleven and at the most seventeen Commissioners was appointed by the President in consultation with the cabinet.[26] The Commissioners were to be fit and proper persons who do not have a high political profile.[27]

The functions of the Commission were to facilitate inquiries into gross violations of human rights, the nature, causes and extent of these violations including the antecedents, factors, context, motives and perspectives which led to the violations, the identity of all persons, authorities, institutions and organisations involved in the conflict.[28] It also had to facilitate

---

[22] 34 of 1995.
[23] 108 of 1993.
[24] Cf also the preamble to the Promotion of National Unity and Reconciliation Act 34 of 1995. For a discussion of the legal developments during the investigation of the Commission cf Du Plessis, Olivier and Pienaar (1995, 488–91; 1996, 284–87; 1997, 235–39, 552–54; 1998, 171–74, 492–95; 1999, 226–30).
[25] 34 of 1995.
[26] 34 of 1995 section 7(1). For a discussion of the Act see Loots and Du Plessis (1996, 154–60).
[27] Section 7(2)(b).
[28] Section 4.

the gathering of information and evidence about gross violations of power to review actions of sub-committees excluding that of the amnesty committee.[29]

Specific principles were laid down in matters dealing with the testimony of victims of gross human rights violations.[30] These principles include that victims had to be treated with compassion and respect for their dignity, they had to be treated equally without discrimination of any kind, procedures for dealing with applications had to be expeditious, fair, inexpensive and accessible, victims had to be informed through the press of their rights, victims had to be inconvenienced to the minimum and their privacy as well as their safety had to be protected, victims had to be allowed to communicate in the language of their choice and informal dispute resolution mechanisms had to be put in place.

The Committee on Human Rights Violations was to consist of not more than ten members. The Committee had to refer all names of victims of gross violations of human rights to the Committee on Reparation and Rehabilitation.[31] The Committee on Reparation and Rehabilitation[32] had to consider all the cases referred to them and made recommendations on how reparation and rehabilitation could be achieved.[33]

The Act provides that amnesty[34] can be granted to persons that revealed relevant facts with regard to an act, omission or offence associated with a political objective[35], which related to an act committed in the course of conflicts of the past.[36] An amnesty committee consisting of a chairperson, vice-chairperson and three other members who are South African citizens, representative of the community, was appointed. The chair is a judge of the High Court of South Africa.[37] Due to the workload, the Act was amended twice — in June 1997 the committee members were extended

---

[29] Section 5(e). The procedures and powers of the Commission during investigations and hearings of the Commission are set out in sections 29, 30 and 32.
[30] Section 11.
[31] Section 15.
[32] Established in terms of section 24.
[33] Section 26.
[34] Cf also 7 hereafter.
[35] 'Political objective' is defined in section 20(2) as 'any act of omission which constitutes an offence or delict which, according to the criteria in subsection (3), is associated with a political objective and which was advised, planned, directed, commanded, ordered or committed within or outside the Republic during the period 1 March 1960 to the cut-off date.' The criteria in section 20(3) include inter alia (i) the motive of the person, (ii) the context in which the act was committed (eg a political uprising, disturbance or event); (iii) the legal and factual nature of act, omission or offence (including the gravity of it); (iv) whether the object or objective of the act, omission or offence was directed at a political opponent, state property or individuals, (v) whether the act, omission or offence was committed in the execution of an order of an institution, organisation, liberation movement, and (vi) the relationship between the act and the political objective pursued.
[36] Section 22(1) read with section 3(1)(a).
[37] Section 17.

to eleven[38] and in December 1997 to seventeen.[39] The work of the amnesty committee was only completed in the middle of 2002. The final report of the Commission was to be published end 2002.

The names and deeds for which amnesty is granted have to be published in the *Government Gazette.*[40] The consequence of amnesty is that a person cannot be held criminally or civilly liable for any of his or her deeds.[41]

3   CAUSES AND MOTIVES

There are various reasons why people act as they did in a situation where they perceived themselves to be threatened. The Commission felt that perpetrators should be examined as 'multi-dimensional and rounded individuals rather than simply characterising them as purveyors of horrendous acts.'[42]

3 1   General Patterns

A number of general patterns are identified that indicate the motivation of certain perpetrators. Some of the perpetrators believe they were at war and that intentional military actions were therefore justified. Senior officers denied that they knew what was happening or that they gave orders even though their followers claimed they were acting under instructions.[43] Different parties to the conflict were prepared to admit errors, mistakes and unintended consequences.[44] Another pattern was the lack of discipline between the state and its security personnel and liberation movements over

---

[38] Promotion of National Unity and Reconciliation Amendment Act 18 of 1997.

[39] Promotion of National Unity and Reconciliation Amendment Act 84 of 1997. For the names of the members cf Truth and Reconciliation Commission (1998a, 268).

[40] Section 20(6).

[41] Section 20(7)(c). Criminal proceedings that have started will be terminated and if a person is serving a prison sentence his or her sentence will lapse. Civil judgements delivered before amnesty was granted, will not be affected. If amnesty is granted a person's list of convictions will be cleared in respect of that particular offence. Cf. section 20(8)–(10) in this regard.

[42] Truth and Reconciliation Commission (1998e, 259).

[43] Cf. Truth and Reconciliation Commission (1998e, 264–65) where former president FW de Klerk is quoted: 'but things happened which were not authorised, not intended, or of which we were not aware ... I have never condoned gross violations of human rights ... and reject any insinuation that it was ever the policy of my party or government.' In contrast colonel De Kock (convicted for killings at Vlakplaas) stated 'Yet the person who sticks most of all in my throat is former State President De Klerk ... It is because, in that evidence, he simply did not have the courage to declare 'yes we at the top levels condoned what was done on our behalf by the security forces." The allegations were made against Buthelezi who denied condoning violence while Inkatha members based their defence on orders received by the IFP.

[44] Truth and Reconciliation Commission (1998e, 266–69).

their members. Especially the United Democratic Front had trouble with their young members.[45]

3 2 Perspectives

Perspectives also played an important role and led to emotions running high. The perspectives of perpetrators and victims were miles apart and would most probably be the major stumbling block in real reconciliation.[46] Some perpetrators, for example, saw themselves as victims as they had to act on orders that they themselves abhorred or because they needed the money.[47]

It is also important to note that the violence of those in power and the powerless differ. Sometimes violence is committed against other oppressed groups or against each other.[48] Human rights violations were committed by all sides to the struggle. The motives and causes of violence were not the same for all the groupings. The struggle was also not an equivalent struggle in terms of forces deployed, members involved or justice applied.[49] The perpetrators were motivated by different political perspectives.

3 3 Apartheid and Anti-Colonialism

Because atrocities have been committed over a long period of time it is important to see them in the historical and political perspective of each time period. *Apartheid*, rooted in colonialism, can be regarded as the main context for the struggle. The cold war and the anti-colonial context, however, also played a role. As a result of the international climate a virulent form of anti-Communism and anti-Marxism took root after 1948 — leaders, the public and security forces were indoctrinated with propaganda in this regard. There was a strong anti-colonial resistance movement in Africa and there still is — this struggle was incorporated into the South African struggle.

---

[45] Truth and Reconciliation Commission (1998e, 269–70).
[46] Truth and Reconciliation Commission (1998e, 271–76). For example the importance of the act is greater for the victim who experienced the horror of it; perpetrators have less emotion about their acts, there are differences in time perspectives — the pain experience by victims lasts longer than the perpetrator's memory of it; moral evaluations differ — victims distinguish clearly between right and wrong while perpetrators see grey areas; victims see violence as a senseless act while the act is justified for the perpetrator.
[47] Truth and Reconciliation Commission (1998e, 274). The Commission stated that although 'acts of gross violations of human rights may be regarded as demonic, it is counter-productive to regard persons who perpetrated those acts as necessarily demonic.'
[48] Truth and Reconciliation Commission (1998e, 274–76).
[49] Truth and Reconciliation Commission (1998e, 276).

Especially the PAC can be identified in this regard as is also apparent from their slogan 'one settler, one bullet.' It was indicated by Afrikaner leaders that the Afrikaner was also motivated by their legacy of anti-colonial resistance.[50]

The policy of segregation, later known as *apartheid*, started very early in the colonial history of South Africa.[51] Both the Dutch and English colonisers introduced segregation legislation during their reigns. After 1910 when the Union of South Africa was established, more and more legislation was passed by parliament constituting a total different administration pertaining to Black people in South Africa.[52] In 1913 the Black Land Act[53] was passed, dispossessing large numbers of people from their land. Blacks were forced to carry passes and if they did not they were sentenced to prison. The pass laws were only abolished in 1986. In terms of the racially based land legislation three and a half million people were forcibly removed in order to ensure separate residential areas for different people[54] and to achieve the homeland system.[55] By making use of legislation, Black people in South Africa were deprived of education, housing, proper health care and their family lives were destroyed by the so-called 'trek'-labour system.[56]

1960 is chosen as the starting point of the investigation of the Commission. It is the year of the banning of the ANC and the passive march against pass laws at Sharpeville, which was violently suppressed by the police. This march led to the eventual conviction and long-term imprisonment of inter alia former President Mandela. Since 1960, the period under investigation of the Commission, more and more laws were passed dealing with the protection of state security and the protection of the state against Communism and Marxism. These measures have given the security forces virtually unbridled powers. Since 1985, with the declaration of a state of emergency, the measures became more draconian making it possible for the security forces to regard themselves as above the law and to commit and hide human rights violations in terms of the law. Opponents to the state were banned from South Africa, others were detained without trial,

---

[50] Truth and Reconciliation Commission (1998e, 278–80).
[51] Cf also Truth and Reconciliation Commission (1998a, 24–28).
[52] By making use of the Black Administration Act 38 of 1927. For a detailed list of such legislation see Truth and Reconciliation Commission (1998a, 449–96).
[53] 27 of 1913.
[54] In terms of the Group Areas Act 51 of 1950.
[55] The homeland system was based on the idea that Black people in South Africa belong to certain ethnic communities — 'independent states' and 'self-governing territories' were created where the different ethnic communities could live and work.
[56] The 'trek'-labour system was based on the idea that people live in the so-called homelands and only provide labour in white areas — they have to go back to the areas where they 'originated'. Women and children were not always allowed to accompany their husbands — they were left behind in the rural areas and had to cope alone with farming, their children and to survive in general. Women sometimes had to leave their children behind to go and work for white people to raise their children. As a result of the *trek*-labour children no longer had their parents to love and teach them skills and discipline.

tortured or sentenced to death. Organisations were banned and press censorship was strictly enforced.

There was always resistance against the *apartheid* laws, but the violence escalated with the uprising of the Soweto youth in 1976. In the 1980s the violence increased and by the 1990s the government of the day had no other solution than to start a negotiation process with the organisation that they banned before. The violence was severe and sometimes not only directed against government itself, but against civilians and people as oppressed as themselves. In Black towns the local government structures were overthrown and young vigilante groups took over, forcing their co-residents to pay them levies. Any person who was seen as a collaborator with the police or did not join them in marches or boycotts were lashed or 'neck-laced'.[57]

The government of the day and the liberation organisations were all guilty of gross human rights violations and within this context the report of the Truth and Reconciliation Commission must be seen.

3 4   Other Motives

Other motives that may motivate people to act violently include human nature, psychological abnormalities, authoritarianism and social identities[58] (it was for example evident that most of the atrocities were committed by men — few women are to be found amongst the perpetrators in the South African case).[59] In other instances certain situations trigger violence by people who are bound by a certain motive.[60] Language and ideology played a major role in South Africa's history. Social categories were constructed, orders were given, people were persuaded, acts were justified and explained and reasons and excuses were given. People were incited to violence.[61] In this regard the role of crowd violence should also not be overlooked.[62] Two factors that are sometimes overlooked are the role of special organisations that actually committed most of the human rights violations — information about these organisations were difficult to obtain and need further research.[63] Disinformation, secrecy and silence were features of the 1994

---

[57] Neck-lacing was the putting of a rubber tyre around a person's neck (while he or she was still alive), petrol/gas was poured over the person and he or she was then set alight.
[58] Truth and Reconciliation Commission (1998e, 283–91).
[59] The Commission found that 'patriarchy and the cult of masculinity has been embedded in each of the various cultural streams: black, Boer, British. Its significance as a contributing factor should not be undermined' — Truth and Reconciliation Commission (1998e, 290–91).
[60] Three motivational processes are identified namely compliance, identification and internalisation — Truth and Reconciliation Commission (1998e, 292–94).
[61] Truth and Reconciliation Commission (1998e, 294–97).
[62] Truth and Reconciliation Commission (1998e, 301).
[63] Truth and Reconciliation Commission (1998e, 297–98).

South Africa that led to the silent affirmation of the violation of human rights.[64]

4   TRUTH AND RECONCILIATION COMMISSION OF SOUTH AFRICA REPORT

4 1   General

The work of the Commission was constrained by various factors. Not only did they have to record the trauma of victims but also had to ensure that there is due process of law — providing the alleged perpetrators a chance to put their case. The Commission's actions were the subject of several court rulings in this regard.[65] As a result of these decisions the Commission could not always obtain information about the past and it caused the members to be more cautious in their findings than they would have preferred.[66]

Due to the historical division of people into races by the *apartheid* government and as 'badges of privilege and deprivation' references to race became a way of life in South Africa — therefore the Commission reluctantly made use of the 'racial branding' as they provide a guide to the inequities of the past.[67]

In many instances the Commission had to rely on oral reports since the 1970s officials in the former government had deliberately and systematically destroyed state records and incriminating evidence against them.[68]

The *Truth and Reconciliation Report* includes a historical background of the process of the institution of the Commission, a description of the various concepts and principles such as 'truth',[69] the relationship between 'truth' and 'reconciliation', *'ubuntu'*, 'restorative justice' and 'responsibility'.[70] In the report an analysis of the most important matters put before the

---

[64] Truth and Reconciliation Commission (1998e, 297–99). Cf also Du Plessis (1986, 1–4, 291–326).
[65] *Azapo and others v The President of the RSA and others (1996)* (8) BCLR 1015 (CC); 1996 4 SA 671 (C); *Truth and Reconciliation Commission v Du Preez (1996)* 3 SA 997 (C), 1996 (8) BLCR 1109 (N); cf Truth and Reconciliation Report (1998a: 179–86); *Niewoudt v the Truth and Reconciliation Commission Case* (1997) 2 SA 70 (SEC) — cf also Truth and Reconciliation Commission (1998a, 186–200) for a discussion of various other court decisions.
[66] Truth and Reconciliation Commission (1998a, 2).
[67] Truth and Reconciliation Commission (1998a, 3).
[68] Cf in this regard Truth and Reconciliation Commission (1998a, 201–43). From 1990–94 the security establishment embarked on a selective but massive destruction of records beyond the parameters of the Archives Act 6 of 1962 — their actions were halted by the organisation Lawyers for Human Rights. The National Intelligence Agency, however, had destroyed records until 1996. Cf also Truth and Reconciliation Commission (1998e, 226–27).
[69] A distinction was made between factual or forensic truth, personal or narrative truth, social truth, healing or restorative truth.
[70] Truth and Reconciliation Commission (1998a, 110–14).

Commission are discussed. These include for example the claims of the Biko and Mxenge families, party-political proposals from the NP[71], ANC and IFP[72] as well as chemical and biological warfare.[73] The background and reasons for the development of the conflict from 1960–90 that led to gross human rights violations are also referred to, as well as specific investigations into the death of President Samora Machel[74] and the Helderberg disaster.[75] A special investigation was lodged into secret state funding to promote the policies of the former government, and to fund operations against opponents of *apartheid*.[76] The Commission found inter alia that

> secret funding was used to promote a political climate that led directly and indirectly to gross human rights violations — before 1991 this fund was used to also promote party political and sectarian political interests.[77]

A special investigation was also lodged into secret burials and a report on exhumations is given.[78] Despite these findings, numerous people still do not know where their family members are buried.

4 2   Former Government

The Commission made several findings with regard to actions within South Africa during the period between 1960 to 1990 which, to its mind, established gross violations of human rights for which for example the former government, cabinet and the ministers of justice and law and order, commissioners of police and chiefs of the defence force are held accountable. These actions include inter alia (a) banning and banishment orders,[79] (b) executions of people convicted of political offences,[80] (c) the needless

---

[71] National Party.
[72] Inkatha Freedom Party.
[73] Truth and Reconciliation Commission (1998b, 510–23). The Commission found inter alia that scientists from all over the world were recruited, that work was done on a 'need to know' basis; the overall co-ordination was handled by Basson; the surgeon-general was negligent in approving programmes for which he had no understanding; the procedures made self-enrichment possible and that the development of the programme would not have been possible without some level of international co-operation and support.
[74] Of Mozambique — Truth and Reconciliation Commission (1998b, 494–502) — the Commission did not make a finding but raised a number of questions about the possibility of the role of South African authorities.
[75] The crashing of a South African Airways Boeing 747 into the sea off the coast of Mauritius — cf Truth and Reconciliation Commission (1998b, 503–9). The Commission made no findings but pointed out some inconsistencies.
[76] Truth and Reconciliation Commission (1998b, 524–42).
[77] Truth and Reconciliation Commission (1998b, 541–42).
[78] Truth and Reconciliation Commission (1998b, 543–54).
[79] Truth and Reconciliation Commission (1998b, 165–69).
[80] Truth and Reconciliation Commission (1998b, 169–74).

use of deadly force during the restoration of public order and the consequent deaths and injuries to civilians,[81] (d) the use of torture and unnatural deaths of detainees in police custody,[82] (e) the extra-judicial killing of people,[83] (f) attempted killings, arson and sabotage and (f) the work of vigilante groups.[84]

4 3   Violence: 1990–94

During the era of negotiations and transition (1990–94), gross violations of human rights still took place. The Commission had difficulty to uncover violations during this period. This period was characterised by an increase in the levels of violence in South Africa.[85] It became apparent that the security forces continued their practice of detention and torture, there were violations associated with public order policing, external and internal killings of political opponents and raids continued. During this time, allegations were made against the security forces that they were involved in political and train violence and that they failed to act against perpetrators. It was also alleged that police supplied weapons to the IFP.[86] Allegations of a third force[87] were made and the Commission found evidence of security involvement in 'third force' activities; it could not find evidence that this so-called 'third force' was centrally directed. It did, however, establish that there was a network of security and ex-security operatives who acted in conjunction with right-wing elements to instigate violence which resulted in gross violations of human rights.[88]

The role of right-wing parties in violence during the 1990s is also described.[89] The Commission found that members of the *Afrikaner Volksfront, Orde Boerevolk, Boere Weerstandsbeweging* and the *Afrikaner*

---

[81] Truth and Reconciliation Commission (1998b, 174–82).

[82] Truth and Reconciliation Commission (1998b, 187–220).

[83] Truth and Reconciliation Commission (1998b, 220–89). The Commission distinguished between four types of extra-judicial killings, namely targeted killings, killing following abduction and interrogation, ambushes with no attempt to arrest and entrapment killings (222).

[84] Truth and Reconciliation Commission (1998b, 289–312).

[85] Truth and Reconciliation Commission (1998b, 583).

[86] Truth and Reconciliation Commission (1998b, 588–613).

[87] The 'third force' central characteristic is violence covertly undertaken or encouraged — Truth and Reconciliation Commission (1998b, 692).

[88] Truth and Reconciliation Commission (1998b, 709). In the 1980s the basis was laid for these networks. Senior security personnel had knowledge of these operations and did nothing to stop it. These 'third force' activities contributed to the high levels of violence of the 1990s. Cf also Truth and Reconciliation Commission (1998e, 237–38).

[89] Truth and Reconciliation Commission (1998b, 642–65). The finding is inter alia based on speeches and orders given by senior leaders that incited violence; supporters were armed in contravention with the law; random attacks on Blacks as well as clandestine collusion between members of the security forces and the Inkatha Freedom Party to train paramilitary forces.

Weerstandsbeweging were responsible for gross violations of human rights against supporters and leaders of the liberation movements during April 1993 to May 1994.[90]

4 4 Liberation Movements

The liberation movements were also guilty of gross violations of human rights during the 1990s. Although it was not the policy of the ANC during this time, it was still held responsible for the violent conflict that consumed the country during this era. Many people were killed in an atmosphere that can be ascribed to political intolerance. The political leadership of the ANC did, however, accept political and moral responsibility for the actions of their members in the period 1960–94 and in the light thereof they are also held responsible by the Commission.[91]

The PAC conducted a war against civilians especially after 1990 when whites (at random) and especially white farmers were targeted. The Commission found that this was not only a gross violation of human rights but also a violation of international humanitarian law.[92]

The Commission grouped the violations by the liberation movements from 1960–90 into the following categories namely:

a) violations committed in the course of the armed struggle by armed combatants,

b) violations of liberation movements against their own members or against suspected spies or dissidents in their own ranks (outside South Africa),[93]

c) violations committed by supporters of the liberation movements during the 'mass struggle' of the 1980s[94] and

d) violations committed by members of liberation movements after their legalisation on 2 February 1990.

The Commission endorsed that the policy of apartheid was a crime against humanity and that the ANC and PAC were internationally recognised

---

[90] Truth and Reconciliation Commission (1998e, 236–37).
[91] Truth and Reconciliation Commission (1998b, 666–85). Cf also Truth and Reconciliation Commission (1998e, 240–43).
[92] Truth and Reconciliation Commission (1998b, 685–92). Cf also Truth and Reconciliation Commission (1998e, 244–45).
[93] Truth and Reconciliation Commission (1998b, 347–66). The human rights violations include killings of individuals by order of a military tribunal, deaths in/after detention, execution and killings and torture.
[94] Truth and Reconciliation Commission (1998b, 345–47).

liberation movements conducting legitimate struggles against the former South African government.[95] The Commission distinguished, however, between a 'just war' and 'just means' and found that both the ANC and the PAC as well as their different sub-committees and organisations committed gross violations of human rights for which they are morally and politically accountable.[96]

In the following instances the ANC or its armed wing or its supporters was for example held responsible: (a) unplanned military operations without proper control resulting in the death and injury of civilians,[97] (b) bombings,[98] (c) landmine operations,[99] (d) killing of individual 'enemies' or 'defectors'[100] and (e) the conflict with Inkatha.[101]

The PAC was inter alia held responsible for deeds committed by their military wing Poqo and later APLA. These deeds include (a) a reign of terror in the Western Cape Townships, (b) the killing of dissident members of the PAC, (c) terrorising of representatives of traditional authorities in the homelands and (d) actions against white civilians in non-combat situations.[102]

The Mass Democratic Movement had members that were not necessarily part of any of the other formal organisational structures. It consisted of various movements that more or less had aligned themselves to the United Democratic Front (UDF) during the 1980s. Although it was not the policy of the UDF to attack and kill opponents, members and supporters of this movement did commit gross violations of human rights. The Commission found that the UDF, through their speeches, slogans and marching incited people to violent actions. The violations included

a) killings ('neck-lacing')[103] and ill-treatment of political opponents, members of state structures such as local authorities, members of the police and the burning and destruction of homes and properties,

b) the violent enforcement of worker stay-aways and boycotts leading to killing or attempted killing, and

c) political intolerance resulting in violent inter-organisational conflict with other liberation organisations.[104]

---

[95] Cf also the findings of the Commission — Truth and Reconciliation Commission (1998e, 222–23).
[96] Truth and Reconciliation Commission (1998b, 325).
[97] Truth and Reconciliation Commission (1998b, 326–28).
[98] Truth and Reconciliation Commission (1998b, 328–33).
[99] Truth and Reconciliation Commission (1998b, 333–35).
[100] Truth and Reconciliation Commission (1998b, 335–37).
[101] Truth and Reconciliation Commission (1998b, 340–45).
[102] Truth and Reconciliation Commission (1998b, 369–76).
[103] From 1984 to 1989, 5707 political violent deaths were recorded and approximately 700 deaths by neck-lacing — Truth and Reconciliation Commission (1998b, 389).
[104] Truth and Reconciliation Commission (1998b, 377–92). Cf also Truth and Reconciliation Commission (1998e, 245–49). The UDF, ANC and MK are also held liable for the killing of 76 IFP member killings.

4 5 Homelands

The Commission also gave an overview of the development of security structures in the homelands that worked alongside the South African security forces.[105] Various gross human rights violations were committed by these forces.[106]

Statistics of gross human rights violations are given on a regional basis.[107] From these it seems that KwaZulu-Natal had the highest number of deaths.[108] The type of human rights violations with the highest statistic differs from region to region.

4 6 Sectorial Investigations

The presentations of the Commission for business and labour,[109] the faith (religious) communities,[110] the legal community,[111] health sector,[112] media,[113] prisons,[114] compulsory military service,[115] children and youth[116] and women[117] are also included in the report. It seems that no sphere of the South African society was left untouched by *apartheid*.

Approximately half of the statements before the Truth and Reconciliation Commission reporting on gross violations of human rights were for example from women. It is apparent that women played an active role in all aspects of the struggle and that they suffered as the men did. In some instances the abuse differ from that of men (less killings and more reports on severe ill-treatment) — 'women are not the only sufferers, they bear the brunt of the suffering'.[118]

---

[105] For a background discussion on the creation and problems in these so-called homelands — cf Truth and Reconciliation Commission (1998b, 400–93).
[106] Cf also Truth and Reconciliation Commission (1998b, 613–42) for a description of violence during the 1990s and the findings of the Commission in this regard — Truth and Reconciliation Commission (1998e, 228–29).
[107] Truth and Reconciliation Commission (1998c, 1–11 (general), 34–154 (Eastern Cape), 155–328 (KwaZulu-Natal), 329–89 (Free State), 390–527 (Western Cape), 528–745 (former Transvaal — Northern Province, Gauteng, Mpumalanga and North-West)).
[108] Truth and Reconciliation Commission (1998c, 324). Cf also Truth and Reconciliation Commission (1998e, 233–34 and 235–36) with regard to specific incidences of violence (operation Marion, Esikhawini hit squad, Mlaba self-protection unit camp) in KwaZulu-Natal.
[109] Truth and Reconciliation Commission (1998d, 18–58).
[110] Truth and Reconciliation Commission (1998d, 59–92).
[111] Truth and Reconciliation Commission (1998d, 93–108).
[112] Truth and Reconciliation Commission (1998d, 109–64).
[113] Truth and Reconciliation Commission (1998d, 165–98).
[114] Truth and Reconciliation Commission (1998d, 199–219).
[115] Truth and Reconciliation Commission (1998b, 220–47).
[116] Truth and Reconciliation Commission (1998d, 248–81).
[117] Truth and Reconciliation Commission (1998d, 282–316).
[118] Truth and Reconciliation Commission (1998d, 316); Truth and Reconciliation Commission (1998e, 256).

5   PROPOSALS: THE WAY FORWARD AND ACHIEVEMENTS BY 2002

The Commission also made some proposals for the way forward. It is proposed that a proper system of accountability be introduced to ensure that the past is not repeated again.[119]

The Commission's point of departure is that there should be no repetition of the past. One of the ways to ensure this is to develop a strong culture of human rights. Other ways to achieve reconciliation is to ensure that the report is widely distributed and that museums have sections with expositions of the past.[120] The culture of human rights is growing in South Africa and more and more people are aware of their rights and are enforcing it. By 2002, however, eight years after introducing the Constitution, some people still claim that they have no knowledge of human rights. Programmes are introduced at school level to ensure the establishment of such a culture from a very young age.

The Commission also recommended that the government should ensure that the gap between the advantaged and disadvantaged be closed as soon as possible giving more attention to education, provision of shelter, access to clean water and health services and the creation of job opportunities as well as the protection of socio-economic rights. In job-creation, the government and the private sector has to play a crucial role. The private sector is urged to initiate a fund for training, empowerment and opportunities for the disadvantaged and dispossessed. Although some progress was made by 2002, the pace of realising socio-economic rights is still slow. There is, however, some realism that such progress cannot be made overnight.

The Commission also recommended that those who benefited from *apartheid* should contribute to the alleviation of poverty by for example the introduction of a wealth tax. This issue was still debated by the end of 2002. Steps should be introduced by both the private and public sector to overcome racism.[121] Although this is taken seriously by both private and public sector, there is an increase in reverse-racism — this time from black to white. Xenophobia is also on the increase. By the end of 2002, radical white wing supporters started a reign of terror again. The reasons for the new racism were not clear as there was no need for anyone at that stage to feel threatened by actions of government.

Government should also adopt measures to address the unacceptable high rate of serious crime and in this regard the Commission proposed a system of community policing. By end 2002, several community policing

---

[119] Truth and Reconciliation Commission (1998e, 308–9).
[120] Truth and Reconciliation Commission (1998e, 308).
[121] In this regard the Equity Act 4 of 2000 was published criminalising for example hate speech based on race.

operations were in place. Corruption is seen as another barrier to the creation of a human rights culture — the Commission proposed that government should take a 'ruthless stand against inefficiency, corruption and misadministration at every level of the public and private sectors.'[122] The government is constantly fighting corruption in their own ranks and persons guilty of corruption are prosecuted.

The Commission also proposed that all the trials instituted in terms of the Report should be dealt with within a period of two years. This seems to be an unrealistic period in the light of the number of trials and the situation in which the legal system finds itself at present. According to experts a ten-year period should be set aside to complete these trials.[123] A decision on prosecutions would only be made after the final report of the truth and reconciliation Commission is published at the end of 2002.

To help with healing and rehabilitation it was proposed that non-governmental organisations should be established to assist victims and to facilitate the rehabilitation of perpetrators. Strategies should also be devised on how to integrate perpetrators into society, for example the introduction of community-based projects.[124] By end 2002 this was not in place.

The Commission proposed that the victims of apartheid should be compensated.[125] The Commission struggled with the question what would constitute reparation or rehabilitation. In terms of section 1(1)(xiv) of the Act reparation includes 'any form of compensation, restitution, rehabilitation or recognition.' The Commission drew up a policy with five components, namely:

a)   urgent interim reparation to people who are in immediate need,

b)   individual reparation grants that are paid over a period of six years,

c)   symbolic reparation to facilitate communal process of remembering and commemorating the pain and victories of the past, a national day of remembrance, erection of memorials and museums, legal and administrative measures to assist individuals to obtain death certificates, exhumations and reburials and ceremonies and the expedition of outstanding legal matters,

d)   community rehabilitation programmes (national demilitarisation, rehabilitation, skills training, family based therapy, education, housing) and

---

[122] Truth and Reconciliation Commission (1998e, 308–9); cf proposals to government how to promote a human rights culture — 311–13.
[123] Truth and Reconciliation Commission (1998e, 309); Fourie (1998, 8).
[124] Truth and Reconciliation Commission (1998e, 309).
[125] Truth and Reconciliation Commission (1998e, 170–95; 312–13).

e) institutional reform to prevent the recurrence of human rights abuses in future. Malan[126] felt that individual reparation would be unwise as it does not distinguish between the harm suffered and the needs of the individuals. He recommended a formula with a multi-layered approach, based on affordability, by the state for example a once off grant to all identified victims and then the state can render services based on the needs of the victims such as medical or psychological treatment. If the violation resulted in the loss of housing, a housing grant could be given or exemption of school fees for children if the breadwinner was lost to the family.

Government allocated an amount of R200 million in 1999 and a further R300 million for 2000 and 2001. Initially it was stated that only symbolic gestures of redress such as water and roads would be given, but later it was said that an amount of R5700 would be given, as provisional subsistence to those who have urgent needs. The Truth and Reconciliation Commission recommended that approximately 30,000 victims be paid R21 600 per year over a period of six years which would cost the state approximately R3.9 milliard. No final decision has been made in this regard.[127]

In February 2000 the following newspaper heading perhaps illustrates the initiative government has or has not taken: 'Official silence on reparations cheats the victims of past conflicts of their rights.'[128] Government claims that they do not have money to make the reparations; no reference is made to the budgeted amounts of 1999. Others argue that the number of people identified by the Commission only constitute a small percentage of people violated by *apartheid* and feel that whole communities should benefit. Hamber (2000) pointed out that the government has R30 billion to buy weapons while the truth and reconciliation budget per year was R100 million. The amount proposed by the Commission was R480 million, which is but a percentage of government expense. By December 2002 the victims were still not compensated.

It was further decided by the Commission not to recommend that any person should be disqualified or removed from public office if they were implicated in violations of human rights. They did, however, suggest that political parties and the state should take these disclosures into account when making appointments and recommendations.[129] It is uncertain whether this happens in practice.

---

[126] Truth and Reconciliation Commission (1998e, 452–53).
[127] Swart (1998, 1).
[128] Hamber (2000, 9).
[129] Truth and Reconciliation Commission (1998a, 3); Truth and Reconciliation Commission (1998e, 310–11).

The Commission also made specific proposals with regard to the business and faith communities, the health sector, the media and prisons.[130] With regard to legal and judicial matters the Commission recommended that the possibility of establishing a serious crimes compensation fund be investigated by government and that a code of conduct be compiled for prosecutors to ensure that the interests of victims are properly considered. Access to justice for all accused persons should be achieved by setting up a public defender system and the possibility that law students do compulsory community service should be investigated.[131] It is also proposed that the racial and gender composition of judges in the high court and magistrates in the lower courts be addressed.[132] With regard to the courts of chiefs and headmen the Commission proposed an audit of these courts and that their jurisdiction be established. With regard to the informal or 'people courts' that were established during the 1980s the government is urged to prevent the reappearance of such a phenomenon.[133] By 2002 the Department of Justice and the South African Law Commission were busy with research on the restructuring of the court system.

Extensive recommendations were made with regard to the various security forces. These recommendations mostly include control and monitoring systems.[134] The Commission also made extensive recommendations with regard to record-keeping and access to information.[135] In both instances new legislation was introduced by 2002 to ensure the recommendations of the Commission.

In the case of the liberation movements, it was proposed that the movements should issue 'a clear and unequivocal apology to each victim of human rights abuses in exile and those detained without trial', as well as those who were detained and then found to be innocent. All allegations against detainees should be publicly withdrawn and their names cleared — the movements should also seek to reconcile and reintegrate the victims of abuses. The liberation movements should also establish the whereabouts of all those people who went missing in exile and should regularly publish information in this regard.[136] As far as could be determined, this was not done.

---

[130] Truth and Reconciliation Commission (1998e, 313–22; 334–43).
[131] Truth and Reconciliation Commission (1998e, 322–25). Provision should also be made for witness protection (325–26). This has already been introduced by the Witness Protection Act 112 of 1998. It is also proposed that juvenile offenders should have extensive probation programmes, secure places of safety for awaiting-trail offenders and the release of juvenile offenders into the care of their parents (326).
[132] Truth and Reconciliation Commission (1998e, 326).
[133] Truth and Reconciliation Commission (1998e, 327).
[134] Truth and Reconciliation Commission (1998e, 328–34).
[135] Truth and Reconciliation Commission (1998e, 343–47). New legislation has been introduced with regard to both these issues namely the National Archives Act 43 of 1996, the Legal Deposit Act 54 of 1997 and the Promotion of Access to Information Act 2 of 2000.
[136] Truth and Reconciliation Commission (1998e, 347).

Government should also ratify all international documents on human rights. An apology should also be given to neighbouring states for past violations.[137] By 2002 South Africa still has not ratified all international documents on human rights and no apology was given to neighbouring countries.

The Commission concludes their recommendations with the following words:[138]

'Reconciliation is a process which is never-ending, is costly and often painful. For this process to develop, it is imperative that democracy and a human rights culture be consolidated. Reconciliation is centred on the call for a more decent, more caring and more just society. It is up to each individual to respond by committing ourselves to concrete ways of easing the burden of the oppressed and empowering the poor to play their rightful part as citizens of South Africa.'

6 CONSEQUENCES OF GROSS HUMAN RIGHTS VIOLATIONS

The Commission found that the consequences of gross human rights violations are numerous. These consequences over a broad spectrum include lingering direct and indirect physical, psychological, economic and social effects on the individual, his or her family, the communities (urban and rural) and the nation.[139]

7 CRITICISM AND SHORTCOMINGS

As has been pointed out by the Commission itself, it would be strange if a commission of this nature was not criticised and did not have shortcomings. The Commission accepted that some of the criticism was legitimate, but in other instances they felt that the criticism was based merely on political rhetoric with the purpose to discredit the work of the Commission.[140]

The criticism included inter alia that the Commission was biased in favour of the ANC and that the Commission consisted mostly of pro-ANC, PAC and SACP[141] members;[142] that amnesty hearings were

[137]Truth and Reconciliation Commission (1998e, 348–49).
[138]Truth and Reconciliation Commission (1998e, 349).
[139]Truth and Reconciliation Commission (1998e, 125–69); cf also Van Wyk (1999, 22) that describe reconciliation as a process in religious context.
[140]Truth and Reconciliation Commission (1998a, 8). The Afrikaners for example stated that the Commission was biased in favour of the ANC and therefore not legitimate and not advancing reconciliation.
[141]South African Communist Party.
[142]The members were, however, nominated and interviewed in public sessions by a panel on which all political parties were represented. The President then chose members in consultation

in public;[143] that only the one aspect of justice (retributive and punitive) was emphasised;[144] the Commission's conciliatory attitude towards PW Botha;[145] the lack of hearings of the ANC camps in Angola;[146] the so-called lenient treatment of Ms Madikizela-Mandela and Dr Wouter Basson[147] and lastly that mostly former security force members were targeted.[148]

The Commission identified what to their mind constituted shortcomings.[149] The Commission felt that they did not devote enough time and energy to matters relating to violence in the 1990s. It were, however, new events that would have required a great deal of further investigation.

with his cabinet of national unity (including the National Party and Inkatha Freedom Party). Some of the members of the committee had no formal political party affiliation — Truth and Reconciliation Commission (1998a, 9).

[143] In some instances it was the first time that the family of the applicant realised that their father/husband was a torturer or member of a ruthless death squad — the price was public shaming and sometimes led to the disintegration of the family union — Truth and Reconciliation Commission (1998a, 9).

[144] The Commission, however, also strove to restorative justice — ie the correcting of imbalances, restoration of broken relationships, healing, harmony and reconciliation — Truth and Reconciliation Commission (1998a, 9).

[145] Botha was sentenced to R10 000 or twelve months imprisonment and a further twelve months imprisonment suspended for five years — *S v Botha Case* GSM 15/98 — cf also Truth and Reconciliation Commission (1998a, 197). The Commission did, however, find that during the period that PW Botha was head of state (1978–89) there were gross violations of human rights and other unlawful acts by the security forces. He also chaired the State Security Council, which was found to be the instigators of gross human rights violations. He ordered the destruction of Khotso house (a building that housed organisations which seemed to Botha to be a threat to the security of South Africa) and thereby endangered the lives of people in and around the building. It is found that in his capacity as head of state he contributed to and created a climate in which gross human rights violations could and did occur and that he is as such accountable for these violations — Truth and Reconciliation Commission (1998e, 223–25).

[146] Only a few people did come forward to testify on human right violations in these camps. At one stage someone did testify in the hearing of then President Mandela; a special hearing on prisons also included evidence on conditions in Quatro, one of the ANC camps. There were also other independent Commissions on these camps namely the Stuart, Motsuenyane and Skweyiya Commissions — cf Truth and Reconciliation Commission (1998a, 10); Laurence (1997, 40–41).

[147] Mrs Mandela's case took nine days to complete, she was cross-examined by lawyers and she responded as she deemed fit. As the Commission is not a court of law, they could not pronounce a verdict, but included their findings in the report. A special investigation was also lodged into the Mandela United Football Club and the alleged abduction, assault and killing of youths — cf Truth and Reconciliation Commission (1998b, 555–82). The Commission held that Ms Madikizela-Mandela is politically and morally responsible for the gross violations of human rights committed by the soccer club — cf also Truth and Reconciliation Commission (1998e, 243–44). At the writing of this paper (February 2000) Basson was being tried by the High Court of South Africa for alleged crimes committed during the years of apartheid. Cf also Truth and Reconciliation Commission (1998a, 11).

[148] It might at the first blink of an eye seem to be the case, but many of the liberation movement's perpetrators were already convicted and sometimes executed. The security forces also had the means to hide their actions as they were able to enforce censorship — the truth, when it was unveiled, shocked and disillusioned the white community — cf Truth and Reconciliation Commission (1998a, 12).

[149] Truth and Reconciliation Commission (1998e, 206–8).

The Commission did not call up all the key actors such as Mangosuthu Buthlezi who was the leader of Inkatha Freedom Party. At that time the Commission feared that his appearance at the Commission could spark flames of violence in KwaZulu-Natal. The Commission realised that this may have been a wrong decision. Civil society was not put under enough scrutiny by the Commission — they felt that Black municipal and local government structures, universities and the different research funded organisations should have been put under the same scrutiny as the business and legal sectors. The security forces of the former so-called homelands where many cases of violence were reported (eg Venda, Lebowa and Bophuthatswana) were not dealt with in detail, due to a lack of resources and time. The Commission could not investigate all the cases put before it and therefore had to focus on, as they called it, certain 'window-cases' representing a number of violations of the same type. The reasons were that in order to propose redress, collaboration for stories had to be found. This limited the investigative resources of the Commission. The investigators were also not allowed access to military archives and classified records and had to rely on the police and non-governmental organisations to help them in their investigations.

The findings of the Commission were not always based on tested evidence. The investigation was mostly based on institutions or structures of society, and in only a few instances findings were made with regard to major political figures. The Commission was not a court of law and therefore it did not come to a verdict — it made findings on the evidence before them on the basis of a balance of probabilities.[150] This resulted in the ANC and FW de Klerk applying for interdicts just before the release of the report. The application of the ANC was rejected while that of FW de Klerk was granted — the finding with regard to him is blacked out in the report.[151]

The Commission was also criticised for their decision to protect informants of the former government as it was seen as biased — on the other hand the Commission felt that it should not be used as a witch-hunt by the ANC.[152]

One of the members of the Commission, Malan, withdrew in the final stages of the writing of the Report and brought out a minority report.[153] He felt that the Act did not put *apartheid* on trial but the violation of gross human rights and also did not deal with matters of morality or ethics. According to him there is no historical evaluation of roles played by the various actors and that the report does not put that in proper perspective. The report does not take into account that in human suffering there will be exaggeration and in the case of the amnesty hearings a perpetrator will

[150] Truth and Reconciliation Commission (1998e, 208); cf also Anon (1996, 47–48); Wilhelm (1999, 34–35).
[151] Truth and Reconciliation Commission (1998e, 225–26); cf also Laurence (1998, 39–41).
[152] Russel (1997, 36).
[153] Truth and Reconciliation Commission (1998e, 436–56).

downplay his or her role — the evidence before the Commission was however not contested and was not even given under oath. He criticises the Commission for including in the report uncontested statements of people whose evidence has never been tested or collaborated. According to him a better position would be to acknowledge the conflicts of the past as is required in the Act and then recognise that there were perpetrators and victims in the conflicts and then in the end recognise that 'both perpetrators and victims were victims of the ultimate perpetrator — namely the conflict of the past.'[154] According to him, there should be an integration of the histories to discontinue the past battles.

In favour of the Commission it must be said that they had to find their way — there was no clear path and no international role models. They had to learn by fault and default — in doing so there was insufficient time to do research on all the matters that they would have wished to do.[155]

8   AMNESTY

The work of the Commission is finished but not that of the amnesty committee. It is still an ongoing process. Amnesty is granted to applicants from all political parties and all ranks.[156] Some of the human rights violations for which people were granted amnesty are quite severe. In other instances amnesty was refused. The families of victims are not always satisfied when amnesty is granted and in their case the healing process will definitely take longer.[157] Blank amnesty is not granted — the presiding officers must be sure that the person acted for a political purpose. By October 1998, 7127 amnesty applications were received.[158] Amnesty was granted to 189 applicants and 4479 applicants were refused. Last-mentioned mostly include people who were already serving sentences. By July 1999, five hundred applicants still had to appear before the amnesty committee.[159]

---

[154] Truth and Reconciliation Commission (1998e, 443–48). See the answer of the Commission to the minority report 457–60.
[155] Truth and Reconciliation Commission (1998e, 208).
[156] For a list of names of people who were granted amnesty at the time of the reporting of the Commission — cf. Truth and Reconciliation Commission (1998e, 119–24).
[157] *Azanian Peoples Organisation, Biko, Mxenge, Ribeiro v The President of the Republic of South Africa, the Government of the Republic of South Africa, the Minister of Justice, the Minister of Safety and Security, the Chairperson of the Commission* CCT 17/96. The applicants approached the Constitutional Court to declare section 20(6) of the Promotion of National Unity and Reconciliation 34 of 1995 unconstitutional. This section provides that a person who received amnesty may not be held criminally or civilly liable for that specific Act. Their application was rejected. Cf also Truth and Reconciliation Commission (1998a, 175–78).
[158] Truth and Reconciliation Commission (1998a, 267). For a detailed discussion on the amnesty process cf. Truth and Reconciliation Commission (1998a, 271–75).
[159] Anon (1998a, 4). The Committee granted blanket amnesty to 37 top ANC members. It gave rise to public uproar and led to court cases. In the end the court decided that the granting of the amnesty was ultra vires — cf also Anon (1997b, 11).

The question of amnesty is still debated. The state fears that it may be sued for damages caused by human rights violations. The 1995 Act grants amnesty to individuals for civil claims but not to the state. President Mandela asked the amnesty committee to investigate the possibility of institutional indemnity in the case of the state and state organs — the Act will, however, have to be amended to provide for such an indemnity. There are various requests that the scope of amnesty be widened — that people who are prosecuted for their actions in the past be allowed to not only plead guilty or not guilty but also amnesty. The courts would then have to decide whether the crime is political or criminal of nature.[160] In December 2002 the ANC (ruling party) was again discussing the possibility of a blanket amnesty. Such a move would negate the work of the Truth and Reconciliation Commission, although this consequence was denied by the ANC. It seems as if this might be a politically motivated move in the light of the general elections coming up in 2005.

9   RESTORATIVE JUSTICE

The work of the Commission is completed. What are the consequences of their efforts in reconciliation or peacemaking?

When dealing with human rights violations, three conditions are to be met according to Zalaquett, namely that the complete truth must be established in an officially sanctioned way, that an authoritative version of the events should be rendered, that the policy of human rights should represent the will of the people, that victims should be heard and that the policy or actions taken by the Commission or state should not violate international law relating to human rights.[161]

The Commission chose restorative justice as their underlying philosophy and point of departure.[162] Their choice was criticised by several critics and applauded by others.

Truth commissions have different aims — two objectives that have been identified are to prevent the recurrence of human rights abuses and to repair the damage that was caused. Judicial punishment is not seen as an aim — truth commissions according to this theory have to move beyond this. Villa-Vicencio[163] defines restorative justice as being aimed at the 'victims, perpetrators and communities in a situation of political transition from undemocratic rule to the first phases of democracy and the affirmation of human rights.' Restorative justice should therefore include

---

[160] Thompson (1999, 4).
[161] Liebenberg (1996, 146).
[162] See 4.1.
[163] 2000, 68.

the following concerns:[164] (i) an organised system of justice based on international standards of human rights, (ii) the administration of justice should benefit all, (iii) the promotion of moral values and shared commitment to create a society based on the rule of law, (iv) to hold violators of gross human rights violations liable, (v) collective criminal guilt — the sharing of political responsibility for the past, (vi) to acknowledge the importance of memory, (vii) to punish where necessary and (viii) to rehabilitate the victims. It boils down to acknowledgement, reparation and reconciliation.[165] The Commission worked with acknowledgement but acknowledgement of perpetrators from all sides was flawed as not all were prepared to accept responsibility for the past. Allen[166] is of the opinion that the idea of restorative justice is further flawed, as perpetrators do not come forward out of uncoerced choice — they come forward out of fear for prosecution. The testimonials in front of the Truth and Reconciliation Commission were also voluntary, which excluded many testimonials that should have been heard.

According to Van Marle[167] the Commission provided space for human beings to 'come together and tell their stories ... a space (an event) where reconstruction and transformation took place.' It restored their humanity and vindicated their humiliation and provides them with an opportunity to be equal before the law.[168]

'Theories of restorative justice also emphasise the goal of harmony and community restoration to the neglect of other aspects of criminal justice'.[169] In divided societies the core element of restorative justice is a minimalist consensus on the unacceptance of political cruelty and injustice.[170] This implies that failed applicants for amnesty and those that did not apply for amnesty should be prosecuted by the criminal justice system.

The Commission tried to maximise the truth while the applicants for amnesty tried to achieve their aim with the minimum truth. It was never possible for the Commission to get to the whole truth as they had to rely on what was told and not necessarily on checked evidence.[171] Justice was not realised, as the concepts of justice are fallible. Some victims felt that telling their stories was not enough — they wanted to see the perpetrators punished.[172] The punishment, however, should not degrade the perpetrator, by proclaiming the previous victim master. *Talio*[173] can never be the

---

[164] Villa-Vicencio (2000, 70–72).
[165] Villa-Vicencio (2000, 73).
[166] (2000, 33).
[167] (2000, 253).
[168] Allen (2001, 36).
[169] Allen (2001, 34).
[170] Allen (2001, 35).
[171] See in this regard Duffy (2001, 66–89).
[172] Allen (2001, 37); Van Marle (2000, 253).
[173] An eye for an eye and a tooth for a tooth.

aim of punishment. Punishment may include for example other forms of restitution, community service and monetary compensation. The victims' hearings tried to achieve something of this (see section 5 above).

Moosa[174] states the following with regard to the work of the Truth and Reconciliation Commission:

> the TRC defied all our accepted conception of justice, law, order and fairness. It requires a faith in the *mysterium* of the event, a faith in the rite of reconciliation, a belief in the rituals of confession, rather than an expectation of the process.

What was expected and what happened were not the same — reconciliation, truth and justice were incomplete as the reality differed from the performance.[175]

Bharghava[176] chooses a different philosophy in that 'where no party abides by norms of basic procedural justice, then we descend' from an *asymmetrical barbaric society* into a *symmetrically barbaric society*. According to him it is necessary to find some mechanism to deal with the gross injustices of the past to move towards 'minimal decency'. He refers to South Africa's fragile situation which may 'walk into two explosive moral land-mines.'[177] If former victims become victors who seek comprehensive retributive justice they may transform former victors into victims. Former victims should also not become perpetrators because their needs are not addressed. According to Bhargava a truth commssion was necessary but it is not sufficient to create a minimal decent society in South Africa. The Commission did not bring about reconciliation 'through the process of collective acknowledgement of grave wrongs-cum-forgiveness, because reconciliation requires profound change in people.'[178] The Commission contributed towards creating conditions for reconciliation — it was not an end of itself. It was an important moment in the transitionary process where human forces took precedence over state politics.

Some regard the work of the Commission as transitional justice — 'the justice that is appropriate to societies undergoing transition,'[179] The proponents of this concept can, however, not demonstrate that justice was complete, distinctive and coherent. If justice is the restoration of the human and civic dignity of victims to give them a chance to be heard, the Commission succeeded. The Commission did not establish the factual truth but allowed the victims to give their truth and to give their stories

---

[174] 2000, 117–18.
[175] Moosa (2000, 121–22).
[176] (2000, 64).
[177] Bhargava (2002, 65).
[178] Bhargava (2000, 66–67).
[179] Allen (2001, 25); see also Duffy (2001, 89).

public attention and respect.[180] According to Allen[181] transitional justice overlook the connection between a truth commission's work and legal justice.

The Commission was a response to violations of human rights. It gave publicity to these acts[182] and 'promoted a conception of social unity mediated by respect for justice and the rule of law.'[183] The Commission helped to have victims dignity restored and managed to fulfil all the Commission's duties as set out in the Act.[184] The establishment of the Commission was sanctioned and their work authoritative, people ware aware of their human rights and had a will to be heard. The actions and the policy of the Commission were in accordance to international human rights law.

The Commission might not have fulfilled all the expectations of the people of South Africa, but managed to ensure that people are aware of human right abuses and that they would try to avoid or prevent them in future.

More is needed and according to Villa-Vicencio:[185] the resources in the country, namely its artists, storytellers, journalists, teachers, religious communities, NGOs and opinion-makers should be used to ensure that a 'honest ownership of the past is acknowledged.' The Commission could only recommend reparation to victims, while it could grant amnesty to perpetrators. According to him facilities need to be made available to all traumatised people over the country and the gap between rich and poor need to be addressed.[186] Human rights and democracy can also play an important role to ensure reparation — the promotion of socio-economic rights and the right of free speech should be cherished and promoted.

Reconciliation includes punitive justice where necessary. The question is how South Africa will proceed with this. Although mention was made that some perpetrators of gross violations of human rights will be prosecuted, nothing has happened two years after the final report of the Commission. As has been stated the major political and ruling party in South Africa discussed the possibility of a blanket amnesty during December 2002. This may result in the work of the Truth Commission becoming obsolete.[187]

The road forward is, however, to establish a community where everyone's rights are respected and protected.[188] Although not the work of the

---

180 Allen (2001, 27).
181 (2001, 28).
182 Allen (2001, 37).
183 Allen (2001, 38–39).
184 See 2 above.
185 (2000.75).
186 Ndungane (2000, 358–364).
187 Villa-Vicencio (2000, 75–6); see also Asmal, Asmal and Roberts (2000, 86–98) who strongly propose the prosecution of perpetrators of gross violations of human rights. See also 5 above.
188 Gerwel (2000, 286).

Commission, certain measures are in place to ensure that gross violations of human rights are prevented.[189] South Africa is in the process of harmonising national legislation with international rights standards, the judiciary is independent, the security forces are trained to respect human rights and a Human Rights Commission and a Public Protector are in place.[190]

10   RECONCILIATION — A PIPE DREAM?

According to a report of government 'Our dreams realised' (published during March 1999) it seems that South Africa is now suffering from one of the other legacies of apartheid and poverty, namely crime. Political violence was substituted by another form of violence, although political violence flares up from time to time. South Africa has some of the highest crime statistics in the world when it comes to violent crimes. Government has put various measures in place to deal with the situation and by July 1999 it was apparent that the number of crimes stabilised. However, these statistics are not different from statistics in other African countries experienced during their transitional phases and should be seen in this light.[191]

A symptom of people tired of crime is the number of self-defence units that are established in South Africa. Women for example organised themselves in the fight against rape and in two instances men were castrated and in another a person was put to fire. In the Northern Province a self-defence unit Mapogo a Mathamaga was established, and in the Western Cape Pagad was established. These units' support grows by the day. These self-defence units themselves sometimes ignore human rights in their vigour to apply justice as they see it. The judicial system in South Africa is presently experiencing a crisis; if the situation is not dealt with urgently South Africa might soon need a new healing process unconnected with political violence.[192]

Whether the whole TRC process brought about reconciliation is a question that only time will answer. It did, however, bring information to the fore that was not readily available in South Africa. To the previous advantaged, the truth as unveiled by the Commission came as a shock and revelation; to the disadvantaged it was a confirmation of what they have fought against all these years. The Commission was a necessary start in the healing process, but if socio-economic and juridical reform does not form part of

---

[189] See also 5 above.
[190] Liebenberg (1996, 143).
[191] Cf Du Plessis, Olivier and Pienaar (1999, 222–25).
[192] Makoe (1999, 3).

the process the good effect of the healing process might soon be lost again.[193] The words of Bishop Tutu (1998a) perhaps best illustrate this:

> Inevitably, evidence and information about our past will continue to emerge, as indeed they must. The report of the Commission will now take its place in the historical landscape of which future generations will try to make sense — searching for the clues that lead, endlessly, to a truth that will, in the very nature of things, never be fully revealed.[194]

> Ours is a remarkable country. Let us celebrate our diversity, our differences. God wants us as we are. South Africa wants and needs the Afrikaner, the English, the Coloured, the Indian and the Black. We are sisters and brothers in one family — God's family, the human family. Having looked the beast of the past in the eye, having asked and received forgiveness and having made amends, let us shut the door on the past — not in order to forget it but in order not to allow it to imprison us. Let us move into the glorious future of a new kind of society where people count, not because of biological irrelevancies or other extraneous attributes, but because they are persons of infinite worth created in the image of God. Let that society be a new society — more compassionate, more caring, more gentle, more given to sharing — because we have left 'the past of a deeply divided society characterised by strife, conflict, untold suffering and injustice' and are moving to a future 'founded on the recognition of human rights, democracy and peaceful co-existence and development opportunities for all South Africans, irrespective of colour, race, class, belief or sex.[195]

It is important to remember that reconciliation does not come easy and takes time — it is based on respect for one another's humanity. If the truth had been hidden, it would have become a cancer that would have been transferred from generation to generation, leading eventually to another bloodbath. Such an action was hopefully prevented by the work of the Commission.

To ensure reconciliation some form of restorative justice, not revenge, is necessary. The disclosure of truth and an understanding as to why these violations happened encourage forgiveness. Parties have to accept responsibility for their part in the violation of human rights.[196]

To reconcile does not mean to forget or even to forgive, but it means to remember 'without deliberating pain, bitterness, revenge, fear or guilt' and to co-exist and work for the peaceful handling of most probably continuing differences. In doing so, all South Africans must be committed to ensure

---

[193] Cf also Tutu (1999, 221).
[194] Truth and Reconciliation Commission (1998a, 4).
[195] Truth and Reconciliation Commission (1998a, 22).
[196] Truth and Reconciliation Commission (1998e, 435).

that a culture of human rights and democracy can exist within political and socio-economic conflicts that may ensue.[197]

REFERENCES

Allen, Jonathan 2001. Between retribution and restoration: justice and the TRC. *South African Journal of Philosophy*, 20(1): 22–41.

Anon. 1996. Enter the Commission, *Financial Mail*, 18 October: 47–8.

Anon. 1997a. The truth will set you free. *Finance Week*, 19 December 1996–98 January 1997: 18.

Anon. 1997b. Who violated Cebeckhulu's rights? *Finance Week*, 11–17 December: 11.

Anon. 1998a. 900 aansoeke om amnestie al afgehandel. *Beeld*, 21 October: 4.

Anon. 1998b. TRC amnesty shenanigans. *Finance Week*, 19–25 February: 39–40.

Duffy, Jerrob 2001. Bargaining for truth and reconciliation in South Africa: a game-theoretic analysis. *South African Journal of Philosophy*, 20(1): 66–89.

Du Plessis, Lourens 1997. Afrikanernegatiwiteit oor die WVK: Viva Rip van Winkel. *Woord en Daad/Word and Action*, 37(360): 14–17.

Du Plessis, Willemien 1986. *Die reg op inligting en die openbare belang*. LLD dissertation. Potchefstroom: Potchefstroom University for CHE.

Du Plessis, Willemien 1995. Afrikareg en godsdiens. In *Festschrift JC Bekker*, edited by P D de Kock and JC Bekker. (Pretoria: Vista University) 53–71.

Du Plessis, Willemien, Olivier, Nic and Pienaar, Juanita 1995. Geweld — nog geen einde in sig. *South African A Public Law 10*: 487–503.

Du Plessis, Willemien, Olivier, Nic and Pienaar, Juanita 1996. Versoening en pogings om geweld te bekamp. *South African Public Law 11*: 283–97.

Du Plessis, Willemien, Olivier, Nic and Pienaar, Juanita 1997. Nog meer maatreëls om geweld en misdaad te bekamp. *South African Public Law 12*: 233–50.

Du Plessis, Willemien, Olivier, Nic and Pienaar, Juanita. 1997. Geweld, waarheid en versoening. *South African Public Law 12*: 550–64.

Du Plessis, Willemien, Olivier, Nic and Pienaar, Juanita. 1998. Beskerming teen geweld of beskerming vir die misdadiger? *South African Public Law 13*: 169–85.

Du Plessis, Willemien, Olivier, Nic and Pienaar, Juanita. 1999. Stortvloed van maatreëls poog orde en stabiliteit — utopia? *South African Public Law 14*: 222–40.

Du Plessis, Willemien, Olivier, Nic and Pienaar, Juanita. 1998. Hoe meer maatreëls, hoe meer geweld. *South African Public Law 13*: 489–501.

Fourie, Corlia 1998. Vervolgings kan eerder tot tien jaar duur. *Beeld*, 21 November: 8.

Goldstone, Richard J 1997. Healing for wounded people: War crimes and truth Commissions. *Woord en Daad/Word and Action*, 37(360): 17–23.

Hamber, Brandon 2000. Official silence on reparations cheats the victims of past conflicts of their rights. *Sunday Independent*, 20 February: 9.

---

[197] Truth and Reconciliation Commission (1998e, 435, 444).

Krog, Antjie 1999 *Country of my skull*. London: Vintage.

Laurence, Patrick 1997. Selective justice in Winnie probe. *Financial Mail*, 5 December: 40–41.

Laurence, Patrick. 1998. Anatomy of a risky gambit. *Financial Mail*, 6 November: 39–41.

Liebenberg, Ian 1996. The truth and reconciliation Commission in South Africa: context, future and some imponderables. *South African Public Law/Publiekreg*, 11: 123–59.

Loots, Jaco 1995. Dilemma rondom vrywaring. *Woord en Daad/Word and Action*, 35(353): 20–22.

Loots, Jaco and Du Plessis, Willemien 1996. Die Waarheidskommissie — Nürnberg-verhore of bevordering van nasionale eenheid en versoening? *Tydskrif vir Suid-Afrikaanse Reg*, 1: 154–60.

Makoe, J 1999. Vigilante group to go national. *Sunday Independent*, 11 June: 3.

Russel, C 1997. One-eyed view? *Finance Week*, 13–19 March 1997: 36.

Sindane, Jabu 1997. The future of traditional leadership, *ubuntu* and nation-building. In *Traditional leadership in Southern Africa*, edited by Konrad Adenauer-Stiftung. (Johannesburg: Konrad Adenauer-Stiftung): 147–62.

Swart, Freek 1998. Ruim belastingtoegewings vind byval. *Beeld*, 12 March: 1.

Thompson, Desmond 1999. Sonder wysigings kan skendings nadraai hê. *Beeld*, 27 February: 4.

Truth and Reconciliation Commission 1998a. *Truth and Reconciliation Commission of South Africa Report. Volume 1.* (Cape Town: Juta).

Truth and Reconciliation Commission 1998b. *Truth and Reconciliation Commission of South Africa Report. Volume 2.* (Cape Town: Juta).

Truth and Reconciliation Commission 1998c. *Truth and Reconciliation Commission of South Africa Report. Volume 3.* (Cape Town: Juta).

Truth and Reconciliation Commission 1998d. *Truth and Reconciliation Commission of South Africa Report. Volume 4.* (Cape Town: Juta).

Truth and Reconciliation Commission 1998e. *Truth and Reconciliation Commission of South Africa Report. Volume 5.* (Cape Town: Juta).

Tutu, Desmond 1999. *No future without forgiveness*. (London: Ryder).

Van Marle, Karin 2000. An 'ethical' interpretation of equality and the truth and reconciliation Commission. *De Jure*, 248–58.

Van Wyk, Amie 1999. Kommentaar op die verslag van die Waarheids- en Versoeningskommissie. *Woord en Daad/Word and Action*, 39(367): 21–23.

Wilhelm, Peter 1999. Slammed as theatre of victims. *Financial Mail*, 30 July: 34–35.

Court decisions:

Azapo v The President of the RSA (1996) (8) BCLR 1015 (CC); (1996) 4 SA 671 (C).

Du Preez v Truth and Reconciliation Commission (1997) 3 SA 204 (A); (1997) 4 BCLR 531 (A).

Niewoudt v the Truth and Reconciliation Commission Case (1997) 2 SA 70 (SEC)

S v Botha Case GSM 15/98.

S v Makwanyane and Another (1995) 3 SA 391 (CC); (1995) 2 SACR 1; (1995) (6) BCLR 665.

Truth and Reconciliation Commission v Du Preez and Another (1996) 3 SA 997 (C), (1996) (8) BLCR 1109 (N).

Legislation:

Archives Act 6 of 1962
Black Administration Act 38 of 1927
Black Land Act 27 of 1913
Constitution of the Republic of South Africa 200 of 1993
Constitution of the Republic of South Africa 108 of 1996
Equity Act 4 of 2000
Group Areas Act 51 of 1950
Legal Deposit Act 54 of 1997
National Archives Act 43 of 1996
Promotion of Access to Information Act 2 of 2000
Promotion of National Unity and Reconciliation Act 34 of 1995
Witness Protection Act 112 of 1998

Part II

Power, Structures, Processes, and History in the Reconstruction of Peace

The Reconstruction of Peace II: Asian Experiences

9

Democracy and Ethnic Conflicts: The Politics of Ethnicity and Conflict Resolution in South Asia

JAKOB RÖSEL

IT IS NOT easy to cover in the space of some twenty pages the experiences, which three experiments in democratisation have accumulated over the span of half a century in South Asia. In order to bring to mind the sheer numbers of men and women involved in and determined through these experiments we have to see that South Asia comprises more than one fifth of mankind. India, for example with a population of one billion, constitutes a democracy, which comprises more citizens and voters than all the established western democracies combined. To understand therefore the magnitude of the Indian, Pakistani and Sri Lankan experiments we have to realise that every single page in this chapter represents at least the equivalent of a country with more than sixty million people, that is a state of the size of France or Great Britain. Given these constraints of space I will concentrate on the shortest possible outline. In the following I will analyse the capacities of containing ethnic conflict in the case of India, Pakistan and Sri Lanka, that is first a successful process of democratisation, secondly a repeated failure at democratisation and thirdly an attempt to establish a pro-sinhalese, an ethnic democracy. In every case I will concentrate on four points of comparison:

I will first demonstrate which balance the respective state and polity have established in those three dimensions, which are essential for the consolidation of democratic power. This is first the balance between the imperative of secularism as against the claims of a dominant religion or religious majority; secondly the balance between civil administration, democratic party control and military power, and thirdly the balance between the ideal of a unitary and the demands for a federal state. I will secondly focus on what party system evolved, as it is the nature and composition of a democratic and bureaucratic mass-party and party system, which determines the outcome of democratisation. I will thirdly concentrate on the type of identities and patterns of allegiances which survived or which evolved during these experiments of democratisation. And, finally, as a consequence of these balances struck, party systems established and identity patterns transformed, I will outline the specific political style and strategy of coping with ethnic conflict, which has evolved in each of the three cases.

It is in this framework, that I hope to address but certainly not to answer three important questions: Why has India, the largest and in terms of ethnic and religious complexity most diverse nation and society successfully prevented, contained or solved so many potential and actual conflicts? Why had (West) Pakistan, an artificial, incomplete and politically and regionally unbalanced state as well as a potential powder keg of ethnic irredentas never to confront any large-scale ethnic uprising — apart from the recent Mohajir revolt? Why has Sri Lanka initially perceived as an example of perfect democratisation succumbed to an ethnic civil war, which has by now become the single most important determinant for its government and state?

1   INDIA: SUCCESSFUL DEMOCRATISATION

1 1   Constitutional Balance

For the Congress party, which gained India its independence there was never any doubt about the primacy of secularism. It was only through the acceptance of the ideal of a secular state that the party could hope to transform itself into a truly national movement and to be capable to challenge effectively the colonial government. Equally Congress had never any doubts about the subordinate position of the military and it already inherited a federal state, that is a state which had unintentionally acquired a federal character, first through the haphazard style by which the East India Company had conquered and organised the subcontinent and finally through the process of decolonisation during which the British in 1920 granted self-determination to the provinces, while keeping control over the central government (RL Hardgrave, 1975: 84–108).

1 2   Party System

As we all know, the Indian experiment in democratisation and political mass-mobilisation was initiated through and controlled within a so-called 'dominant one party system'. This structure has survived to the present day, although the system has for me last twelve years witnessed the decline of its founding organisation, the Congress, and the ascent of two political alternatives, which compete for the inheritance of the dominant one party position and the control of its inevitably centrist policies. These competing alternatives are constituted by the Hindu-nationalist but by now increasingly centrist Bharatiya Janata Party and their un-orthodox allies and by multi party coalitions comprising the major regional parties, the true yet regional successor organisations of Congress. Congress first dominated and advanced democratisation and finally declined because of its very success in democratisation. The Congress-initiated advance and consolidation of democratisation and sadly enough its own demise was the result of several factors: Congress was willing to give through a process of states-reorganisation, every major linguistic group its own state. It thus initiated the so-called 'vernacularisation' of Indian democratic politics, which, accompanied by 'membership drives', transformed the regional Congress organisations into powerful political machines and turned the All India Congress into a genuine microcosm of all the social, cultural, sectarian and regional complexities of India. Through the same process Congress was capable to defuse separatist regional or ethnic movements. Under the strategy of '(secular and political) Unity in (regional and religious) Diversity' regional Congress organisations de-politicised regional movements, incorporated their followers, corrupted their leaders, folklorised their contents and marginalised their steadfast adherents. Even when the regional Congress organisations lost their power to dominate the provincial arena, their political rivals and successor organisations were moulded in the Congress image and they had to operate according to the federal rules. In the long term they emerged as secular, pragmatic and folkloristic regional movements and parties. In the very rare instances, when separatist organisations or militant social movements could not be bribed through patronage and 'tokenism' or emasculated through the buying over of its voter- and caste groups, such organisations were destroyed by the security forces or hunted down by the dominant castes (J Manor, 1991).

1 3 Patterns of Identity

Five decades of political but only limited social and economic modernisation have led to a configuration of identities, which contributes to the consolidation of a federal democracy. Although at the eve of independence there existed several long-established separatist regional movements, apart from the open warfare between Hindu- and Muslim-communities, they have all been accommodated and contained in their respective regional arenas. What we find now is a configuration of modern as well as traditional identities. The province, its politics and patronage resources, its language, culture and historical traditions, attracts the interests and the political and cultural attachment of the average Indian citizen and voter. Beyond this regional horizon and political identity there is only a dim and episodic awareness of an Indian state and of the ideal and demands of an Indian nation. But apart from this political as well as folkloristic identity, there exist social and religious identities, which focus on one's regional caste and caste-status and on one's village temple, regional pilgrimage centre or sectarian group. These are localised or at the utmost regionalised social and religious identities, they are not yet based on a clearly defined notion of caste as class or of Hinduism as a definable and pan-Indian religion. The only identity circle, which truly transcends the boundaries of village and locality, is thus a political and cultural identity focused on one's region. It is an identity which is constitutionally acknowledged, eminently practical and legitimate and, as long as Congress, the BJP or multi party coalitions respect the political rules it carries no secessionist threat (W Morris-Jones, 1967: 40–49).

1 4   Dealing with Conflict

In every social group or political system, based on a substantial degree of individual self-determination, we should expect the social and political styles of compromise, bargain and confrontation. As the aforementioned facts already imply, it is a style of bargaining, which characterises this dominant one party system. The regional Congress organisations and by now their successors, the dominant regional parties certainly know how to compromise on demands put forward by new movements, interest groups or parties. If these groups, parties and movements constitute a major challenge the established parties can fall back on five decades of experiences in coalition building and 'log-rolling'. They know how to plagiarise and immediately to defuse popular as well as subversive party platforms, to coopt dissidents and marginalise their party-vehicles. In the case of intransigence, that is in the case of cadre-parties — very rare because they cannot organise a mass following — or in the case of secret organisations and terror groups — which up till now constitute only local threats — they follow a policy of benign neglect, they will tolerate a shadow war waged by the high ranking peasant castes or they will call in the regional security forces (J Rösel, 1998: 37–45).

2   PAKISTAN: FAILED DEMOCRATISATION

2 1   Constitutional Balance

After three attempts at democratisation and by now three military coups and dictatorships this artificial state has not yet established the constitutional equilibrium necessary for a self-sustaining process of democratisation: Pakistan's ruling classes have not arrived at an informed consensus whether this artificial state should be a secular, a Muslim majority or a Muslim theocratic state. Equally, there is no consensus on the legitimate roles and tasks, which the military, the civil service and the political parties can and should perform in the maintenance of a democratic Pakistani state. Finally no consensus has emerged whether Pakistan's structure should tolerate the emergence of regional parties and political subcultures or whether its Federalism should operate under remote control by two national parties, an authoritarian civil service and the army. The failure of democratisation in Pakistan is therefore the consequence as well as the cause of a constitutional imbalance. Questions, which the political process and constitution of India had already decided and laid to rest some five years after independence, continue to undermine any future attempt at democratisation and they prevent the consolidation of the Pakistani state. This capability of postponing instead of solving the most fundamental challenges for the process of democratic state-, nation- and party building is closely connected with the structure of the Muslim league and the development of the Pakistani party system (A Jalal, 1990: 194–276).

2 2   Party System

In contrast to the Congress party, the Muslim league — the only force that was capable to demand and established a separate Muslim state — was not a democratic and bureaucratic mass-mobilising party. Further more it was dominated by a North Indian Muslim elite and it had no significant following in those provinces which were to form the future (West-) Pakistan. The new state was therefore forced upon provinces and Muslim majority populations, which were either unaware of or indifferent and hostile to the creation of Pakistan. Transplanted into Pakistan the Muslim league during a first attempt at democratisation (1947–58) was never capable to reinvent itself as a democratic and bureaucratic national party. Instead it was taken over by the various regional landholding elites of the Punjab, the Sindh and the North Western Frontier Province. This take-over fractured the already weakened party-apparatus and it pushed the established party elite, the 'Mohajir' refugees, who had been driven from India and who had identified with this party and its vision of Pakistan into the background. Under the first phase of dictatorship, under Ayub Khan (1958–70), the Muslim league became further discredited, as Ayub Khan was able to persuade league politicians to create a so-called 'Convention Muslim League' and co-operate with his regime. It was only in the twilight of the Ayub Khan regime, that a second party with national and secular pretensions emerged, the Pakistan People's Party, established and completely dominated by Ayub Khan's former foreign minister

Zulfikar Ali Bhutto. Like the Muslim league before the PPP never evolved into a genuine democratic and bureaucratic party. From the beginning it was capable to exploit regional, Sindhi resentments against the Punjab's predominance in population numbers, economic preponderance and political influence. At the same time it portrayed itself as a genuine national party to gain enough votes in the Punjab and thereby power in the centre. Thus during a second attempt at democratisation under Bhutto (1970–78) — with the unforeseen emergence of independent Bangla Desh in the East and Bhutto's ascent to power in West Pakistan — and under the second dictatorship under Zia Ul Haq (1979–88) there emerged a de facto two party system.

This two party system consolidated its control on the national level and it began to extend into provincial politics during a third phase of democratisation (1988–99), which started with Zia ul Haq's death. Yet this de facto two party system far from strengthening democratisation undermined and discredited the democratic process. Both parties are dominated by landed elites, merchant groups, newly established 'industrial houses' and prominent (Sufi) saints, which control huge landholdings and networks of followers. As both parties have been and continue to be controlled by regionally or nationally entrenched ruling families, the PPP by the Bhutto clan and its affiliates, the Muslim league by the Punjabi elite, both parties continue to operate without the bureaucratic and democratic framework, procedures and checks and balances of a modern party organisation. Instead both parties are characterised by a feudal as well as outwardly modern style of family politics. These families demand and receive the absolute allegiance of their dependants, tenants, day labourers, clerks, lower officials or lay disciples. On the other side these families are entrenched and they operate in the modern structures and arenas of party politics, the civil administration, an industrialising economy and a system of higher education. It is in these sectors and on the basis of these networks of co-operation and competition that these families pursue their intrigues, contract marriages, construct alliances, coopt business partners and form friendships. Thus this ruling elite, operating under a veneer of modernity is not fractured by regional, ethnic or ideological cleavages: The interethnic interests of a ruling class always prevail over the demands of intra-ethnic solidarity, that is solidarity with the interests of one's local or regional ethnic group (I Talbot, 1999: 287–374).

2 3   Patterns of Identity

Pakistan is replete with combustible material for widespread ethnic and in addition sectarian and socio-economic conflict. Yet, with two exceptions, the secession of East Pakistan and the Mohajir insurrection in

Karachi, it has never encountered ethnic uprisings on a mass scale. This artificial state was enforced on indifferent or hostile regional ethnic groups. All endogenous groups, the Punjabis, the Pashtuns, the Sindhis and the Balutch resented the prominent role, which the refugees from India, the Mohajirs, played in the setting up this ramshackle state. In addition Sindhis, Balutch and Pashtuns out of different reasons and with different degrees of resentment feel themselves threatened by the Punjabis, which constitute nearly two third of the population of Pakistan and control most of its industry and irrigated land. A tiny Balutch intelligentsia has, since the end of the First World War cultivated the vision of a 'Greater Balutchistan' comprising most of the Sindh and extending into Iran and Afghanistan, meanwhile the Pashtun leadership in the North Western Frontier Province has been influenced by the project of a Greater Afghanistan or Pashtunistan extending to the Indus River. Thus the legitimacy of the whole western border of Pakistan is contested and this artificial state is confronted with two potential secessionist movements, Balutch and Pashtun, and the demand for greater autonomy on the side of the Sindhi population. Yet there has never been — apart from a localised uprising by several Balutch tribes — any protracted and widespread ethnic irredenta. The answer to this surprising fact lies in the lack of political and social modernisation. Democratisation facilitates the emergence of ethnic ideologues, entrepreneurs and parties and it provides the institutions and mechanisms for the politicisation and radicalisation of ethnic demands and party programs. But neither a process of political nor a process of social and cultural modernisation has yet occurred. Ethnic identities as they exist in Pakistan are still traditional identities. As traditional identities they are experienced as the rather remote and outlying identity circle, which incorporates the smaller, and concentric identity circles of one's family, lineage, caste and tribe. This ethnic identity has not been the object of scientific research, ideological elaboration and propagation by modern mass media. Thus ethnic identity coexists and competes with other traditional identities. It is not yet a unifying and levelling force percolating from the top, from a modern ethnic party elite into the interior of an ethnic group. Instead it subsists and coexists with other traditional yet crosscutting identity patterns of sect, caste and feudal obligation. Crosscutting traditional identities and cleavages, of sect, caste, village, tribe and ethnic group therefore tend to balance and fracture each other. This contrasts with cases where political mobilisation already during colonial times led to the emergence of modern ethnic ideologues, entrepreneurs and parties. Such ethnic elites as they existed in India were capable to modernise and idealise ethnic identities, but in the framework of Indian's dominant one party system they could be depoliticised, they were transformed into regional movements and by now they constitute a source of strength for the Indian Union. In contrast to

Pakistan India has therefore succeeded already first in the modernisation of ethnic identities and finally in the regionalisation and de-politicisation of these potentially subversive movements.

Ethnic strife in Pakistan, if it occurs, tends to be localised, it involves antagonistic tribes, castes or interest groups, and the 'ethnic identities' projected and the 'ethnic demands' expressed are derived from ad-hoc interpretations of a vernacular image of the honour and dignity of one's ethnic group, but not from a modern and ideological construct of the 'tradition', 'culture' and 'historical rights' of the respective group. The failure of democratisation and a lack of modernisation have therefore prevented the emergence of a systematic, politicised and to the outside as well as to the inside uncompromising concept of ethnic identity. In other words, the challenge of modernised ethnicity, which India due to successful democratisation and federalisation has already confronted and solved, will probably threaten this incomplete state in a not so distant future, as a consequence of renewed democratisation and accelerating modernisation (A Jalal, 1995: 100–21).

2 4   Dealing with Conflict

Due to the absence of modern forms of ethnic identity, which can be propagated, exploited and radicalised by parties, ethnic conflict has been marginal and localised in nature. Therefore the Pakistani ruling elite's capacity of dealing with widespread ethnic violence never developed and never has been tested. Yet, these ruling families and the family dominated two party system had to confront localised ethnic conflicts either in the form of rural unrest or urban riots. A specific style of dealing with these conflicts can be observed, which does not bode well for the capability of this families, parties and the Pakistani state to control future, more violent, politicised and extended conflict. This is a style of intrigue: In confronting such conflicts the Pakistani polity and state cannot rely on an informed consensus, on shared experiences and on established democratic routines, which clearly set out the margins of compromise, the limits for possible political bargains and the boundary line which separates political negotiation from confrontation. Instead the political actors have to operate in an atmosphere and arena of suspicion, lawlessness and unrestrained competition. This cannot endanger the functioning of institutions and the stability of state as long as these conflicts are local in nature. If local warlords, militant sheikhs, prominent racketeers, tribal sardars or rural agitators are killed in police custody, lured into a trap, bribed with patronage, elevated to party offices or coopted into the local political machines, then these manoeuvres will corrupt a district administration and they will further undermine the credibility of parties. They will not destabilise the provincial governments or the state. But such a mode of conflict resolution must endanger the functioning and the cohesion of the state, if it is applied to large-scale ethnic uprisings as it is occurred during the Mohajir insurrection in Karachi.

Yet, for the near future, there is no alternative to deal with these conflicts other than in the style of political intrigue. Political intrigue must be the strategy of choice in a political system in which ruling families jockey for influence and power and where their behaviour cannot be disciplined due to the absence of bureaucratic party organisations, a competent civil administration, an independent judiciary and a constitutional consensus — in other words a functioning system of the separation of powers. Political intrigue means that the age-old strategy 'my enemy's enemy is my friend' now imposes itself on all the actors concerned. Confronted with local or sectarian conflicts some of the competing local or regional families have to align themselves with local ringleaders, agitators or demagogues, while others will attempt to confront and destroy them. As long as these uprisings are local in nature these strategies will tend to split and marginalise these movements. Absence of institutional constraints and mutual suspicion and competition among ruling families will therefore not result in unlimited escalation. Even when local families outbid each other in self-interested support of agitators the prevalence of traditional and crosscutting identities and interests will confine such conflicts to the local arena. Yet, a completely different development will set in, when this traditional style of the politics of power and intrigue has to address politicised ethnic groups relying on a modern and ideological variant of ethnic identity. In this respect the Pakistani state lives on borrowed time (E Duncan, 1989: 135–237).

3   SRI LANKA: ETHNIC DEMOCRACY

3 1   Constitutional Balance

Sri Lanka confronts us with the paradoxical case of a seemingly successful, yet in the long-term self-destructive process of democratisation. The institutional causes as well as indicators of this self-destructive development we can find in a constitutional imbalance tilted in favour of an ethnic majority, its religion and its self-proclaimed ideal of a unitary state. Democratisation in Sri Lanka — on the basis of full franchise and nearly complete political control by the Sri Lankan parliament, parties and government — was initiated in 1931 by the British government. At that time the leaders of all Sri Lankan parties had to be coerced into accepting the chances and dangers of democratic mass politics. While the leaders of the Tamil Minority Party with good reasons opposed the establishment of a majority-based democratic system — as it threatened them with the majority rule of the Buddhist sinhalese, which comprised roughly two third of the population — the sinhalese gentlemen politicians were in fear of not being able to control the new voting-power of an impoverished population, which they had ages since oppressed with impunity. In order to maintain control these honoratiores quickly embraced a virulent and xenophobic Sinhalese-Buddhist nationalism. Through this stratagem they shifted internal conflicts — over adequate wages and land reform — to the outside and laid the blame for the 'Nation's' poverty and the scarcity of land on the British 'imperialists' and their Tamil 'allies'. When Sri Lanka gained independence in 1948 a Sinhala-Nationalist party, first the Ceylon National Congress, then since 1946 the United National Party had been in power for 17 years, ethnic mass politics were firmly established and the party system had split along ethnic line.

With the Sinhalese majority's hold on power never in question a constitutional imbalance developed which over three decades furthered the tensions between the Sinhalese majority and Sri Lankan-Tamil minority. Finally in 1983 these tensions turned into an ethnic civil war. Even before as well as after independence the maintenance of a unitary and centralised state was never in doubt. Thus the suggestion of a high ranking British official like Leonard Wolf, Virginia Wolf's husband, to give this small but highly heterogeneous and multi-ethnic Island a constitution modelled on the 'Cantons' of the Swiss Republic never received a serious discussion. For the Sinhalese power elite Ceylon had been predestined by the Buddha himself to be ruled by the Sinhalese and to be converted to the Buddhist faith. Equally these ruling circles were adamant in their belief — based on a traditional and by now ideologically and scientifically embellished historiography — that this Dharma dhipa, 'Island of the (Buddhist) Law' had always been kept under 'one umbrella of (Buddhist) rule', that is one central and centralising monarchy. Federal concessions to minority groups as, for example to the small Tamil based 'Federal Party' were therefore seen as tantamount to treason and the second constitution of independent Sri Lanka (1972) prohibited any attempt at federalisation as unconstitutional. Equally, the Sinhalese ruling elite insisted since the beginnings of this 'democratisation from above', that Buddhism should be entitled to occupy a privileged although largely undefined position in the affairs of the state. Against their critics these Sinhalese politicians would insist that the privileged treatment of Buddhism did not run counter to the principle of a secular and multi-religious state: as Buddhism was no religion but a universalistic philosophy of tolerance, the original and unsullied manifestation of what the west considered as secularism. It was only in the second constitution that this privileged position of Buddhism was constitutionally enshrined. Yet, while mass politics, that is politics for and by the ethnic majority, created a constitutional imbalance in favour of the majority's ideal of a unitary Buddhist state in a third constitutional dimension, in the realm of political, administrative and military relationship, Sri Lanka evolved as a democratic state in which the army was kept under firm command and the administration under corrupt political control by the respective party in power. Before sliding into civil war Sri Lanka therefore established a democratic system, which to outsiders appeared as exemplary and exceptionally well consolidated, while to insiders, from the minority groups, the same experiment appeared as unjust, dangerous and self-destructive. The emergence of this constitutionally flawed, ethnic as well as consolidated democracy was initiated and determined by a peculiar party system (J Manor, 1989: 125–67, 254–318).

3 2   Party System

The first two pro-Sinhalese political parties, the Ceylon National Congress and the United National Party had been dominated by a tiny Sinhalese ruling elite comprising plantation owners and proprietors of merchant houses, transport companies, law firms etc. These honoratiores were incapable to exert a strong leadership, to establish a network of party offices or collect membership-fees. The UNP thus, according to a contemporary observer, resembled a bus into which any local leader could enter to drive to parliament. During elections in many constituencies several UNP candidates would compete against each other. The structure of parties began to change when SWRD Bandaranaike, the son of the richest plantation family on the island, after conflicts within the UNP decided to found his own party in 1952, the Sri Lankan Freedom Party. Bandaranaike, an Anglican by faith and English speaking by family tradition had since the 30s converted to Buddhism, started to learn Sinhala and had embraced a virulent variant of Sinhala Buddhism. His party from the beginning embraced a more radical version of Sinhala nationalism and in the election of 1956 he promised to established 'Sinhala only', that is only the majority's language as Sri Lanka's new official and national language — to the detriment of the minority's Tamil and the UNP's elite families' English. In addressing the resentments of the Sinhala-speaking middle classes and in mobilising the lower Buddhist clergy Bandaranaike had, with his mixture of welfare state-socialism, anti-elitepopulism and anti-Tamil nationalism not so much created a political party, than a millenaristic movement. After his election victory Bandaranaike was now in a position to completely 'Sinhalize' the state and to transform the SLFP into a modern mass party. These developments impressed upon a divided UNP the need to embrace the same virulent and populist Sinhala nationalism to outbid the SLFP with pro-Sinhalese development and nationalisation programs and to transform itself into a competitive mass party, again based on the Sinhalese majority. Thus a decade after independence there emerged an ethnic, a pro-Sinhalese two party system in which two parties outbid themselves in anti-Tamil demands and promises, while the Tamil minority vote, split between two small and hostile parties was unable to influence the politics of patronage and minority discrimination. This ethnic party system and its consequences of ethnic exclusion and radicalisation had a strong homogenising impact first on the Sinhalese and then, in reaction, on the Tamil's interpretation of their community's identity, historical rights and destiny (J Rösel, 1997: 95–154).

3 3   Patterns of Identity

Three centuries of Portuguese, Dutch and British rule over the Sinhalese lowlands had practically destroyed Buddhism as an organised religion practised and propagated by the Buddhist clergy and venerated and funded by the court and the peasant castes. Yet, what survived the destruction of this 'Great Tradition' was a localised 'Little Tradition' not so much of genuine Buddhism but of the veneration of village gods and the practise of exorcism and ceremonial dances. It was only in the nineteenth century that, in reaction to the British missionaries' efforts, a Buddhist revival began, the invention and implementation of a 'Protestant' variant of orthodox Theravada Buddhism. Still, even this revival of Buddhism had of necessity to accept the presence of this in essence pre-buddhist village and folk religion. The forms of religious and social identity, which we find in the late nineteenth century, were therefore still traditional and the recently re-established Protestant Buddhism would constitute the outer rim of a concentric identity circle in which individuals would define themselves in the traditional terms of family, caste, village and region. Yet, already at the turn of the century a 'Saviour of the Nation' — in the eyes of his Sinhalese followers, and an ethnic demagogue — in the eyes of the British — transformed Buddhism into an ethnic creed. Anagarika Dharmapala, a self-styled, secular monk now defined the concept of the 'Sinhala-Buddhists', thus transforming a universalistic religious category into an ethnic concept. In conformity to this interpretation he preached a nationalist crusade to defend 'the land, the race and the faith'. This new concept of ethnic Buddhism was simultaneously extensive and restrictive: It claimed that the whole land by tradition, predestination and faith belonged to the 'lion race', the Sinhalese (Sinha: lion) and it ignored, marginalised or criticised the traditional identity patterns based on villages and local cults and on castes and caste obligations.

Anagarika's variant of religious ethno-nationalism would have remained ineffective, if the Sinhalese ruling elite, threatened with the advent of mass politics, had not embraced this xenophobic doctrine. Yet, it was only with the SLFP's assumption of power that this ideology was transformed into a political program and that it could operate as a self-fulfilling prophecy: transforming through message and believe a disparate electorate into a homogeneous 'lion race'. With the help of massive alphabetisation and school construction programs the SLFP as well as the UNP succeeded to teach two generations of Sinhalese pupils that Sinhala-Buddhism was and is the true foundation of the nation's history, destiny and identity. With official funding and middle class laymen's assistance Buddhist temples could be constructed in the remotest villages. They would marginalise or coopt, reinterpret and transform village cults and local traditions. This process was facilitated by the fact that the government and the school teacher could easily convince the peasant population, that what they received was not by any means an ideological innovation, but the rediscovery and reestablishment of a creed in which they and their ancestors had been brought up since more than two thousand years (J Brow, 1988).

The Sinhalese government not only succeeded in submerging diverse and crosscutting traditional identities in a unitary and by now highly visible and suggestive Sinhala-Buddhist identity, they were even capable to suppress and then to transform the concept and identity pattern of caste — at least in the nationalist discourse. The Sinhalese society was and is a caste-society and individuals would traditionally define and perceive their identity not only in terms of family, village and region but in most transactions and contexts in terms of caste. Yet, the mention of caste is taboo in national politics and official discourse. 'Caste' has been transformed to and is now substituted by 'Class', yet this new concept has again tended to level internal (caste) differences and to strengthen the belief in a uniform, Sinhala-Buddhist 'lion race'. In the eyes of Bandaranaike Sinhalese society consisted only out of two classes, the suppressed Sinhala-Buddhists and the westernised, anglophone and partially Anglican UNP-elite. After the SLFP's assumption of power and the UNP's tactical embrace of Sinhala-Buddhism, both parties now describe, during election campaigns, the whole Sinhala Nation as a suppressed class, exploited and threatened by various other neo-colonial classes as the Sri Lankan Tamils (in league with South Indian Tamils), India (operating as a sub-imperialist power) or the West (trying to impose alien, materialist values on this pristine spiritual society). Both variants of 'class-oppressions' were first elaborated by young, urban and lower ranking monks in the 1940s and this view was integrated into the SLFP's program as it helped to further homogenise a sinhala identity and as it offered a socio-economic justification for the discrimination of minorities, for opposition to India and for non-alignment.

The construction, propagation and finally implementation of this new identity — through education, village-development, election campaigns and 'cultural programs' — was no benign exercise. It created the ground support and mass following for the UNP and SLFP, which at least form the seventies onward, became the prisoners of their own ideology, promises and voters. Legislative acts, which discriminated against ever-broader sections of the Tamil minority, now transformed ethnic antagonism, which had been entrenched in the party system even before independence, into ethnic conflict. Such acts initiated violent riots and demonstrations and since 1983 ethnic conflict escalated into civil war. This is not the place to detail this descent into violence, equally it is impossible to detail how in reaction to sinhalese identity-, nation-, and state-building, the Sri Lankan Tamils reacted with a modernisation and politicisation of their hitherto traditional and diverse concepts of a Tamil identity, history and destiny. Instead, what we have to observe is how this perfectly functioning, yet ethnic, seemingly consolidated yet radicalising democracy coped with the inevitable result of its mode of operation: ethnic conflict (J Rösel, 1996: 86–121).

3 4   Dealing with Conflict

In addressing ethnic conflicts, caused by minorities or regional movements, characterised by an already modernised but politically moderate concept of regional, cultural or social identity, the Indian polity will prefer and it can practise bargaining. In addressing ethnic conflicts caused by local lineages, tribes or interest groups characterised by traditional, crosscutting and in the long term mutually blocking loyalties, the Pakistani polity will and must rely on intrigue. In addressing ethnic conflicts, caused not so much by the reaction of the Tamil minority, but by the Sinhala State itself, characterised by a modernised, politically aggressive and exclusive concept of identity, the Sri Lankan polity employs casuistry and subterfuge. It opts for this strategy, because it has to reconcile constitutionality and legal process with the self-imposed demands of ethnic exclusion and discrimination. The structure and the demands of ethnic democracy impose on the Sinhalese polity the necessity to advance its ethnic majority interests, while maintaining the decorum of democracy and constitutionality — even in times of crises and civil war.

Comparable to India, but in contrast to Pakistan, there exist an informed consensus, broad experiences and a general acceptance of the rules of the constitution in dealing with ethnic conflict. The only difference is that this consensus, experiences and rules all point into the direction of confrontation and suppression, not of negotiation and bargaining. Yet, negotiation and bargaining have increasingly become necessary with the rise of Tamil militancy resistance and power. This constraint has imposed on the Sinhalese polity its specific style of political casuistry and legal subterfuge. Under pressure from the international community or from India negotiation are offered in principle but obstructed in practise — through the manipulation of protocol or agenda and the construction of legal loopholes in drafts for a settlement. If the Tamil and the Sinhalese side conclude, against all odds, a bargain — which was the case with the Banderanaike/ Chelvanayakam-Pact and the Senananayke/ Chelvanayakam-Pact — the Sinhalese government, after extracting concessions, later reneges on its side of the bargain. Yet, while doing so, it will cite constitutional constraints, its inability's to secure parliamentary support or the obstruction by an independent judiciary. This style of dealing with ethnic conflict has enabled successive sinhalese governments to pursue two different aims at the same time: On the one side it was able to accelerate the 'Sinhalisation' of state and society, to side-track reform proposals and finally to wage an internal war; on the other side it could portray itself as a democratic power, circumscribed by the rule of its constitution, but prepared to negotiate with minorities and willing to accept some of their demands — as long as the rules of the constitution, the maintenance of the democratic process and the self-respect of the Nation would not be compromised (J Manor, 1979).

4   SUMMARY

We have focused in this chapter on India, Pakistan and Sri Lanka — a consolidated democracy, a failure at democratisation and an ethnic democracy. Against the fairly widespread assumption, which regards democracy as a means to either prevent, contain or negotiate ethnic conflict, we have described democratisation as a process which, if successful, can in the long term manage or solve those conflicts which it has initiated, politicised or radicalised in the short term. Democratisation is thus a deeply ambivalent process, which in all probability will offer new scope, techniques, platforms and arenas for ethno-political demands, but which can, not out of necessity and only from itself, develop the antidote to contain ethnic ideologues, entrepreneurs or parties. In order for democratisation to succeed in such containment, it is necessary that democratisation is aligned with or based on other processes among which figure most prominently a secularisation of politics and a federalisation of state. Yet, such processes are neither necessary functional requirements or elements of democratisation nor can they be decreed and implemented through a simple 'fiat' of party politics. It is therefore of interest to observe to what degree, successful or failed, democratisation is accompanied by processes of secularisation and federalisation.

In India we could observe a democratic experiment, which had already set in decades before independence, a democratic experiment, which evolved in a federal, first a colonial, then in a reformed postcolonial structure of state; furthermore due to the convictions of a western orientated Congress leadership and because of the trauma of the partition, this democracy was from the beginning based on the principle of secularism, on the theory of 'one (secular) nation'. Federalisation and secularism thus provided this democracy with a framework, in which those ethnic, religious, sectarian conflicts, generated or enhanced through democratisation, could be contained and accommodated in provincial arenas or controlled and marginalised in a secularised political public and party system.

In contrast to India, Pakistan constitutes a case in which neither a democracy nor this framework was ever firmly established. Yet, Pakistan, an artificial state, characterised by an enormous potential for ethnic, secessionist and sectarian conflict and incapable to develop democratic means and strategies for conflict resolution has — apart from the secession of East Pakistan and the Mohajir uprising — not experienced widespread ethnic irredentas and separatist conflicts. This is because a general lack of political, social andcultural modernisation has prevented the emergence of those broad based and region — or nation-wide movements and parties, which could challenge the Pakistani state — incapable to solve or negotiate such conflicts. Pakistan's stability thus rests on borrowed time, because its failure to initiate genuine democratisation, secularisation and federalisation will not in the long run prevent the emergence of mass-based ethnic movements. Such movements may emerge, because Pakistan's army apparatus and oligarchic parties cannot isolate forever and everywhere these still localised and traditionalist societies from the outside world and the lure of ethnic or regional self-assertion and mobilisation. Yet, when this authoritarian state will finally have to confront such movements, it will lack the means of democratic consensus-building and control.

With Sri Lanka we encountered a case of successful, of text-book democratisation operating against any serious attempt at secularisation and federalisation. It can even be said, that the entrenchment of this broad-based, highly competitive, yet, ethnic, pro-Singhalese two-party-democracy necessitated the change from a formal and British inherited secularism to Buddhism — as a de facto state religion, official 'culture' and national 'identity'. Parallel to this transformation the Singhalese majority, polity and government defended the (over)centralised state against any serious attempts of decentralisation or federalisation to preserve their 'historic' claim and their control over the whole island. The result of this (in contrast to India) democratisation without secularisation and federalisation was and is an ongoing civil war between the Singhalese majority and the Sri Lanka Tamil minority.

Looking back on these three experiments in state- and nation-building in multiethnic societies, we can therefore conclude: Successful democratisation, without secularisation and federalisation carries the danger of initiating widespread and uncontrollable ethnic and religious conflict. It is only when we find a convergence of these three processes, that we can expect a development in which democratisation on the one hand may exacerbate conflict, while it, on the other hand, due to secularisation and federalisation, acquires the necessary rules, routines and institutions to contain or negotiate such conflicts. Finally, in the absence of these three ideally self-enforcing processes, we can observe a paradox:

We find still traditional, highly segmented societies and authoritarian, yet not necessarily strong states, which, although they comprise and rest on an enormous potential for ethnic and religious conflict are not (yet) challenged by mass-based secessionist, regionalist, sectarian or fundamentalist revolts or movements. Yet, in the short or in the long term these laggards in modernisation will have to confront such movements without the means and experience of democratic conflict resolution. In this case and at this late hour, such states can only choose between three options, all of which are equally difficult and unsatisfactory: they can attempt to suppress such movements and thereby they will risk to become embroiled in endless conflicts; they might finally initiate democratisation and thereby they will contribute to the politisation and radicalisation of these conflicts; they can finally try to decree and (kick)start democratisation, secularisation and federalisation at the same time. Yet, this dismantling of the authoritarian state carries the risk, that it might implode before it is transformed.

Therefore, if ethnic and religious conflicts should be prevented, contained and controlled there seems to exist only one in the long term reliable strategy. This strategy is easier to define, than to implement: it is based on an early and earnest commitment, by a political elite or polity, to engage itself in an open, a democratic state- and nation-building. And this strategy must include the willingness to democratise, to secularise and to decentralise at the same time.

REFERENCES

Ali, Chaudhri Muhammad 1967. *The Emergence of Pakistan.* (New York: Columbia University Press).

Andersen, Walter; Damle, Shridhar 1987. *The Brotherhood in Saffron: The Rashtriya Swayamsevak Sangh and Hindu Revivalism.* (Boulder: Westview Press).

Bernard, J 1985. *L'Inde, le Pouvoir et la Puissance.* (Paris: Fayard).

Brass, Paul Richard 1994. *The Politics of India since Independence.* (Cambridge: Cambridge University Press).

Brow, James 1988. In Pursuit of Hegemony. In *American Ethnologist,* 15: 311–27.

Duncan, Emma 1989. *Breaking the Curfew. A Political Journey Through Pakistan.* (London: Arrow Books).

Hardgrave, Robert Lewis 1975. *India: Government and Politics in a Developing Nation.* (New York: Harcourt, Brace & World).

Jalal, Ayesha 1985. *The Sole Spokesman: Jinnah, the Muslim League, and the Demand for Pakistan.* (Cambridge: Cambridge University Press).

Jalal, Ayesha 1990. *The State of Martial Rule: The Origins of Pakistan's Political Economy of Defence.* (Cambridge: Cambridge University Press).

Jalal, Ayesha 1995. *Democracy and Authoritarianism in South Asia.* (Lahore: Sang-E-Meel Publications).

Kohli, Atul (ed) 1991. *India's Democracy: An Analysis of Changing State-Society Relations.* (Princeton: Princeton University Press).

Lipset, Seymour; Rokkan, Stein (eds) 1967. *Party Systems and Voter Alignments: Cross National Perspectives*. (New York: Free Press).

Manor, James 1979. The Failure of Political Integration in Sri Lanka. In *Journal of Commonwealth and Comparative Politics*, 17: 21–46.

Manor, James 1991. Parties and the Party System. In *India's Democracy: An Analysis of Changing State-Society Relations*, edited by A Kohli. (Princeton: Princeton University Press).

Manor, James 1989. *The Expedient Utopian: Bandaranaike and Ceylon*. (Cambridge: Cambridge University Press).

Morris-Jones, Wyndraeth 1967. *The Government and Politics of India*, London: Hutchinson.

Rösel, Jakob 1998. Aufstieg und Niedergang der Congressherrschaft. In *Bürger im Staat, 48(1):* 37–45.

Rösel, Jakob 1998. Demokratie unter scheinbar aussichtslosen Bedingungen. In *Bürger im Staat, 48(1):* 33–6.

Rösel, Jakob 1997. *Der Bürgerkrieg auf Sri Lanka: der Tamilenkonflikt: Aufstieg und Niedergang eines singhalesischen Staates*. (Baden Baden: Nomos).

Rösel, Jakob 1996. *Die Gestalt und Entstehung des singhalesischen Nationalismus*. (Berlin: Duncker & Humblot).

Singh, MP 1992. Bharativa Janata Party: An Alternative to the Congress? In *Asian Survey, 32/4:* 303–17.

Smith, Donald (ed) 1966. *South Asian Politics and Religion*. (Princeton: Princeton University Press).

Talbot, Ian 1999. *Pakistan, a Modern History*. (Lahore: Vanguard Books).

Thakur, Ramesh Chandra 1995. *The Government and Politics of India*. (Basingstoke: Macmillan Press).

Tinker, Hugh 1966. *India and Pakistan. A political analysis*. London: Pall Mall Press.

Wolpert, Stanley 1993. *Zulfi Bhutto of Pakistan: His Life and Times*. (New York, Oxford: Oxford University Press).

10

Law, Violence and Peace Making on the Island of Ambon*

KEEBET VON BENDA-BECKMANN

O N JANUARY 19, 1999 an Ambonese[1] taxi driver got into a fight
with a Buginese tricycle rider in Ambon town. Similar fights often
occur in the tough neighbourhood of Batu Merah, where people
from many different ethnic and religious backgrounds live closely packed.
Emotions run high, often resulting in one or more wounded and sometimes
even death. But usually as quickly as a fight flares up, it cools down again,
but not this time. This was to be the beginning of a long period of intense
fighting and rioting that has developed into something close to civil war. At
first it was confined to Ambon-Lease, the central Moluccan islands with
Ambon as the provincial capital, but it has spread to the North Moluccan
islands and to the Southeast Moluccas around Key and Tanimbar. Many
people have died, more have lost their homes and fled, houses have been
burnt down and mosques and churches have been burnt to ashes.[2] For
almost a year the only road to the northern part of the island of Ambon
was literally blocked by a brick wall, and nobody, especially not Christians,
was allowed to pass. After the road over the hills was opened again, transport from Ambon town to the northern part of the island by road remained
difficult. Only Moslems live behind the wall, both Ambonese and Butonese,
though the number of Butonese has decreased. All Christians have fled the

---

* An earlier version of this paper appeared in Dutch: K von Benda-Beckmann 2000.
[1] I use the term Ambonese for someone who belongs to the autochthonous population of
Ambon-Lease, which includes the islands Ambon, Haruku, Saparua, Nusa Laut and Eastern
Ceram, in order to distinguish them from other ethnic groups on the island of Ambon. In the
Dutch literature the term Moluccan is more current. However, strictly speaking this term
would also refer to people from the Northern Moluccas (Ternate, Tidore, Halmahera) and
South-Eastern Moluccas (Key and Tanimbar). On Ambon, these groups would not be considered autochthonous inhabitants: for them other *adat*, ie customs and customary law, would be
applicable.
[2] Manuhutu 2000, 16 reports that 1,200 deaths and 160,000 displaced have been registered,
but that estimates are a lot higher.

area, after the *kampong Kristen* in Hila/Kaitetu was attacked and set up in flames. The oldest Protestant church in Eastern Indonesia was destroyed, a beautiful building with a tiled floor vaguely showing the symbols of the ancient and long abandoned secret male societies. The centre of marine studies, a research site of Universitas Patimura, in which a number of Christians worked, was also attacked and looted and the Christians chased away. Many Butonese, though Moslem, have fled as well. Other Butonese, who used to live peacefully in Christian villages, fled to the Moslem northern part of the island, where they felt safer. Nobody knows exactly how many moved in and out of the area, and it is not quite clear where they went. Some went back to Buton, their land of origin on the southeast tip of Sulawesi, where a meagre existence is waiting in an overcrowded, barren area. Others have gone to other parts of Sulawesi, notably Macassar. The rest lead a quiet but uncertain life alongside their Ambonese Moslem neighbours largely cut off from the rest of Ambon. The north coast of Ambon no longer obtains its products through Ambon city, but directly through Macassar. Hitu, until recently a small, sleepy and insignificant harbour, is booming and expanding rapidly.

Many have attempted to create peace and reconciliation: religious leaders — both Christian and Moslem — local leaders, influential intellectuals, and high politicians and even former president Abdulrahman Wahid and the current president Megawati Sukaronoputri, but all in vain.[3] Moluccans in the Netherlands are also trying to think of ways to de-escalate the violence and create reconciliation. Some look to *adat* procedures as a way of creating peace. Others have more faith in the rule of law: the military should return to the barracks, take a neutral position in the conflict, and refrain from infiltration, and a public administration together with a judiciary that have been cleansed of corruption must reinstall good governance. Still others hope the 'international community' might play an enabling role. And finally there is a small group that believes violence and armed force is the only way to reach any solution. In fact, nobody really knows what to do and most people are rather desperate for creative ideas.

Over the past years there have been several periods in which there was hope that the riots belonged to the past, but this hope was shattered over and over again. Every time, violence flares up, only to settle down and continue smouldering beneath the ashes. Since it has become clear that agitators from outside have been active, probably with support from high political circles, there are voices that say that the troubles are externally initiated and are not really an internal problem within the Moluccan community. This is very unlikely. Troublemakers from outside may have intensified violence; it would not have reached the level and intensity in the Moluccas if there had

---

[3] See also Manuhutu 2000, 14.

not been serious problems in the region. However, agitation and the import of weapons have definitely increased the level of violence. During the first months people fought with knives and home made weapons. Nowadays a large number of guns and highly modern automatic weapons is in the hands of civilians, bought or 'borrowed' from the armed forces, and illegally imported from outside. The navy has confiscated many transports, but many manage to get into the area.

The Moluccas are in a situation where peace has not yet been re-established. Unfortunately it is still impossible to know when and how peace will be achieved. To say something about the peace-making process is therefore necessarily somewhat speculative. We can only look at the process while it is taking place, without knowing for sure which direction developments are taking. Yet I believe it is of crucial importance to document and analyse the process as well as possible while it is going on, and see where things go wrong and where there may be an inroad towards possible peace. Explaining the process leading to peace with hindsight, when peace has been established, runs the risk of overlooking with what hopes, expectations, information and (mis)understanding of what is going on, people search for possible ways out of a dreadful situation.

I hope to contribute to understanding a process the outcome of which is still completely unclear. I do not pretend to be able to look into all factors, but shall confine myself to two points, which I consider to be of vital importance. I shall try to unravel the various constellations of parties in which the conflict is situated and I shall look at how state law and *adat* law play a part in the conflict. What is often presented as an inter-ethnic or an inter-religious conflict is in fact a vastly complex set of overlapping conflicts that are expressed in different constellations of parties.[4] I shall discuss the main constellations, describe the dividing lines along which the parties have been formed and ask what role various kinds of law play in the formation of parties. Then I shall describe what constitutes the conflict in each of these constellations. I shall draw attention to the lack of traditional institutions that reach beyond the level of villages. Furthermore, it is of crucial importance to understand the role of the youth in the processes of violence, and I shall argue that traditional mechanisms to break through cycles of violence have disintegrated. Finally I shall discuss to what extent the various legal systems carry possibilities for re-establishing peace. I shall suggest that *adat* and a common religious past might be re-activated as an important symbolic support to other methods of establishing trust between Ambonese Moslems and Christians. However, in constellations with other parties, such as Butonese or Buginese migrants, *adat* is unlikely to serve for peace making. Too strong an emphasis on *adat* may even deepen the conflict.

---

[4] For a similar analysis of 'ethnic conflicts' in the Transcaucasus, see Yamskov 1991.

My analysis does not apply to the whole region, but will be confined to the island of Ambon. The situation there is complicated enough in itself. Besides, the problems and causes of violence and riots in the North- and Southeast Moluccas differ from those in the Central Moluccas and require different explanations and perhaps different modes of peace making than Ambon-Lease, which forms a single socio-political region.

1   REGION AND CENTRE

Since Indonesia became independent, the Moluccas have played a special role within the Indonesian state. Attempts to found the independent state of the South Moluccas after Independence have not been forgotten, let alone forgiven. The wish for an independent state was especially strong among Christian Moluccans, who feared the Moslem dominance from Western Indonesia. But it was by no means an entirely Christian dream. Many Moslem leaders backed the struggle for independence. These plans were supported by the Dutch government, who distrusted Sukarno and his political supporters and had been in favour of a Federal Indonesia in the first place. Besides, the Dutch government promised its support for an independent South Moluccan state in recognition of the loyalty of the Moluccan soldiers in its colonial army. When it became clear that the Netherlands would lose the Dutch Indies, it put the majority of the Moluccan section of its army together with their families on transports to the Netherlands, where they should await more peaceful and secure times to return to the Moluccas. Things turned out differently. The Moluccas did not obtain independence and Indonesia quickly turned into a centralist state and they never did return to the Moluccas. The dream of an independent state was kept alive in the Netherlands for many decades, reaching its summit in the mid seventies, when violent outbursts and train hijacking symbolised the frustration at broken promises by the Dutch government and poor integration in Dutch economy and society. During that whole period, connections with the Moluccas were very infrequent. It was only from the 1980s on that it became possible for Dutch Moluccans to travel to Indonesia and the Moluccas on a regular basis. And it was only then that people started to realise how much had changed, and how far they had grown apart from their relatives on the Moluccas. The political struggle for an independent state was not abandoned, but it lost much of its overall support and rallying power. Instead, people started to think of other ways of supporting their relatives and home communities.

This history was in part Dutch history, a history of a particular migrant community in the Netherlands, but it also remained part of Indonesian history. Despite the fact that the Christian church and the Christian public at large had supported the unitary Indonesian state from the very beginning of the Republic,[5] the Moluccas continued to be regarded as potentially disloyal to the Indonesian state and its unity and therefore needed special control. It was not by chance that Ambon became the most important naval port of Eastern Indonesia, from where it defended its territory towards the Pacific. This way the navy could also keep control over this unruly province. Besides, the navy, together with the civil government, created quite a lot of jobs. Jobs were scarce in that area of the archipelago and the central government hoped it would keep the population satisfied. Of course, it overruled its own policy by reserving the lucrative clove trade for one of Suharto's sons, who had secured for himself a monopoly on the trade and owned one of the largest cigarette factories producing clove cigarettes. Thus, the government took with one hand what it had given with the other: the possibility of making a decent living.

The unrest in Ambon is therefore part of the overall political developments in Indonesia. The struggles for power that started between the new civilian government of President Wahid and the military elites, who are divided amongst themselves, continued under President Megawati. It is reported that disloyal high officers try to create unrest to enhance their position with the help of *preman*, semi-militia and groups of militant youths trained and led by high politicians or military officers, who enter regions of unrest stirring up trouble and violence.[6] While the police is reported to be siding with the Christians and the military with Moslems, the navy stays in contact with both and seems to have had a mitigating effect on the conflicting parties. The reports about armed forces who are kindling the fire and support or even send infiltrating militia, refer to the military and the police, not to the navy. The navy has remained remarkably reserved in the present conflict and managed to maintain an independent position among the parties.[7]

These are all part of the general political developments that are going on in Indonesia, with its decentralising policies and the development towards a more federal structure. Different parts of the state apparatus and different political groups have different interests and try to use these local upheavals to their own ends. These ends have only partially to do with regional politics, and are primarily inspired by what is going on in Jakarta, at the centre of power. But they do have a deep impact on the political constellation and the development of the struggles in the region. Unless this struggle at central level cools down, there will be no peace in the region. Whether the new law on decentralisation that allows for more regional autonomy is going to help in this process remains to be seen.

---

[5] Bartels 2003.
[6] Meuleman 2000, 22.
[7] Manuhutu 2000, 13.

This is also part of a struggle between those who want to establish a nation state based on Islam, and those who are in favour of a secular state. The three presidents Indonesia has had since the demise of the Suharto regime have all strongly supported a secular state that offers room for all religions. However, militant Moslems from Java, belonging to the organisation of *Laskar Jihad*, have entered the Moluccas and call for a *jihad*, in the sense of a religious war. And they propagate a Moslem Indonesian state. Below, we shall come back to the religious factor in the conflict.

The situation escalated so much during the months of May and June 2002, that President Wahid decided to withdraw the Moslem commander of the army and substitute him with a Hindu, who was expected to take a more neutral position than his predecessor. He announced a state of civil emergency on 26 June 2000, on the basis of the Law of National Security.[8] Since May 2000, the situation has worsened, and the army has played a central role in this disintegration. While locally-made weapons were predominantly used in the initial phase, from May 2000, more and more professional weapons were imported into the region. There are strong indications that the army has provided Moslem groups with arms. It certainly has done little to de-escalate the conflict or to contain the import of weapons. Some politicians are calling for intervention by the UN, though it is unclear what such an intervention at this moment could do to re-establish order and peace. In the meantime, several international donor agencies have sent experts in peace making to the region. It is not clear yet whether these attempts have had any success.

2   CITIZENS AND GOVERNMENT

One of the greatest problems in the central Moluccas is great dissatisfaction with a failing, corrupt government. It is beyond the scope of this chapter to explain every way in which the government fails. But some factors are specific to the Moluccas, and they deserve to be mentioned here. The Moluccas have no industry of any importance. Economically they depend to a large extent on the production of spices, especially cloves for the cigarette and pharmaceutical industries, and nutmeg. Because of the monopoly in the hands of the inner circle around the former president Suharto, possibilities to sell these spices are very limited. Income from spices has been insecure throughout history, as a result of great fluctuations on the world market and, in addition, as a result of these monopolies. In the middle of the 1980s there was an economic boom in the Moluccas due to high prices and good harvests. Since that time, prices have dropped dramatically and no longer compensate price increases in rice and other basic food products that have

---

[8] *Keputusan President* (Presidential Decree) 88, 26 June 2000. See Jakarta Post, 27 June 2000.

to be imported into the region. The economic and monetary crisis has exacerbated the problems. The 1990s were a period of economic stress. The feelings of dejection were enhanced by a civil government that after a long period of expansion for the first time had to cut down. Till then, the government had managed to accommodate the majority of the young high school and university graduates with a good education, but this became increasingly difficult towards the end of the decade. The prospects of these well-educated youths who had completely turned away from the agriculture and horticulture of their parents, had crumbled. Going back to the village and the life of a peasant would mean disillusionment, loss of face and dissatisfaction. Many opted for an equally unsatisfactory attempt to survive in Ambon town on odd jobs. This development increased feelings of resentment towards the government.

The armed forces also no longer offered these youths the prospect of a job. The old ideal, to have at least one child in every family with the armed forces, no longer was a viable option. This increased the criticism on the side of the population, who had until then had a somewhat ambivalent attitude towards the armed forces. Those who had secured the protection of the armed forces because they had close relatives in its service tempered their critique. But those who had no relatives with the military or police voiced their ciriticism more freely.

There is a general feeling of dejection, and great distrust towards the government and towards 'Jakarta', which does too little for the Moluccas, is capricious and authoritarian and which creams off the profits from the spices through patronage and corruption. Growing youth unemployment especially under the better educated, and a town that is splitting at its seams with a very diverse population highlight these developments. The new regime has not managed to change this. Habibie was still identified with the Suharto regime and did not bring any real change to the situation. Only one thing really changed: it became possible to express one's discontent openly without having to fear the police, and people have done so increasingly and loudly. Under these conditions former President Habibie's attempt at reconciliation was bound to fail. The short visits by President Wahid and by President Megawati were not able to produce any results either, and the present government has not managed to gain the trust of the local population. Much more radical change is needed. The longer the conflict lasts, and the more people die, the longer the process leading to conciliation is going to last. The road from honesty to corruption is a lot shorter than the other way around.

3   VILLAGE AGAINST VILLAGE

It is remarkable that most reports and debates on the Moluccas conflict do not mention the age-old tensions between neighbouring villages. What is involved is more than ordinary rivalry between neighbours. Three centuries of colonial government and fifty years of centralist Indonesian government have not fully erased pre-colonial structures. The VOC, the Dutch East Indies Company, at the beginning of the seventeenth century forcibly resettled the population that lived in the mountains on the coast, in order to make them easier to control. What today are regarded as *adat* structures and *adat* positions, in fact were largely fabricated by the colonial government for these new settlements.[9] Often, families who under the old structure had occupied little land and a lower position, and now were willing to cooperate with the Dutch and to take the lead in resettling on the coast, were rewarded with more land and leading positions. In this restructuring, the territory was redistributed, leading to disputes over land between neighbouring villages that have lasted until the present. The Dutch seizure of hegemony in the region aborted the fragile political structures that surpassed the village level and that might have been the first steps towards state formation in a region of autonomous villages. From then on *adat* structures were confined to the village level. Beyond that, there was colonial authority and later state authority, but no *adat* authority that could intervene in case of disputes. The colonial literature is full of lamentations of colonial officers whose attempts to settle quarrels and disputes between neighbouring villages remained unsuccessful. They complained about lacking clarity and the impossibility to reach a definitive settlement.

In the course of the nineteenth century Butonese migrants were encouraged to settle in the border regions between villages, and to act as a buffer between the rivalling parties. Below we shall come back to the position of the Butonese to discuss the tensions and conflicts of these migrants with the Ambonese population. Here it is important to note that these old rivalries have continued to exist even today. They are as vicious between neighbouring villages of the same religion as among those of different religions.[10] The quarrels and disputes are largely a result of the confrontation of colonial laws and *adat*, despite the fact that *adat* itself has been deeply affected by the colonial administration. But there are hardly any *adat* procedures and structures beyond the village level that could be called upon to deal with the larger issues we are confronted with today. And that is an immediate inheritance of the Dutch colonial experience.

4   CHRISTIAN AND MOSLEM AMBONESE

Christianity and Islam came to the Central Moluccas around the same time in the late sixteenth and early seventeenth century. It was a period of great

---

[9] F von Benda-Beckmann 1999, 138 ff.
[10] Historically, the choice for Christianity or Islam was always made by a whole village. There have been a few cases where the village was split and one half became Christian, while the

turmoil in the region, during which several trading powers tried to gain control over the profitable spice trade. Islam came from Ternate and Tidore in the Northern Moluccas, who were attempting to expand their hegemony to Ambon, Ceram and further. The Portuguese at first profited from these hegemonic claims, by supporting the local leaders who were in a process of state formation themselves and established themselves as the main traders. When the Portuguese became too greedy, the Dutch saw an opportunity to get rid of their rivals and to take their place as partners in the clove trade. Those who supported the Dutch became Christians, while their rivals, who lived mainly on the north coast of Ambon, opted for Islam, though the old religion was never fully abandoned. Throughout the colonial period this division of the Ambonese population into a Christian and a Moslem section continued to exist.[11] This resulted in a highly skewed access to positions in the colonial administration and colonial education. Upon Independence only children of the *rajas* and other *adat* officials had been able to follow Dutch education in Moslem villages, while Dutch education was far more common in Christian villages. The Indonesian state inherited an administration that was almost exclusively Christian. This advantage continued long after Independence. Only in the 1980s a growing Moslem self-consciousness allowed for pressure, with support from Jakarta, to appoint more Moslems in the provincial administration. From the mid 1980s onwards this policy was strongly implemented. Schulte Nordholt reports that from 1992 onwards members of the Islamic Organisation of Moslem Intellectuals (ICMI) were systematically appointed to all vacant high positions of the provincial administration.[12] But contrary to what Schulte Nordholt seems to suggest, replacement by Moslems had started many years before. This policy created a strong sense of insecurity among Christians, a feeling that was enhanced by reports that 'Christian capital' was disadvantaged in the financial world and was running the risk of being confiscated, while it became increasingly difficult for Christian companies to attract capital. Moslems point out that the new policy was only a long overdue correction to the imbalance that was an artefact of colonial policy. The issue is still very sensitive on both sides and each side reacts passionately to policy changes. President Abdurrahman Wahid was strongly opposed to the replacement policy, but was unable to prevent it. The substitution of Christian civil servants by Moslem has continued under President Megawati.

The conflict here is in part a socio-economic and political conflict over access to profitable positions in the state administration. These positions

other opted for Islam. As a result, two villages by the same name were founded, such as Siro Sori Serani (Christian) and Siri Sori Islam.

[11] Chauvel 1990.
[12] Schulte Nordholt 2000, 36.

are all the more profitable because of all the extra income made possible by a corrupt administration. Of the local population only ethnic Ambonese are eligible for a position in the administration. Other local communities are barred due to a common unwillingness on Ambonese side to let them in. In that respect there is great unity between Christian and Moslem Ambonese. To be sure, there are non-Ambonese civil servants, especially in higher positions. They are highly educated people from Java and Sumatra. The divisions run along religious and ethnic lines, each with its own alliances. But while Moslem and Christian Ambonese fight for a position in the administration, members of other ethnic groups hardly make any attempt to do so. They are focused on the private sector, where each ethnic group used to have its own economic niche.

During the year 2000 the conflict among the population groups has changed in character. There are several reasons for this change. In the first place people have started to vent their anger on buildings of worship: mosques and churches have been burnt. Secondly the role of the armed forces has become increasingly problematic. The army reportedly supports and even actively sends agitators from outside to increase religious tension. Whether or not the first churches and mosques were set on fire at the instigation of these agitators is unclear. What has become clear is that *pre-man*, semi-militia and groups of militant youths have encouraged these actions. With that, the conflict has obtained a new dimension. Setting fire to buildings of worship touches upon the heart of religion because it is a sign that one wants to destroy the religion. This is seen as something fundamentally different from harassing people of another religion. It has led to great frustration, anger and especially to immense fear. It has been an important reason why relatively simple fights have developed into armed conflict. A conflict in which the army and the police are increasingly taking sides, which at the end of June 2000 led the President to force the army to replace the divisions with other, hopefully more neutral divisions. Several attempts have been made to improve the situation by replacing the leadership.[13] But the army and the police are still accused of taking sides in the conflict and neither has been able to stop violence.

In such a constellation it is hardly suitable to attempt to create peace with a single conciliation mission from Jakarta, as happened in 2000 with the visit of the President and the Vice-President. In order to decrease the mutual fear among Christians and Moslems, several conditions must be met. First and foremost the armed forces have to maintain a neutral position instead of taking sides. They also must stop providing arms to the civilian population. Secondly, the current appointing policy of the government has to be replaced by one based on meritocratic principles, where religion

---

[13] Tempo, 10 July 2000; Tempo, 11 July 2000; Antara, 11 July 2000 (1).

and ethnic background are not relevant features for an appointment. A credible beginning needs to be made to do away with corruption. Meeting each of these conditions on their own is difficult enough. In combination the task is truly formidable.

The question is what legal instruments are available. In principle, state law could provide the measures to deal with these issues. However, the practice of the Indonesian legal system is not promising. The judiciary, itself thoroughly demoralised, poorly salaried and highly corrupt,[14] is, under the present conditions, not capable of redressing the current discriminatory policies. The armed forces are even more problematic. The President, though perhaps in theory having supreme authority, does not seem to have the necessary control over them. This is primarily a political battle the outcome of which is highly uncertain.

Some have suggested that *adat* might play an important part in recreating peace. Possibilities seem rather limited, however, because this problem has to do with a realm of social life where traditionally *adat* had no role to play. There were no viable *adat* institutions to deal with such serious conflicts beyond the village level. Public administration has always been beyond the reach of *adat* and will continue to be that way.

However, there might be a role for *adat* as a symbolic universe to find a way out of violence. In a recent publication, Bubandt has called attention to the force of symbolic discourse as a stimulus for starting and continuing violence.[15] As in the North Moluccas, narratives of violence and of super-human invulnerability have a long tradition on Ambon as well. But it seems that they may not point as unequivocally towards violence between Moslems and Christians as in the North Moluccas. In the Central Moluccas these narratives of violence seem not to have been associated with clashes between Moslems and Christians, but rather with clashes of Moslems and Christians jointly against the colonial oppressor and against the central state. Moreover, as Bartels suggests, Moslems and Christians share a common religious past.[16] Symbolically, this unity has been represented by the institution of *pela*, old alliances between villages that established ritual blood relationships, also between villages of different religions. Though such alliances are of limited practical value, symbolically they may serve as a possible way out of violence among Moslems and Christians. Since the outburst of violence, Moslems and Christians have forgotten that it was not long ago that they recognised each other's God.[17] Nevertheless the joint religious past and *adat* could symbolically be reactivated and help Moslems and Christians find peace together.

[14] Bedner 2000.
[15] Bubandt 2000, 17.
[16] Bartels 1977, 2003.
[17] Bartels 2003.

5   AMBONESE AND URBAN MIGRANTS:
BUGINESE, MACASSARESE AND TORAJAS

The fight between the taxi driver and the *becak* driver was a fight between an Ambonese and a Buginese. The Ambonese happened to be Christian, while the Buginese was Moslem, but religion in that particular constellation was of marginal importance. Like the conflict mentioned above, this conflict, too, is a socio-economic conflict, but now between an autochthonous population and a group of relatively recent migrants living in a densely populated neighbourhood in Ambon, Batu Merah, where most of the *becak* drivers live. Until violence broke out, Buginese and Macassarese dominated this economic sector, while Moslem and Christian Torajas occupied the furniture sector. Torajas are considered to be less aggressive and threatening. The differences are no less, but they are more moderate and perhaps economically less important.

But in contrast to the conflict between Christian and Moslem Ambonese mentioned above, we are here dealing with a conflict over access to sectors in the private economy, not to government positions and the related patronage-economy. The economic depression certainly has exacerbated the conflict. While in the past the economic sectors in which different ethnic groups dominated were rather sharply separated, the boundaries have recently begun to dissolve because Ambonese have tried to enter into these sectors and claim a dominant position for themselves. Manuhutu points out that Ambonese who until recently looked down upon a *becak* driver, now want to drive one themselves to make a living.[18]

State law can do little here as long as the economic situation remains problematic and as long as the police has little authority and remains corrupt. For this type of conflict in an urban setting, *adat* has little to offer. On the contrary, *adat* enhances some of the conflicts in so far as it gives only Ambonese people a position of full citizenship placing migrants in a subordinate position.

6   AMBONESE AND RURAL MIGRANTS: BUTONESE

In rural Ambon there is another ethnic conflict, but this time between Ambonese and Butonese people.[19] Since the second half of the nineteenth century there has been a constant stream of Butonese migrants to the central

---

[18] Manuhutu 2000, 12.
[19] See von Benda-Beckmann and Taale 1992, 1996 and F and K von Benda-Beckmann 1999 for a detailed analysis of the relationships between Ambonese and Butonese in Hila, on the north coast of Ambon.

Moluccas. This migration is spontaneous and has nothing to do with transmigration programs of the government. As mentioned before, these Butonese were welcomed and were assigned a place at the border between neighbouring villages where they acted as a buffer between rivalling village communities. They remained second-rate citizens, which throughout history repeatedly led to violent conflicts. Until the beginning of the 1980s they were prevented from participating in the *raja* elections for the traditional village head who at the same time has the position of mayor in the state administration. But more important was that their second rate position also put them at an economic disadvantage. They were not allowed to own land or trees — especially not the profitable clove and nutmeg trees. An exception was made in the case of land for housing and only for old migrant families. As a result, Butonese people could not participate in the production of the most profitable crops of cloves and nutmeg and could only partake in the profits in sharecropping relationships. During the boom years of clove prices in the 1980s this led to serious disturbances between Ambonese and Butonese inhabitants in dispute over the division of the harvest and trees. The trees had been planted by migrants who thought they would acquire half of the trees as soon as they started to produce. In this conflict several people died, among them a police officer.

Because they were not allowed to own land and trees, many Butonese were forced to grow annual or biannual crops. Many have become successful vegetable growers, while commercial coastal fishing is largely in the hands of Butonese fishermen. When clove prices dropped dramatically in the late 1980s, many Ambonese also turned to growing vegetables. They became dependent on the knowledge and seeds of Butonese experts.

The struggle around the spices also had another economic background. Planting a clove or nutmeg tree, which only starts to produce after at least six years, means a long-term commitment of the land on which the trees stand. The Ambonese feared that planting trees would after some time result in a claim to the land. Ambon *adat* recognises a division of ownership between the land and what is on the land, but this rule has been contested throughout history. There is an inherent tension between the formal legal division and the economic unity of land and tree ownership. This tension has resulted in violence many times in the past, especially when prices on the world market happened to be high.

In this constellation of parties within the conflict *adat* appears to be as much part of the problem as a way to solving it. It is not by chance that Butonese people always have called for state law to defend their position. They base their claims on civil rights laid down in state legislation. But in practice things have been different. They have had to submit to the dominant position regarding land and administration, as embedded in *adat*.

7   AMBONESE ON AMBON AND THE MOLUCCAN COMMUNITY IN THE NETHERLANDS

As the upheavals on Ambon acquired a more and more religious character, this came as a great shock to the Moluccan community in the Netherlands. For more than forty years they had lived with the idea that relationships between Moslems and Christians were good on the Moluccas. Relations in the Netherlands had been strained in the beginning. Moslems had been tormented so badly during the initial period in which they lived in camps that a Moslem camp had been created. And during the first years in which they had started to live in Moluccan neighbourhoods, there had been fights among Christians and Moslems in Waalwijk and Ridderkerk, where Moslem Moluccans were concentrated. But overall there was the idea that there were no real contradictions and that the religions lived peacefully side-by-side, because of their common pre-Christian and pre-Moslem religion.[20] The fierce battles that have driven Christians and Moslems on the Moluccas apart came as a great surprise and meant an enormous blow to the image they had of themselves. This image had been symbolised by their common ancient religion and by the institute of *pela*. These features were important markers of their ethnic identity. It is clear to most Moluccans in the Netherlands that *pela* is not sufficient to help bring the parties together.[21] What might help, but only as one element in a much larger process of reconciliation, is a reference to the common ancient religion, as a way of emphasising commonality in otherwise diverse religions. This could offer a symbolic support for other and more difficult means necessary to re-establish mutual trust.

Many Dutch Moluccans have lost relatives or friends. And almost everyone has been asked for help by relatives and village members on Ambon, either through relatives or through *kumpulan*, organisations based on common descent from the same village. These requests create grave dilemmas for them. For in as far as support is asked for food, clothing, housing, medical treatment, and rebuilding religious centres, people are eager to help and large amounts of money are sent. But requests for money to buy arms are an entirely different matter. They are faced with the question whether to help relatives defend themselves, at the risk of encouraging violence. There is only a minute, but radical minority that is prepared to support armed defence. The large majority is radically against any support for arms. But the pressure is high and heated debates are going on over the question as to what support from the Netherlands could be most effective. There are many initiatives and ideas floating around, but the situation on the Moluccas does not allow for any concrete projects yet.

[20] Bartels 1977.
[21] Bartels 1977, 1989; Strijbosch 1986; Manuhutu 2000, 11.

The Moluccan Historical Museum started an initiative to provide information on Internet and E-mail. At first, the Moluccan community thought that the upheavals were all initiated from outside the Moluccas. They could believe that violence among Christians and Moslems was an external thing. However, it turned out that more was at stake and that the violence had become an internal issue that cannot be fully explained by infiltration. The Dutch Moluccans find it difficult to get a proper insight into what is going on. In part this is due to the internal structure of the conflict itself: the more rigid the religious divide and the more segregated society on Ambon is becoming, the more difficult it is to get reliable information on all sides. The Moslem Moluccan community in the Netherlands is small and by far the most information comes from the side of Christian Moluccans. The Moluccan Historical Museum is doing its utmost to develop initiatives that bind people from both religions together.

Support from the Netherlands is complicated by the historical distrust on the side of the Indonesian government towards the Free South Moluccan movement. This is particularly the case in military circles, though President Wahid did not seem to be much intimidated by this history. Laskar Jihad and other radical Moslem organisations continue to stress that Christians are seeking an independent state. This history does hinder the Dutch community from contributing to reconciliation.

The Moluccan community in the Netherlands is not the only Moluccan migrant community. There are many Moluccan migrants in Jakarta employed in government service and in private companies, well educated and with a high income. They have also organisations that resemble the *kumpulan* in the Netherlands. However, their relationships with Ambon seem to be far less emotionally loaded than those of the Dutch Moluccans. Much material support is provided to relatives, but it is unclear in what way and to what extent there are attempts to de-escalate the conflict.

8 YOUTH AND LEADERSHIP

One of the aspects that has received relatively little attention is that the actual violence is predominantly committed by young, usually unmarried men. In small groups they plan raids, make weapons and go out every time there is a rumour that a mosque or church has been burned down. They operate independently and seem to be living in a restricted awareness where they can only think of the next operation, how to get hold of arms and who or what to attack next. Some speak of 'tunnel vision', typical of such violent groups of young men who increasingly become incapable of thinking about the wider issues involved. Of course there is nothing new to this fact. But there is little known about the social field in which these youth operate. It is not quite clear who these young people are, whether they are largely unemployed, what their level of education is, etc. There are rumours of bandleaders who have gathered groups of youth around them. Some even talk about 'war lords'. However, there is very little inside information and what can be said is necessarily somewhat speculative. Though there are some strong leaders, group formation seems to be very loose and youths seem to operate predominantly in shifting ad hoc associations.

Some of the violence that is occurring now resembles a traditional pattern of violent conflict management. If a close relative is wounded, for instance in a traffic accident, brothers and cousins set out to catch the presumed perpetrator. If they succeed, he will be severely beaten, sometimes even to death, whereupon a counterattack may follow. But if the perpetrator is not immediately caught, violent retaliation will no longer be sought and another mode of conflict regulation takes its place: negotiation and reconciliation by elderly relatives. This form of violence is very common, and the practice of immediate violent reaction is constrained as elderly men and women take over. But in the present violence the social restrictions and constraints that prevent serious escalation of the conflict seem to be failing. Youths still follow more or less classical patterns of immediate violent reactions to real or presumed violence against their relatives. But there are three important differences. The amount and quality of available weapons have raised the violence to a previously unknown level. The military leadership claims that the weapons used by civilians are often of higher quality than the weapons of the army itself. Besides, there seems to have been an extension of the classical pattern in the sense that not only relatives and village members, but also all members of the religious community have to be defended. But rather than having undergone the same extension, traditional constraining mechanisms seem to be rapidly disintegrating. The elderly would not know whom to talk to in order to negotiate a solution and they are totally at loss as to how peace might be re-created.

9   CONCLUSIONS

One of the biggest problems is how to find a way out of violence that is increasing at a frightening speed. The government, being the only structure of authority that surpasses the village level, is too much part of the problems to be an acceptable independent third party. It is very doubtful whether the substitution of the military commanders will be sufficient, though it is an important first step.

Most ideas and attempts to create peace start out from the assumption that the parties should be reconciled in order to establish mutual trust so that they can start building up their society again. But how should one envisage this? The above analysis shows how complex the conflict is, or rather, that what is presented as one conflict in reality is a complex of related conflicts with different constellations and alliances of parties. This complicates the task of identifying the parties that should be reconciled. Yet this may turn out to be the easiest part of the problem. Far more problematic is the fact that many attempts hinge on the idea that there is a clear leadership, while in reality there is a striking lack of leadership. As explained before, there are no *adat* structures beyond the village level. Furthermore the religious structures on Ambon make it difficult to find religious leaders with sufficient authority.[22] Islam on Ambon-Lease is virtually exclusively locally organised. In rural areas, mosque functionaries are appointed locally and are intimately tied up in *adat* positions. They have rarely received religious training outside their village, nor do they form part of a wider hierarchy of authority beyond the village.

Christian church organisations show different characteristics. There is a more centralised authority with a synod and pastors have received church-related training. The problem here is that the embedding in *adat* has only partially taken place. Many pastors are considered to be outsiders in villages where they have been appointed, because they usually have not been born there and therefore have no position in *adat*. Though there is clearer religious leadership in Ambon than in the Islamic community, the church structure is also a problematic basis for solving the kind of complex problems we are dealing with here.

This means that all attempts to re-establish the kind of trust necessary to finish violence have to start out from an extremely diffuse social field with many conflicting interests and a complex of conflicts with many and diverse features. Attempts to come up with solutions within a short period of time with a relatively small number of leaders are bound to fail. Far more is needed than the mere promise of greater autonomy. Much time, energy, patience and careful listening to all involved must be invested in order to find modes and procedures that cannot be directly derived from one set of norms, regulations and institutions, be it *adat*, religion, or the state.

Trust has to be built at many levels. An interesting approach has been suggested by a former village head, who, besides trying to set up some overall Ambon projects that explicitly link Moslems and Christians, pleads for an incremental approach, in which neighbouring village leaders, together with groups of young people start discussing and doing things together. Once they have built up some trust and common projects, the next village has to be approached to collaborate. What makes the approach interesting is that it is not confined to one single level, but operates at different levels at the same time. In bringing Ambonese Moslems and Christians together again, reactivating their common religious background, symbolised by the institution of *pela* may help, as a powerful symbol of unity, to lead the way out of violence.

[22] F and K von Benda-Beckmann 1988, 1993.

Many other laudable initiatives are going on by local and international organisations for peace making. One of the problems is the lack of co-ordination between these projects and initiatives. This again is a feature that shows remarkable persistence throughout history: projects are started but rarely reach a state of permanence and co-ordination that makes them viable over a longer period of time.

Change is needed in so many ways: the civilian government has to make a credible start to banning corruption, so that people can begin to believe that its government and legal system has something valuable to offer. The military has to take a neutral position instead of encouraging unrest and start collecting arms instead of providing the civilian population with arms. People from different religions have to start collaborating in providing help to the dislocated refugees and create forums of common discussion, while the calls and support for *jihad* from Java have to be stopped emphatically. The fact that Laskar Jihad has finally been forced to withdraw from the region is a welcome beginning. Additionally, all initiatives have to take the younger generation seriously, both in binding it into immediate tasks and projects, as well as providing it with prospects for a meaningful existence instead of a future as marginal horticulturists for which young people have not received an education and in which they do not believe. It is indeed a formidable task to establish the beginning of trust that is needed to finish the state of terror. The signs at this moment are not promising. Violence is still rampant, the import and spreading of arms are not under control. And there is still a great distrust in the police and the military and civilian leadership.

REFERENCES

Bartels, D 1977. *Guarding the invisible mountain: intervillage alliances, religious syncretism and ethnic identity among Ambonese Christians and Moslems in the Moluccas.* (Ithaca: Cornell University Press).

Bartels, D 1989. *Moluccans in exile: a struggle for ethnic survival.* (Utrecht: COMT/IWM).

Bartels, D. 2003. Your God is no longer mine: Moslem-Christian fratricide in the Central Moluccas (Indonesia) after a half-millennium of tolerant co-existence and ethnic unity. In *Proceedings of the 5th Maluku Conference*, edited by S Pannell. Darwin, Australia, July 1999. (Darwin, NTU Press) (in print).

Bedner, A 2000. *Administrative courts in Indonesia: a socio-legal study.* (Leiden: Van Volenhoven Institute).

Benda-Beckmann, F and K von. 1988. Adat and religion in Minangkabau and Ambon. In *Time past, time present, time future: perspectives on Indonesian culture; Essays in honour of PE de Josselin de Jong*, edited by HJM Claessen and DS Moyer. Verhandelingen van het Koninklijk Instituut voor Taal-, Land- en Volkenkunde 131: 195–212. (Leiden: KITLV Press).

Benda-Beckmann, F and K von. 1993. Eine turbulente Geschichte im Verhältnis zwischen Religion und Volksrecht: die Molukker in Indonesien und in den

Niederlanden. In *Sprache, Symbole und Symbolverwendungen in Ethnologie, Kulturanthropologie, Religion und Recht. Festschrift für Rüdiger Schott zum 65. Geburtstag,* edited by W Krawietz, L Pospisil and S Steinbrich. (Berlin: Duncker & Humblot).

Benda-Beckmann, F and K von. 1999. A functional analysis of property rights, with special reference to Indonesia. In *Property rights and economic development: Land and natural resources in Southeast Asia and Oceania,* edited by T van Mijl and F von Benda-Beckmann: 15–56. (London: Kegan Paul International).

Benda-Beckmann, F von. 1999. Multiple constructions of socio-economic spaces: resource management and conflict in the Central Moluccas. In *Frontiers and borderlands: Anthropological perspectives,* edited by M Rössler and T Wendl: 131–58. (Frankfurt a/M: Peter Lang).

Benda-Beckmann, F von and T Taale. 1992. The changing laws of hospitality: Guest labourers in the political economy of rural legal pluralism. In *Law as a resource in agrarian struggles,* edited by F von Benda-Beckmann and M van der Velde: 61–87. (Wageningen: Pudoc).

Benda-Beckmann, F von and T Taale. 1996. Land, trees and houses: changing (un)certainties in property relationships on Ambon. In *Remaking Maluku: Social transformation in Eastern Indonesia,* edited by D Mearns and D Healey: 39–63. (Darwin: NT University).

Benda-Beckmann, K von. 2000. Recht en geweld op Ambon. In *Libris Satiari Nequeo: Afscheidbundel voor Kees Boender,* edited by H Elffers: 7–21. (Rotterdam: Onderzoekschool Maatschappelijke Veiligheid. Erasmus University Rotterdam).

Bubandt, NO 2000. Conspiracy theories, apocalyptic narratives and the discursive construction of 'the violence in Maluku'. *Antropologi Indonesia* 63: 15–32.

Chauvel, R 1990. *Nationalists, soldiers and separatists: The Ambonese islands from colonisation to revolt 1880–1950.* (Leiden: KITLV Press).

Manuhutu, W 2000. Een jaar geweld op de Molukken: een terugblik. In *Maluku Manis, Maluku Menangis: de Molukken in crisis,* edited by W Manuhutu, J Meuleman, N Schulte Nordholt, and J Willemse: 7–17. (Utrecht: Moluks Historisch Museum).

Meuleman, J 2000. Islam in het hedendaagse Indonesië. In *Maluku Manis, Maluku Menangis: de Molukken in crisis,* edited by W Manuhutu, J Meuleman, N Schulte Nordholt, and J Willemse: 19–27. (Utrecht: Moluks Historisch Museum).

Schulte Nordholt, N 2000. De Molukken als oefenterrein voor de machsstrijd in Jakarta. In *Maluku Manis, Maluku Menangis: de Molukken in crisis,* edited by W Manuhutu, J Meuleman, N Schulte Nordholt, and J Willemse: 33–44. (Utrecht: Moluks Historisch Museum).

Strijbosch, F 1986. Het pelarecht van Molukkers in Nederland. *Nederlands Juristenblad* 1986/6: 177–83.

Yamskov, AN 1991. Ethnic conflicts in the Transcaucasus: the case of Nagorno-Karabakh. *Theory and Society* 20: 631–60.

11

The Search for New Sources of Legitimacy in Indonesia after Suharto

JOHN R BOWEN

FROM WHAT SOURCES can legitimacy be derived when a bankrupt political order falls? Indonesia after Suharto seems plagued by both a massive failure of social order and a severe crisis of political legitimacy. The two are connected, and have been exacerbated by the failure of the 'New Order' (the regime under President Suharto that lasted from 1966 to May 1998) to create a legitimate and effective legal system.

Local social conflicts have been massive and widespread in the period since early 1998, and each has had a different character. In East Timor, a region never recognised by the international community as part of Indonesia, the army and its civilian militias waged a campaign of terror against civilians, in a vain effort to prevent the referendum on independence. In various parts of Java, well-organised (and probably army-related) campaigns of terror were carried out against Chinese populations, and included the rape of Chinese women (an unusual occurrence in Indonesia). In the north-eastern region of Maluku, where separate communities of Muslims and Christians have been the basis for vertical networks of patronage and support, gang wars, probably originating in Jakarta, escalated into all-out communal massacres, and these massacres have led to 'copycat' killings elsewhere in the eastern half of the country, as well as to polarisation of Islamic and Christian media. In West Kalimantan, indigenous Dayaks joined forces with Malays and even with Chinese to attack Madurese settlers. In the northwestern most province of Aceh, the liberation army and Indonesian troops pick off each other's men daily, others die, and someone is terrorising Javanese transmigrants. Aceh is only one of several provinces where demands for independence, or autonomy, have been made by groups claiming to represent the people of the province.

How do we make sense of these distinct violent events and suggest ways of resolving them? I think that the way not to understand them is to label them as 'ethnic conflicts', a phrase that smuggles into discussions a pseudo-analysis of conflict as caused by the sheer presence of ethnic differences (Bowen 1996). One might do better by beginning from the complaints, demands, and explanations put forth by people involved in these conflicts.

In what follows, I explore current debates within Indonesia about the legitimacy of various proposed legal and political responses to the legitimacy crisis. These responses consist of specific types of tribunals to deal with crimes committed under the Suharto regime, reforms in the justice system, and a devolution of authority to regions, ethnic groups, or religious communities. I am particularly interested in the potential tensions between two types of demands: one for a more effective and impartial nation-wide legal system, the other for greater recognition of the rights of ethnic and religious communities and the autonomy of regions. This tension, I argue, has its roots in a basic contradiction between two competing Indonesian ideas of the political community.

1   TRUTH AND TRIBUNALS

The overwhelming response to recent events of violence is to demand an investigation, sometimes with a 'truth and reconciliation' body in mind, after what Indonesians presume to be the successful experience in South Africa (*Jakarta Post,* 17 February 2000). The phrase 'truth and conciliation' often appears in English in the Indonesian reports. It is unclear what the phrase means to key government actors, but the international provenance of the institution clearly contributes to, if not constitutes the sole foundation of, its legitimacy. Indonesian Human Rights Commission members have called for a truth and reconciliation commission, and the government plans to submit a draft bill to Parliament that would establish such a body (*Kompas,* 20 February 2000).

Everyone agrees that 'truth' is a desired end-point of whatever legal processes take place; the question is whether truth is better than, or at least an acceptable substitute for, criminal prosecution. But truth is not easily found, and in at least one case some have urged abandoning the quest for truth. One of the most explosive sets of accusations concerned the rape of Chinese women during the anti-Chinese violence and destruction of May 1998. The destruction is thought by many to have been part of a systematic campaign to destabilise the country, either to keep Suharto in power or to enable a military coup. Even the commander of the armed forces, General Wiranto, admitted (on 21 August 1998) that soldiers were involved in the destruction, and a government fact-finding team chaired by the human rights leader Marzuki Darusman declared that November that it had found evidence of rapes, including interviews with victims.

But in January 2000, after no prosecutions had begun, Marzuki Darusman reported that no testimony had been obtained from victims, only from 'third-party informants', and the State Minister of the Empowerment of Women, Khofifah Indar Parawansa, declared that the government would open a new investigation. The reaction from feminist activists was mixed. Some welcomed the new investigation but at least one leading activist, Rita Serena Kalibonso, said that the government had already stated that many suffered from the May 1998 riots, and that it should focus instead on programs to compensate these people and legal measures to prevent the recurrence of such violence. The reasoning was best expressed in a Human Rights Watch report of October 1998, that

> the more the debate focuses on the issue of whether or not rapes occurred, the less likely it is that serious investigations will be pursued to establish the extent of, and reasons behind, attacks on ethnic Chinese (HRW 1998).

The problems of proof with respect to the rape accusations were also used by Islamic groups (and by the Saudi government) to discredit the broader charges of organised anti-Chinese violence as designed to discredit Muslims (Tempo, 28 August 1998). The credibility of the accusations was further weakened when it was revealed that photos alleged to be of raped Chinese women that had been posted on the Internet were taken from pornographic sources and from East Timor by a Chinese association based on San Francisco.

In this case, the kind of proof demanded by police and prosecutors — public testimony by victims — is especially difficult to procure in a climate of widespread military intimidation of civilians. A continued drive to find out the truth would only further add credibility to those parties who denied that the rapes took place (or could biologically have happened — an especially strange debate took place for a short period over the conditions under which erections are possible [Detik 4 September 1998]). Truth would not set free the victims, given the conditions for proof established by the authorities.

But it is also unclear which courts ought to try the perpetrators of these and other crimes. Indonesia faces the general problem of bootstrapping its judiciary into legitimacy. The general courts have generally been seen as corrupt, and its judges at all levels subject to bribes and to midnight telephone calls from a spokesman for the executive branch indicating that a certain case should be dropped. To whom, then, does one turn for judgement in sensitive cases involving human rights violations?

The issue is currently posed most visibly with regard to East Timor, where the Indonesian government has stated that it will set up an Indonesian tribunal. Kofi Annan recently blessed this proposal, but held out the prospect of an international 'human rights tribunal' should the Indonesian efforts prove unsatisfactory. The Indonesian court will therefore have to be developed 'in the shadow of' other such courts so as to prevent United Nations action.

To investigate allegations of abuses by the military in the province of Aceh, the government has created an interjurisdictional tribunal (peradilan koneksitas), apparently first proposed in 1998 by Marzuki Darusman on grounds that the dualism of military justice and civilian justice could only be overcome if abuses by military were tried in civilian courts with some military judges on the panel.

Finally, wholesale revisions of the court system are being proposed, with special attention to the problem of legitimacy. If, it is argued, the Supreme Court is empowered to exercise judicial review of laws and of Presidential decrees, then not only will it gain in authority, but the courts in general will gain in legitimacy. The argument rests on the unfavourable comparison between the Indonesian and the United States Supreme Courts, the judicial review powers of the latter being taken as a reason for the relatively lawful behaviour of US presidents.

Each of these proposals draws on the legitimacy of an international or foreign institution as a reason for adopting a particular reform. Each of the various types of institutions that are proposed within Indonesia — truth and reconciliation commissions, human rights tribunals, interjurisdictional tribunals, judicial review — relies for its legitimacy on its foreignness. Indeed, 'the rule of law', a phrase much heard (in the English) in Indonesia in recent years, is seen as an international idea and for that reason a good thing.

The international origins of these legitimating legal concepts stands in contrast to the general thrust of political arguments since independence. Indonesian political rhetoric has always been strongly 'indigenising'. Supposedly indigenous concepts and institutions were taken as the foundations of a truly Indonesian political system. In particular, the capacity to work together to form consensus was declared to be the Indonesian genius, opposed to the 'free-fight liberalism' of the West.

Two concepts were particularly ubiquitous in this rhetoric. 'Working together' (gotong royong) characterised village forms of co-operation and also the way national leaders did and should cooperate. 'Consensus through deliberation' (musyawarah mufakat) is one of the five components of the state ideology, the Panca Sila, first formulated by Soekarno in 1945. The phrase is invoked daily in national political life to justify a broad range of measures, some of them intended to suppress debate in Parliament, others intended to suppress popular dissent. It is ideologically effective because it resonates with long-standing local norms that decisions should be reached through consensus; indeed, in his essay on law and culture, Clifford

Geertz (1983) took Indonesian norms of arriving at consensus through harmonious speaking as the defining feature of indigenous social norms, or *adat*, in the archipelago (Bowen 2000).

In contrast to this indigenised political rhetoric, talk about law eschews the local for the global. In some cases, notably that of East Timor, this preference may be the result of external pressure: labelling a court a 'human rights tribunal' and following procedures similar to those followed elsewhere will make the Indonesian trials look more like what the United Nations would have created on its own — and still could create — should the Indonesian response not prove satisfactory. And yet the phenomenon also is in response to an internal problem of legitimacy: against a record of corrupt courts and a military free to commit abuses — where, as in the rape cases, truth is hard to prove — searching outside Indonesia for legal forms may bring a new reservoir of legitimacy into the country's political and legal life.

2   LAW AND LOCAL VIOLENCE

But law needs to treat highly local problems. One major condition for the escalation of local incidents into large-scale violence in various parts of Indonesia has been the absence of effective means of resolving disputes across ethnic or religious lines. By 'effective means' I mean, very broadly, legal institutions, social institutions, and social norms of cross-group toleration. One would then argue that the new architecture of law and politics ought to be effectively supra ethnic, and, in general, universalist.

Consider, for example, the massacres in West Kalimantan in early 1999 that pitted indigenous Dayaks against immigrants from Madura. Conflicts between these two groups date back to 1950, and had erupted frequently since 1968. The presence of Madurese in Kalimantan is due largely to the government's transmigration program, which moves people from crowded Java and Madura to other islands. Tens of thousands of Madurese were settled in West Kalimantan, many of them in the past twenty years.

Some of these immigrants Madurese controlled jobs and land areas that had been enjoyed by Dayaks. Madurese were able to gain title to land that had been used by Dayaks and local Malays for rotation subsistence farming. At the same time, local farmers had come under increased pressure from state-backed private enterprises seeking to control large tracts of land for logging.

But local commentators cited social factors as even more important in generating enmity between Madurese and others, specifically a tendency to keep to themselves and to behave generally in a 'harsh' (kasar) manner. Madurese, like some other ethnic groups in Indonesia (notably Makassarese and Bugis, both groups from Sulawesi) make much of the importance of 'honour' in social life, and are quick to retaliate against tarnishing of that honour. By contrast, Malays and Dayaks in Kalimantan have been said to intermarry and to 'get along' generally. In the 1999 clashes, Chinese, Malays, and Dayaks joined to fight against the Madurese (*Forum*, 3 September 1999).

The tensions, therefore, were not 'immigrant versus local' and also not 'ethnic conflict' in general, but rather a specific tension between one group and all others that had to do with the demographics of immigration, conflicts over jobs and land, and the culturally specific ways in which the Madurese responded to inter-group incidents. These tensions might have resolved themselves over the long term, but for the absence of institutions to prevent conflicts between the groups.

Two relatively minor incidents turned this long-standing tension into a deadly conflict. In January 1999 after a Madurese man had been caught stealing from a home in a Malay village. The man was beaten by the villagers and let go. About two hundred Madurese returned shortly thereafter and attacked the village, killing two Malays and a Dayak man. The response by the police was critical in what followed. They arrested eight villagers who had taken part in the original beating, and the father of the theft suspect (who had turned himself in), but they arrested no one else in connection with the three murders.

About a month later, a second incident occurred: a Malay bus conductor was stabbed by a Madurese man who refused to pay the bus fare. The latter was arrested, but within six hours, word of the stabbing had spread widely, and groups of Malays, Bugis, Chinese, and Dayaks had begun to attack Madurese settlements (*Forum*, 3 September 1999; TPK Sambas 2000).

The resulting killings quickly became known abroad as 'Dayak headhuntings', but one American environmental expert working in the area (Judith Mayer, borneo@igc.org, 21 March 99) observed Dayak leaders vowing to protect Madurese and organising '*adat*-style ceremonies' to try and keep the peace. These improvised efforts have no legal force, however, and cannot counterbalance the major shortcoming, namely the absence of social norms or legal institutions capable and willing of resolving disputes between these groups.

The story is a familiar one (compare the Serbs in Croatia): the migration, or state-induced movement, of large numbers of people into an area previously exploited by another, with resulting conflicts over land and jobs, and, in this case, a cultural style on the part of the immigrants that meant quick escalations of particular incidents. No supra-ethnic social norms existed to mediate between groups (despite the efforts of those Dayak chiefs to improvise '*adat*-style' rituals), and the legal authorities, the police and army, did little to prevent the violence from escalating upwards.

A similar situation led to the violence in the Maluku region of eastern Indonesia, where Muslim newcomers have been fighting local Christians.

Christianisation is a centuries-old phenomenon in eastern Indonesia, but much of the conversion in Maluku took place in the nineteenth century under Dutch rule. Some Muslims had lived in the region, especially in the city of Ambon, for centuries, but many more began to arrive from South Sulawesi in the past ten years. The newcomers took over many informal sector jobs, such as market-place sellers and pedicab drivers; their own social networks allowed them to dominate these sectors. Tensions between Muslims and Christians rose after the economic crisis of 1997, when the control of jobs became a matter of survival. In Ambon, patronage networks stretch all the way up to the highest offices, with the governor, high-ranking army officials, and a former mayor of Ambon controlling both employment opportunities and local gangs.

In 1998 (and just as in Kalimantan) a small incident involving a bus conductor and an obstreperous passenger touched off fights between rival gangs (whose numbers had swelled with recent arrivals from Jakarta). The major difference for the nation between this event and those in Kalimantan was that the lines of social cleavage here corresponded to nation-wide divisions between Muslim and Christian communities. Christian networks throughout Indonesia began to warn of plots to Islamise all of eastern Indonesia. (Detailed versions of this story continue to appear on the Internet in 2000.) Islamic groups reminded their supporters of long-standing efforts at Christianisation, and warned that warriors from the 1940s Republic of South Maluku were waiting for a chance to launch a separatist movement. Some pro-Suharto factions of the armed forces may have supported calls for Muslims to fight in defence of their co-religionists.

In both Kalimantan nor Maluku conflict came about when large-scale immigration of people who differed in some marked way from longer-term residents (in Kalimantan, the cultural style of the Madurese; in Maluku, the Islam of the Sulawesi immigrants) coincided with struggles over resources (land, jobs). Local social norms and legal institutions were unwilling or unable to prevent minor incidents from escalating into large-scale conflicts. Specific policies and tensions from the Suharto era were involved: state-induced transmigration, pressures on local land resources from state-backed logging enterprises, the virtual monopoly of local authority by police and army (and thus the absence of other supra-ethnic mechanisms for resolving conflicts), and the conflicting interests of rival factions of the army.

These cases thus point toward some of the elements that must be part of a new legal and political structure that can win legitimacy in the eyes of Indonesians by providing the needed mechanisms. They suggest that in general law and politics must be independent of ethnic and religious allegiances, so as to effectively broker relationships among communities. An effective and impartial police power is required. Rules for land use must be general, thus supra ethnic, but also must make allowances for local practices of resource use.

This direction of reform is, however, precisely what the New Order said it was trying to accomplish: to create a unified, supra-ethnic legal and political framework. If reform were entirely about making political life live up to New Order rhetoric, then these measures would attract broad support. But much of what we might call the second wave of reform, characteristic of 1999, has consisted of calls for greater self-determination: of provinces or districts, of *adat* communities, and of the Muslim community. This direction of reform is in tension with the other: law would be more specific to a territory, an ethnic identity, or a religious affiliation.

3   MASYARAKAT ADAT

Beginning in the late 1990s, Indonesian news media begin to use a category of masyarakat *adat*, '*adat* community' or 'people who live according to *adat*'. The term '*adat*' itself has a breadth of historically sedimented meanings. Most generally, it can refer to a way of life, a sense of propriety, social norms. Dutch administrators, seeking some regularity in social norms (and anticipating a law-and-society tendency to merge law and norms), divided the Indies into distinct areas based on '*adat* law' (adatrecht). In general, the relationship of kinship ideas to political structures was the major criterion for grouping societies into a single '*adat* circle'. Under the New Order, '*adat*' was used by judges in the Dutch sense of *adat* law, but in other government contexts to refer to 'tangible culture': the dress, wedding practices, and house styles typical of a province.

The more recent references to masyarakat *adat* bring the '*adat* law' meaning of *adat* to the surface, but disentangled from the court system. The term is used most frequently with respect to local efforts to resolve disputes, often land disputes, by calling an '*adat*-style' assembly. For example, in February 1999 a group of Dayak people in East Kalimantan held an '*adat* tribunal' to resolve a conflict between a logging operation, PT Anangga (a subsidiary of Barito Pacific Timber), and local residents. The latter claimed that the loggers had destroyed forest that they relied on for food and medicines, and to which they had rights as their tanah ulayat. The Indonesian legal category of hak ulayat refers to rights enjoyed by a collectivity by virtue of their history of using the land in question (Evers 1995; Moniaga 1993). The Dayaks also claimed that company-set fires had destroyed some of their gardens and houses. The company said it was ready to pay a small amount, but that the government had given them the right to log the land and that they knew nothing of traditional rights.

In the end, the company agreed to pay an amount higher than their original offer, though less than the residents had demanded. The session, acting in the name of the *adat* community, was presided over by the government district head, the Camat, and attended by seventy armed members of the police or military. It combined state power and state legal categories with the legitimising categories of the '*adat* community': the local language, references to the sanctions of ancestors, and traditional land use practices (*Kompas*, 22 February 1999).

The success of several such events in the general climate of political reform led to the creation of the Alliance of Adat Communities in the Archipelago. Although their initial attempt in March 1999 to meet en masse with legislators failed, the delegates used the occasion to convey their demands to reporters. The North Sumatran delegate stated:

> Long before the state existed, *adat* communities in the archipelago already had succeeded in creating a way of life; the state must respect the sovereignty of the *adat* communities (*Kompas*, 22 March 1999).

The delegates to the Alliance were generally affiliated with local councils, which may give them so degree of local legitimacy, but certainly facilitate their entry into national politics. For example, the Majelis Adat Dayak Kalimantan Barat, Dayak Adat Council of West Kalimantan, has proposed that one of its leaders, Drs AR Mecer, be selected as a representative of the Dayaks to the MPR, in the category of 'group delegate' from an ethnic minority. But this very idea of an 'ethnic minority' grates on others' ears: two other Dayak leaders, one a Council officer, the other described as an 'informal leader' (tokoh masyarakat), argued that Dayaks should not be represented as 'ethnic minorities', both because on Kalimantan they are the majority, and because it is control of local resources, and not representation in national forums, that is important (*Kompas*, 9 August 1999).

Translating 'local aspirations' onto the national and international stage has involved the efforts of NGOs, who make it possible for statements to circulate worldwide as representative of the opinion of an ethnic group. For example, the Drs Ar Mecer mentioned above wrote in November 1999 that 'the Dayak *adat* community' demanded that a federal system be put into place. His statement was initially posted on a 'civil society discussion' Web site run by PACT (Private Agencies Co-operating Together), which is headquartered in Washington, DC, funded by USAID, and involved in civil society, HIV/AIDS, and civil-military dialogue projects; it was then emailed by the site's editor to the free apakabar list server, and in that way ended up on the computer screens of many Indonesians and Indonesianists throughout the world as well as in Indonesia. However, left unexamined is the relationship of his claims about federalism and Dayak 'ethnic minority' status to the broader universe of Dayak opinions on these topics.

Brought into being in the climate of reform, as a political entity that could be opposed to the government, the '*adat* community' is current represented as a body capable of resolving conflicts over resource use (when allied with state officials), as a channel for the people's aspirations, and as the appropriate group to manage collective resources, principally forested areas. Certain individuals manage to speak for these bodies in the public space of newspapers and Internet sites. This speaking-for, claiming to represent the *adat* community, depends on a succession of mediations involving local councils, Indonesian NGOs, their foreign supporters, 'coffee-house discussions', and the Internet.

4   REGIONAL AUTONOMY

As the Dayak example shows, demands for *adat* self-determination are sometimes linked with the idea of a federal system, and with the claim that *adat* communities preceded the state and have preserved certain political rights. Demands for autonomy, or even independence, have come from all corners of the country. They have led to a national debate about the relative merits of 'autonomy' (otonomi), a 'federal state' (negara federal), and the current 'unitary state' (negara kesatuan). These debates draw on experience of other countries — both the United States and Malaysia are mentioned as successful federal systems — but they are more strongly shaped by Indonesia's own history.

Indonesian history contains competing ideas about the political community, which in their most polarised form depict Indonesia as a nation-state, on the one hand, and as an association of self-sufficient communities, on the other. The idea of an Indonesian nation-state posits a unitary and centralised state that has a monopoly of legitimate authority, principally in the form of positive law enacted by the legislature serving as the voice of the people. It also posits a unified people-nation (bangsa), possessing common cultural characteristics, declaring themselves to be a nation, coming together to form a nation-state, and together fighting off the Dutch and their allies during the 1945–50 period of revolution.

The nation-state idea was a foundation of the dominant ideology of the New Order regime. The cultural, legal, and political policies of Suharto were directed at strengthening the capacity of the central executive power to monitor and shape social life throughout the country, and at the same time strengthening the idea of Indonesia as a collection of similar 'cultures', each defined as an assemblage of comparable traits (dances, languages, etc.)

The entire weight of political and legal reform of the past three decades — the effective period of New Order control — has been to centralise politics and law in Indonesia. Centralisation has meant both creating uniform structures and codes, and grasping effective central control of everyday life, the étatisation of social life. This process has involved either abolishing or rendering subordinate alternative structures of authority. Even in the 1970s, many Indonesian provinces had specific political structures that long predated the Indonesian republic. These structures drew their legitimacy from local social norms, not from Jakarta. Their structures included 'dat councils' of local notables; hereditary rulers whose positions lay somewhere between the administrative district (kabupaten) and the village; and multiple, overlapping ideas of 'village'(desa), including residential unit, a unit of governance, an irrigation or other functional unit, and so forth. These were gradually abolished in the 1970s and early 1980s in favour of a uniform, three-tiered administration.

Courts were regularised under the Supreme Court, in a process that lasted through the 1980s. General courts, Pengadilan Negeri, were successors to courts created by the Dutch, and likewise drew their legitimacy from central state authority. Matters of marriage, divorce, and inheritance, however, were often brought to local Islamic tribunals. The legitimacy of the latter did not depend on Jakarta: they were seen as enforcing sacred law. Although in the 1970s the Islamic court justices were civil servants, and thus technically under the control of the central Ministry of Justice and the Ministry of Religion, only in 1989 did the national legislature pass a bill setting out a uniform structure for these courts — in effect, claiming to be the source of their authority. In the early 1990s, President Suharto declared that a uniform code of Islamic law should be followed by all the Islamic court judges and indeed by all civil servants. This code dealt with family law matters only. The President's declaration removed the process of legal interpretation from learned Islamic men and women, whether judges or other learned persons, and gave it to the new Islamic law code and the process by which it had been created. Judges were officially understood to only apply the law, not interpret it.

The second, associational idea about the Indonesian political community depicts distinct regions and communities as coming together to form Indonesia. Each such community had, and still has, its own set of social norms, some of which have legal standing. One such community is the masyarakat adat discussed above. But a region may also be represented as a self-sufficient community, especially when past kingdoms may be cited as proof of self-determination. For some Muslims, the entire Islamic community also has its own social norms, and its own history, in which Dutch suppression of sharî`a plays an important role.

The provinces into which Indonesia was divided at independence did not correspond exactly to colonial adat areas or to precolonial states, but they usually bore a relationship to colonial administrative boundaries, and thus the provincial governments could draw on habits of 'administrative pilgrimage' (Anderson 1991) that were made by representatives of various parts of the province to the provincial capital. In addition, the political instability of the five years of revolution between the proclamation of independence (1945) and the final emergence of the unitary Indonesian state (1950) left the provinces as often the effective unit of political control, responsible for creating new institutions and resolving conflicts among them. Many, indeed most, of these provinces later resisted Jakarta's politics or policies on various matters, and some formed coalitions, or independent states. The first few decades of independence thus involved provinces acting qua provinces to negotiate with the central government, thereby strengthening provincial identities as political entities.

In the current (early 2000) political climate, many provinces are calling for autonomy or independence, and subprovincial units are calling for provincial status. And yet these calls again raise the question of how 'the people's aspirations' are to be discerned. One such debate has concerned the relative cultural appropriateness of consensus (musyawarah) and 'voting' (in English). 'Voting' refers to counting votes in an assembly, and as such is a recent idea and is perceived as a foreign procedure. It is to be distinguished from pemungutan suara, counting votes (literally 'voices') in an election or pemilihan, election. Voting became a topic of discussion during the 1998 session of the MPR, the Majelis Permusyawaratan Rakyat, the 'super-assembly' composed of the elected Parliament plus appointed members that selects the President and Vice President. Voting factions, roughly corresponding to political parties, had always arrived at a common position behind closed doors and then made that position known openly; 'voting' was a proposal to allow individual representatives to vote in open session on issues.

Although it continues to be condemned by some commentators as a foreign practice (Budiono 1999), it has become increasingly difficult to oppose 'voting', lest one be seen as anti-democratic. One by one, the political parties have come to accept it as the procedure to be used in the 1999–2004 MPR (*Kompas*, 22 June 1999). As in the case of tribunals, it may be the very foreignness of the idea and the word that is proving attractive.

If 'voting' has become an increasingly legitimate way for bodies of elected officials to make decisions, 'referendum' (in English) has taken on increased importance as the way for the people to assert their will. It was the fighting over the East Timor referendum that brought the term into general Indonesian consciousness. Indeed, when some Acehnese leaders demanded that they, too, be allowed to vote in a referendum, President Abdurrahman Wahid's reaction was that if the East Timorese had been given the opportunity, why not the Acehnese?

It is from Aceh that the strongest voice for independence now comes. Aceh, on the northwest tip of Sumatra, has known periods of greatness as an Islamic sultanate, mainly in the sixteenth and seventeenth centuries. The Acehnese continued to resist Dutch efforts at colonial rule right up to the Japanese invasion of 1942, and they gave a great deal of assistance, in fighters and in supplies, to the people of northern Sumatra in their efforts to prevent the Dutch from re-establishing control after 1945. Acehnese provincial ideology has combined the Islamic-state legacy with the recent experience of support for the Revolution and the Republic. However, shortly after independence many Acehnese supported an armed rebellion against the central government over what were felt to be broken promises: to give militiamen positions in the army, to support religious schools, and to allow Aceh a degree of self-government. In addition, Javanese soldiers stationed in Aceh were seen as a morally corrupting influence, for a time Aceh was part of a larger province centred in Medan, a city populated by Christians, and Soekarno was seen as in the control of the Communists.

Although this rebellion, called the Darul Islam movement, was ended in the early 1960s, a newer version of the rebellion took off in the 1970s. The overall complaint was again that control was in the hands of Jakarta, but this time the specific complaints were that highly valuable oil, gas, and forest resources were exported to Jakarta, and that, since the mid-1980s, the (mainly Javanese) troops engaged in a campaign of terror against the Acehnese people. After 1998, the Acehnese Liberation Movement began to operate more openly, and more violently, against Indonesian troops. Javanese transmigrants have also been targeted for killings — although it is not yet known whether the killers are the liberation movement or the military.

A number of distinct futures for Aceh are currently being discussed within the province. These range from full independence, to independence with a Commonwealth-type relationship to Indonesia, to continued membership in Indonesia but with more autonomy than that currently planned for all Indonesia's provinces — a distinct judiciary, for example. Those calling for Acehnese independence justify their demands on grounds that Acehnese desire to have their own country, and they supply reasons for that desire which include Aceh's pre-Indonesia political autonomy, the abuses committed by the Indonesian military, the small percentage of oil and gas revenues kept by the province, and Aceh's religious difference (as an all-Islamic area) from multi-confessional Indonesia.

Would an independent Aceh (or Riau, or Papua) lead to more freedom or autonomy in general than under a regime of autonomy or federalism? The question is complex; it involves such issues as the effect on the personal development and social toleration of individual Acehnese of living in a drastically smaller and more homogeneous country than today. Let me mention just one issue, however, that of minorities within a minority region. Aceh includes other ethnic groups: the Gayo (where I conduct fieldwork) consist of about 250,000 people, linguistically and culturally very different from the Acehnese; other, smaller indigenous groups (Alas, Kluet), and large numbers of immigrants from Java, West Sumatra, China, and elsewhere. Gayo have generally found that Acehnese monopolised trading networks and political power in the province, and found it necessary to leapfrog over the provincial capital to Jakarta to win contracts, export licenses, and government positions. Javanese, many of whom have lived in Aceh since the 1920s, consider themselves even more marginalised by Acehnese. Chinese are, of course, far more culturally different.

As with the myth of the nation-state ('once we get the borders right ... '[Brubaker 1996]), the myth of provincial autonomy conceals the internal heterogeneity of even this relatively homogeneous province. Of course, issues of tolerance and freedom go beyond ethnic differences. Acehnese differ among themselves on questions of religious practices, attitudes toward outsiders, the proper content of schooling, and so forth. Religious movements and Sufi orders on Aceh's west coast have been prohibited by the provincial religious leadership, for example. Would an independent Aceh begin to enforce a religious orthodoxy that was deemed improperly divisive in New Order Indonesia?

The major difference in legal and political structure proposed for Aceh has been the development of a legal system based on Islamic law, shari'a. Now, Aceh already has a system of Islamic courts (as does Indonesia as a whole) that handle all cases involving marriage, divorce, and reconciliation. Furthermore, in Aceh, unlike in every other Indonesian province, Muslims must take inheritance disputes to the Islamic court. In other provinces they may choose the general courts or the Islamic courts. No signs of support for Islamic penal laws have surfaced. What, then, are the substantive changes that Acehnese would hope for would the province base its legal system on shari'a?

Most likely, measures regarding women's clothing, the sale of alcohol, and the closing of restaurants during fasting month would be introduced in a shari'a-based Aceh. But shari'a also functions for many Acehnese as a sign of self-determination, as it has for many Indonesian Muslims for much of this century. This issue of shari'a thus brings us back to the national level, and the degree to which the 'Islamic community' ought to enjoy legal status within Indonesia.

The political significance of labeling one's legal system 'Islamic' is due in part to colonial efforts to limit the applicability of Islamic law. In 1937 the Dutch revoked the right of religious courts on Java and Madura to decide inheritance cases, thereby making Islamic inheritance law a symbol of the fight against colonial rule (Lev 1972). These jurisdictional issues also have become arenas for post-colonial debate about national identity. In the 1970s, for example, Parliament considered allowing the general courts, and not just the Islamic courts, to validate the marriages and divorces of Muslims. Heated debates ensued in the national press and in the streets on topics of national identity and religious freedom: some argued that the measure would contribute to creating an integrated, national legal system; others, that it would abrogate the rights of Muslims. The proposals were abandoned, and a much different bill passed, one that preserved the monopoly held by the Islamic courts over Muslim marriage and divorce. When in 1989 the government successfully proposed expanding the overall jurisdiction and enforcement powers of the Islamic courts, a similar debate took place, with some parties warning that the bill heralded the creation of an Islamic state; others, that it finally undid the colonial wrongs perpetrated against Indonesian Muslims.

Many, though certainly not all, Indonesian Muslims today see the presence of strengthened Islamic courts as guarantors of their religious identity within a pluralistic, non-sectarian national context. From the many new political parties to have emerged in the wake of Suharto's fall in May 1998 have come a wide variety of platforms for Indonesia's future, but those put forward by the major parties agree on a view of a multi-confessional and legally pluralistic Indonesia.

And yet Muslim groups have urged that stronger barriers ought to be put in place between the Muslim and Christian communities, regarding mixed marriages, conversion, and adoption, all seen as attacks on the Muslim community of a package with the violence against Muslims in Maluku and elsewhere.

5   CONCLUSION: RIGHTS VERSUS RECOGNITION?

Indonesian efforts to reconstruct a legal system combine (a) references to international standards of rights and legal processes with (b) demands for recognition of subnational communities, based on *adat*, cultural distinctiveness, or religious affiliation. These two tendencies are, of course, found elsewhere. On the one hand, rights increasingly are defined by transnational bodies and are distinguished from nationality (Soysal 1994). Forms of justice, such as the South African Truth and Reconciliation Commission, also 'travel' outside the borders of a country or region. On the other hand, some of these 'travelling' ideas involve a rejection of universal, or even nationwide, laws and norms. NGO-fuelled calls for the recognition of indigenous peoples' rights to land or to enforce their own social norms have received support in the United Nations. This second trend looks toward an increasingly pluralistic legal structure within states.

These two trends come into conflict when legally-enforced social norms of a subgroup violate international standards — one thinks of women's rights under Islamic law, or the rights of religious dissenters in Native North American tribal communities, or the problems posed by Israeli state support of Orthodox against Reform versions of Judaism. Local legal institutions can also pose questions of representation — who speaks for the 'indigenous community'? But rights and recognition, if I may so refer to them, can also come into conflict in a negative, less easily noticed way, if a weakening of universalist legal institutions reduces the protections offered individual citizens against violence or discrimination.

In the Indonesia case, this problem of protection has already been at the root of some current local conflicts, as I noted in the discussion of the Kalimantan incidents, where no effective forums were available to resolve conflicts between ethnic groups. This problem receives continued attention by Indonesian commentators. But the issue is less often discussed concerning the problems that minorities might face within newly autonomous regions. Would urban, Muslim residents of Kalimantan be more likely to recognise the validity of ways of life pursued by non-Muslim, small-scale groups engaged in shifting cultivation than was Jakarta? Is it not possible that Jakarta will be better able to produce cosmopolitan activist groups (such as WALHI) that would campaign for social tolerance? Will Gayo traders have more or less access to export markets in a country dominated by Acehnese than they do today?

The two ideas of the Indonesian political community — the nation-state and the association of communities — rise and fall in relative strength, and in early 2000 it is the associational view that at last enjoys free expression. Social peace and political justice in Indonesia probably depend on maintaining both ideas at the same time. The greatest degree of political and legal legitimacy for a future government may well depend on its capacity to achieve this balance.

REFERENCES

Anderson, Benedict 1991. *Imagined Communities*. Revised edition. (London: Verso)

Bowen, John R 2000. Consensus and Suspicion: Judicial Reasoning and Social Change in an Indonesia Society, 1960–1990. *Law and Society Review 34 (1)*.

Bowen, John R 1996. The Myth of Global Ethnic Conflict. *Journal of Democracy 7(4)*: 3–14.

Brubaker, Rogers 1996. *Nationalism Reframed*. (Cambridge: Cambridge University Press).

Budiono, Kartohadiprodjo 1999. Pemungutan Suara dan Kepribadian Bangsa. *Gatra 48 (5), 16 October*.

Ellen, Roy F 1983. Social Theory, Ethnography, and the Understanding of Practical Islam in South-East Asia. In *Islam in South-East Asia*, edited by MB Hooker (Leiden: EJ Brill).

Evers, Pieter J 1995. Preliminary Policy and Legal Questions about Recognising Traditional Land Rights in Indonesia. *Ekonesia 3*: 1–24.

Geertz, Clifford 1983. Local Knowledge: Fact and Law in Comparative Perspective. In Geertz, Clifford. *Local Knowledge: Further Essays in Interpretive Anthropology*. (New York: Basic Books).

HRW Human Rights Watch. 1998. *The Damaging Debate on Rapes of Ethnic Chinese Women*. (www.hrw.org/hrw/reports98/indonesia3).

Kell, Tim 1995. *The Roots of Acehnese Rebellion 1989–1992*. Ithaca, NY: Cornell Modern Indonesia Project, Monograph No 74.

Lev, Daniel S 1972. *Islamic Courts in Indonesia: A Study in the Political Bases of Legal Institutions*. (Berkeley and Los Angeles: University of California Press).

Moniaga, Sandra 1993. Toward Community-Based Forestry and Recognition of Adat Property Rights in the Outer Islands of Indonesia. In *Legal Frameworks for Forest Management in Asia,* edited by Jefferson Fox. (Honolulu: East-West Centre Program on Environment). Occasional Paper No 16: 131–50.

Soysal, Yasemin Nuhoglu 1994. *Limits of Citizenship.* (Chicago: University of Chicago Press).

TPK Sambas 1998. Tim Pencari Fakta (Fact-finding team), DPD, Kabupaten Sambas. *Kronologis Kerusuhan di Kabupaten Sambas (Chronology of Uprising In Sambas District).*

Conclusion

At the Heart of Legal Anthropology: Analyses of Peace Processes

MARIE-CLAIRE FOBLETS AND BARBARA TRUFFIN

Can we find, in societies that are very different from ours, exact equivalents to our own notion of 'violence', with its connotations of bestiality, illegitimacy and disorder? This fundamental question cannot be dismissed out of hand, any more than can its counterpart: can the researcher avoid his or her study being hijacked by the popular concepts and theories that are current in the society being studied?

Pierre Centlivres[1]

1   PROCESSES OF RESTORING PEACE AS THE OBJECT OF ANTHROPOLOGICAL ANALYSIS

THE CONTRIBUTIONS IN this volume were conceived as the continuation of the studies previously presented at the French-German meetings of legal anthropologists. Each meeting sought, from a particular angle, to explore the question of violence.[2]

The problem of violence is one of the most important — and long-standing — questions raised by anthropologists concerning the ongoing (re-)constitution of human societies. Just like the topic of pain, it is one of the most difficult to consider and to resolve, precisely on account of its destructive potential.[3] By its very nature, violence engenders and is constituted by relationships arising from such great tensions and instabilities that rules alone are unable to reduce them. Under the effects of violence, power relations replace social ones.[4]

---

[1] P Centlivres (1997), 'Violence légitime et violence illégitime — A propos des pratiques et des représentations dans la crise afghane,' *L'Homme* 144 (1): 55.
[2] See, among others, T von Trotha and J Rösel, eds (1999), *Lokale Repräsentanten und locale Repräsentation von staatlicher Gewalt im Prozess der Dezentralisation*. Köln: Rüdiger Köppe.
[3] In this regard see, among others, V Das (1997), 'Souffrances, théodicées, pratiques disciplinaires, récupérations,' *Revue internationale des sciences sociales*, 611–21.
[4] See, among others, M Osiel (1997), *Mass Atrocity, Collective Memory, and the Law*. (New Brunswick/London: Transaction Publishers).

If the question of violence is a troubling one, there is, however, no shortage of anthropological analyses of it. Each analysis, in its own manner, seeks to explore the specific causes of eruptions of social violence, as well as the different ways in which societies live with this violence, organise themselves in relation to it, adapt to it, and integrate it into their daily functioning.[5] The potential for violence seems to be inherent in human society.[6] Countless studies have drawn attention to the importance of the anthropological study of the phenomena of violence for a good understanding of the political, ideological and legal functioning of social relations, whether these concern relationships between individuals or between groups, either within or outside of states.[7]

The purpose of the meeting at Oñati was to take this anthropological reflection a step further. On this occasion, we decided to underline and document the multiplicity of ways dynamic processes of restructuring human communities, struck by periods of overt violence, are taking place all over the world on both small- and medium-scale levels.

Indeed, the knowledge and expertise of anthropologists need to be more developed when it comes to the question of peace processes. This is especially true with regard to the study of contemporary processes for restructuring societies. For example, one can observe the (re)appearance of fortune-tellers[8] and informal justice, as well as, at the opposite end of the spectrum — namely at the international level — the intervention of (international) tribunals for peace[9] and the creation of electoral mechanisms under the aegis of international authorities.[10] What about our (anthropological) knowledge concerning the restoration of lasting

---

[5] See, among others, G Balandier (1978), 'Anthropologie de la violence,' *Revue des sciences morales et politiques* 131 (4), 527–45. P Clastres (1977), 'Archéologie de la violence: la guerre dans les sociétés primitives,' *Libre* 1: 137–73. P Menget (1985), 'Guerre, sociétés et vision du monde dans les basses terres de l'Amérique du Sud. Jalons pour une étude comparative,' *Journal de la Société des Américanistes*, LXXI, 131–42. F Heritier (1996), *De la violence*. (Paris: Odile Jacob).

[6] See, among others, E Fromm (1975), *The Anatomy of Human Destructiveness*. (Harmondsworth: Penguin). K Lorenz (1966), *L'agression, une histoire naturelle du mal* (French translation of *Das sogenannte Böse, zur Naturgeschichte der Agression*. (München: Borotha Schoeler). D Szabó (1976), 'Agression, violence et systèmes socio-culturels: essai de typologie,' *Revue de sciences criminelles et de droit penal comparé*, 377–98. Y Michaud (1985), 'Violence,' *Encyclopedia Universalis* 18: 914–20.

[7] On this subject, see among others, P Bohannan, ed. (1967), *Law and Warfare: Studies in the Anthropology of Conflict*. (New York: Natural History Press).

[8] See, among others, H Malkki (1995), *Purity and Exile. Violence, Memory and National Cosmology among Hutu Refugees in Tanzania*. (Chicago: University of Chicago Press).

[9] See, among others, PJ Magnarella (2000), *Justice in Africa: Rwanda's Genocide, its Court, and the UN Criminal Tribunal*. (Aldershot: Ashgate). Y Beigbeder (1999), *Judging War Criminals: the Politics of International Justice*. (New York: St Martin's Press). P Akhavan (1998), 'Justice in The Hague, Peace in the Former Yugoslavia? A Commentary on the United Nations War Crimes Tribunal,' *Human Rights Quarterly* 4, 737–816.

[10] There are, on the other hand, excellent analyses by political scientists who discuss mechanisms of conflict resolution, referring principally to contemporary history. See, among others,

peace? A restoration which often has to come to terms with the memory of traumatised societies. A restoration which, without putting at risk the processes of re-establishing power, may be more or less democratic, and is often very fragile.

The problem at stake concerns recent history. There are many communities today which, after a time of overt violence, and even of full-scale war, are engaged in reconstruction by setting up mechanisms intended to re-establish effective power structures.[11] These structures are set up to allow societies to reconnect with the foundations of their social reproduction and to re-establish, in the terminology of Pierre Legendre, a 'logic of symbolic transmission.'[12] They sometimes do so under constraint of the international community,[13] or occasionally under the threat of their own collapse,[14] for better or for worse.

2   THE MULTIDISCIPLINARY APPROACH

Questions concerning the restoration of ideological and social equilibrium within societies consumed by explosions of violence call for an interdisciplinary approach that extends over different areas of expertise: law, political history, sociology, international relations, to name but a few. This is what we have done: we have endeavoured to work together as anthropologists, historians, jurists. The processes of restoring social order, which we examined during the two days of workshops, are often complicated by a phenomenon of shifting solidarities, by the emergence of new actors, by political transformations and by numerous repositionings. Paradoxically, all those episodes that constitute the dynamics of restructuring are very often opaque and inconsistent. The interdisciplinary approach has allowed us to devise a procedure that borrows elements from distinct but complementary

DJ Whitaker (1999), *Conflict and Reconciliation in the Contemporary World.* (London/New York: Routledge), as well as GJ Mitchell (1999), *Making Peace.* (New York: Alfred Knopf). ChW Kegley (1999), *How Nations Make Peace.* (New York: St Martin's Press).

[11] See especially AJ McAdams, ed (1997), *Transitional Justice and the Rule of Law in New Democracies.* (Notre Dame/London: University of Notre Dame Press). GM Sorbo and P Vale, eds (1997), *Out of Conflict: From War to Peace in Africa,* (Uppsala: Nordiska Afrikainstitut). JP Lederach (1997), *Building Peace: Sustainable Reconciliation in Divided Societies.* (Washington, DC: United States Institute of Peace Press). B Hudson (1998), 'Restorative Justice: the Challenge of Sexual and Racial Violence,' *Journal of Law and Society,* 2: 237–56.
[12] P Legendre (1999), *Sur la question dogmatique en Occident.* (Paris: Fayard).
[13] IW Zartman and JL Rasmussen, eds (1997), *Peacemaking in International Conflict: Methods and Techniques.* (Washington, DC: US Institute of Peace Press). For a recent example of international constraint, see especially F Webber (1999), 'The Pinochet Case: the Struggle for the Realization of Human Rights,' *Journal of Law and Society* 4: 523–37, as well as J Rehman (1998), 'The Role of the International Community in Protecting the Physical Existence of Minorities: A Case Study of Pakistan,' *Liverpool Law Review* 2: 201–27.
[14] For an example, see T Lyons (1999), *Voting for Peace: Postcolonial Elections in Liberia.* (Washington, DC: Brookings Institution Press).

perspectives. In doing so, it has invited us to challenge certain fixed notions concerning violence and its analysis, and, eventually, to suggest new paths for reflection.

Our aim was to put together a series of studies, a selection of informed 'facts' — taken largely from contemporary history — that would enable us to take a truly anthropological, that is, comparative, turn to study mechanisms of restoring peace which, for the peoples involved, would lead in the medium or long term to political stabilisation. The various contributions cover a large geographical area. Although our attention was focused mainly on Africa (Rüdiger Köppe / Wilhelm Möhlig and Dieter Neubert), in particular on northern Mali (Georg Klute / Trutz von Trotha and Barbara Rocksloh-Papendieck / Henner Papendieck), South Africa (Willemien du Plessis) and Uganda (Dirk Beke), the volume contains papers dealing with India (Jakob Rösel) and Indonesia (John Richard Bowen and Keebet von Benda-Beckmann) as well.

3   THREE PERSPECTIVES

The studies presented at our meeting approached the question from a wide range of viewpoints. To some extent this was the consequence of the polysemic nature of the notion of violence. This polysemy results both from the multitude of situations studied and the diversity of theoretical perspectives guiding the different analyses.

We have distinguished three types of analysis: conceptual analysis; empirical analysis; and finally, what could be called a normative approach. We have chosen for this chapter to present only those contributions that belong to the first and/or second perspective. We shall later return to this subject.

Moreover, certain analyses combine the conceptual and the empirical perspectives, which makes them difficult to classify.

The first type of approach, the conceptual one, attempts to clarify conceptual categories that are useful for the study of peace processes. This might involve, for example, seeking to define the concepts of social peace, of society, of violence, and even of law itself.

Although it was not covered in all the chapters, one of the most basic questions underlying all restructuring of any kind is that of identifying the conditions of violence within a particular social context. Before one can speak of restructuring, one must examine the conditions that give rise to violence in a given situation.

Legal anthropology, the object of which is precisely to understand the development of what Pierre Legendre has called 'foundational representations'[15] in various societies, must trace the question of violence

---

[15] P Legendre (1999), above n 12, 72–73.

back to these underpinnings. These foundational representations fashion, in a manner that is different in every society, the boundaries of humanity. They are, as Clifford Geertz would say, 'constructive of social realities,' naming in a symbolic way what is possible and what is forbidden. It is within the framework of these foundational representations that the anthropologist seeks to understand the causes of violence, which are either constitutive of, or on the contrary lead to the disintegration of human beings as subjects.

In his opening remarks, Trutz von Trotha appeals to the concept of 'fundamental narrative,' the complex structure of which is intended by its nature to give meaning, to discuss and to integrate an event — whether individual, social, symbolic, or political.[16] The complex issue of the constitution and mobilisation of the collective memory of a group or of a society seems to be closely linked to the principle of a foundational image of the sort discussed by Legendre. The question of the confrontation of concurrent foundational representations has probably been the most provocative issue in the papers presented at Oñati.

This preliminary linking of the experience of violence with the foundational representation(s) identified as acting upon a group, and by the same token with its foundational narrative, can help clarify from a conceptual point of view the vast problematic being examined in the course of our meeting. It allows one to take into consideration, in *emic* terms, the interpretation and the use of violence by a society and its members.

A second illustration of a conceptual approach is to be found in the analysis provided by Wilhelm Möhlig and Rüdiger Köppe. These two authors examine, through the use of linguistics, what they describe as cultures of violence in Africa, and more particularly in Kavongo, Rendille and Swahili societies. This foray into the field of semantics clearly tends to approach the question of violence as much as possible from an internal perspective. It tackles the question of the 'socialisation' of violence through its semantic and cultural enunciations. When violence is culturally assigned a 'language', a set of practices and representations — whether important or not — it becomes possible to understand how violence is regulated, circumscribed and treated within this framework. The officially sanctioned treatment of the violence of the Rendille warrior through the rites of purification, reported by Möhlig and Köppe, illustrates this point.

George Klute and Trutz von Trotha offer a third example of conceptual clarification. They describe how, most ingeniously, the victors in a

---

[16] On the elaboration of a facet of the 'fundamental narrative' of German society, as well as on the evolution of these conditions, see F Etienne (1998), 'Ecrire une histoire des lieux de mémoire allemands: Pourquoi? Comment?' In *Travail sur la figure, travail de la mémoire*, *Avancées* 4 (Strasbourg: Presses universitaires de Strasbourg) 57–66.

'fratricidal' struggle within Tuareg society carefully mobilise the language of filiation/affiliation in their effort to reconstruct both a new social memory capable of giving meaning to their new power, and a place to the vanquished.[17]

The second type of approach is the empirical one, which allows us to discover various social contexts — contemporary and historical — but also the constraints of the environment, of the particular territory and of the ideology that weigh upon the peace process. The empirical approach, by means of ethnological accounts, recalls the extraordinary diversity of situations in which the question of restoring and securing peace may be posed.

John Richard Bowen, for example, describes in detail the competition that is currently taking place in the Indonesian archipelago between, on the one hand, the state's efforts to monopolise violence and its schemes — by 'domesticating' what appear to be threatening particularisms — and, on the other hand, the demand for a recognition of autonomy on the part of provincial and local entities. Bowen identifies local violence as principally resulting from the absence of effective means, institutions and norms for conflict resolution that would help manage the demography of immigration, a very tight labour market and a situation of interethnic tension. He then points to the state and holds it responsible for the events. The state's claim to a monopoly on violence and to the domestication of society has ended up weakening local public authorities. The latter no longer seem to have the capacity to channel social violence (migration policies, pressures of state enterprises on local resources and the bureaucratisation of daily life), or to resist a political rhetoric of the state that has been strongly 'indigenised' (gotong royong/musyawarah mufakat). This insistence upon a monopoly on violence on the part of state authorities, and the total lack of tools for creating new forms of coexistence among diverse groups within society has, according to Bowen, exacerbated the tensions between the two conceptions of Indonesian political community: on the one hand, the nation-state, and on the other, an association of communities. In this sense Bowen's account is close to that of Bogumil Jewsiewicki concerning African society:

> [...] the bloody divisions do not aim to eradicate the postcolonial state as an institution, but to appropriate it, domesticate it, to turn it into the instrument for realising local and regional objectives. The institution of the state is not

---

[17] It is not rare for filiation to be used as a mechanism permitting a group to reconnect with the foundations of its social reproduction. Pierre Centlivres noted that at the capture of Kabul, initially there seemed to be no massacres, no revenge between communist partisans and mujaheddin. The author attributes this fact to the role of family lineages among the adversaries. He notes that the latter, having never buckled under the antagonism of its members, permitted Afghan society to develop, initially, 'a certain ability to pursue, to reinterpret the rules of the game of tribal culture' (P Centlivres, 1997, above n 1, 62).

the victim but is itself at stake, even if the radical challenge to its monopoly on violence, its monopoly on killing, torturing, mutilating necessarily leads to the reformulation of the political order and its legitimation.[18]

George Klute and Trutz von Trotha, who analyse the second Tuareg rebellion of Northern Mali, propose a similar type of contextualised and case-oriented approach. The authors illustrate the manner in which the end of the conflict, which pitted Tuareg society against the Mali state in crisis, was used by the Ifoghas in their effort to impose and develop new forms of local norms, a new regional political order and a quasi-state. Klute and von Trotha concentrate their analysis on the way in which, in a context of generalised violence in a local arena that has been 'internationalised', the local political idiom of the 'chefferie' of colonial administration is, as it were, reinterpreted in favour of the creation, by the Ifoghas, of a para-State and para-sovereign 'chefferie'. The authors observe that acts of violence have developed with such intensity that the regulatory gates, traditionally constituted by the norms of protection and of tribute, were swept away. The new power demands and seizes the monopoly on violence, both from the central State and from its internal opponents.

These chapters invite us to continue to raise questions about the use of violence, its meaning and its monopolisation as the 'law of the group,' in Pierre Clastres' terms, that is a signpost laying down the boundary between life and death, between good and evil. It sometimes happens that the cultural and normative framework, in which violence expresses itself at a particular moment and in a particular form, goes so far as to imperil the future of a society. Violence may even legitimate madness.[19] The infliction of suffering can also, in extreme conditions, go as far as to appear '...as much a manifestation of the illegitimacy of society as of its legitimacy.'[20] A painful question thus arises: what will happen if a rule, a foundational representation that allows the individual to think and to live his or her human condition in society, no longer seems able to mobilise a narrative and a set of norms capable of regulating violence?[21] Taking into account — empirically or ethnologically — the elements that shape the polysemic reality of violence in a given society allows us to understand the meaning that an act of violence can take on in the eyes of a group. This is a type of approach that should continue to stimulate anthropological research.

Finally, the third type of approach presented at Oñati, which we will not treat here (for the purposes of a typology of the various points of view that

---

[18] B Jewsiewicki (1998), 'Pathologie de la violence et discipline de l'ordre politique,' *Cahiers d'études africaines. Numéro special: Disciplines et déchirures. Les formes de la violence*, 216.
[19] DE Apter, ed (1997), *The Legitimation of Violence*. (London: Macmillan).
[20] V Das (1997), above n 3, 614.
[21] A Mulcahy (1999), 'Visions of Normality: Peace and the Reconstruction of Policing in Northern Ireland,' *Social & Legal Studies*, 2: 277–95.

have been represented at our meeting) as normative, stresses the need to put into perspective the phenomenon of violence and the restoration of peace. This approach to some extent presupposes what is desirable: punitive justice, reference to human rights, and an insistence upon the requirements of democracy. These analyses[22] certainly deserve attention, insofar as they participate — in their own way — in the central questions posed by legal anthropology concerning the way in which a society ensures its own reproduction.

4 TAKING FURTHER THE ANTHROPOLOGICAL ANALYSIS OF THE PROCESSES OF PEACE AND RECONSTRUCTION OF THE SOCIAL FABRIC

How and with what consequences does legal anthropology reconstruct experiences which permit societies to overcome or to transcend violence, even when violence challenges the limits of humanity?

Do the chapters collected in this volume truly allow us to push further the anthropological reflection on the process of restoring peace? Undeniably the collection as a whole addresses a vast number of questions which, each in its own way, help clarify an aspect of the vast problematic under scrutiny.

The problem of reconstructing the social fabric — after a period or several periods of violence — by means of repositioning and of redefining identities, encompasses a number of great themes in legal anthropology. These are well-known themes: the search for justice in its many forms; the meaning given by a group or by individuals to the community of reference and its foundations; the question of the legitimacy of the existing order or of one yet to be established; the study of the process ('process analysis') of development of crises and conflicts, and of their resolution; the elaboration through these processes of a normative system; the notion of normalcy and/or of normalisation (normalisation of violence or of peace?), to name only a few themes.

The anthropological study of peace processes revives, in a sense, key notions elaborated by the discipline in the domain of conflict resolution, and places them back at the heart of the discussion. The various authors who present a contribution in this volume have sought to put into perspective

---

[22] In particular, the following three presentations not included in this volume for editorial reasons: C Younes, 'De la proximité dans le conflit à la proximité dans la relation: à propos du conflit israélo-palestinien/From Proximity in the Conflict to Proximity in a Renewed Relationship: Taking the Israelo-Palestinian Conflict as an Example.' S Liwerant, 'De l'impensable du génocide aux impensés du droit/From the Unthinkable of Genocide to the Unthought of in Law'. C Eberhard, 'Ouvertures pour la paix. Une approche dialogale et transmoderne/Opening up Spaces for Peace. A Dialogical and Transmodern Approach'.

recent experiences of restoring peace, which sometimes draw on the classic juridical model, and sometimes are more closely related to political-administrative purification, pardon, revenge, amnesty, or impunity. The different models or mechanisms put in place vary according to whether it is an external conflict (between different reference groups) or an internal one (within a community) that requires resolution. A conflict is external when violence erupts between independent units, when violence is directed against an external enemy. A full-scale war, for example, can be a way to conquer territory, gain access to merchandise or to symbolic goods from a clearly defined enemy. In the case of internal conflict, it is primarily the perpetuation of the group's identity, or the maintenance of good order within a society, that is at stake. The mechanisms for conflict resolution — internal or external — vary as well, according to the nature of the power relations involved (conquerors and/or the vanquished; the absence of a conqueror), or the presence of third parties.[23]

In a sense, the analyses collected here seek to put into place the elements of an anthropological enquiry into the restoration of peace which draws its inspiration from a body of knowledge acquired over the course of the history of the discipline. This enquiry provides the occasion for giving a new vitality to anthropological expertise in the field of reconstructing societies that have been torn apart by more or less conventional forms of violence.

Gordon Woodman suggested two directions for research: on the one hand, a project concerned with the task of providing immediate assistance to victims of violence, and, on the other hand, one that takes as its object the reconstruction of society. The study by Willemien du Plessis on the function assigned to the South African Truth and Reconciliation Commission belongs, at least in part, to the first group. But it is also true that the line of demarcation is not absolute. It would seem that in South Africa, the Truth and Reconciliation Commission, by expressing and elaborating a collective memory based on individual sufferings, made possible, to a certain extent, the creation of a new public space.[24]

---

[23] Certain forms of violence are in fact induced by power mechanisms put in place in colonies or after their independence, or are encouraged from outside, for instance by means of the code of human rights. The paths to peace and the role played by third parties in its eventual achievement are not the same in cases where the intervention of the third party dates back to a time before the conflict — sometimes in fact provoking the conflict in the first place — and in cases where external intervention comes after the outbreak of the conflict.

[24] Some have, moreover, seen in it a sort of reappropriation and a transformation of traumatic personal experiences for the benefit of the state, which, for Veena Das, allows the '... individual to transform that which has hurt him or her into a vision of the common good' (V Das, above n 3, 614). Concerning the process of reconciliation in South Africa, see also G Werle (1996), 'Without Truth, No Reconciliation. The South African Rechtsstaat and the Apartheid Past,' *Law and Politics in Africa, Asia and Latin America* 1: 58–72. D Nina (1997), 'Panel Beating for the Smashed Nation? The Truth and Reconciliation Commission, Nation Building and Construction of a Privileged History in South Africa,' *Australian Journal of Law and*

The majority of the contributions to this volume concentrate largely, directly or indirectly, on the second area of research mentioned by Gordon Woodman: the reconstruction of the social fabric and the reconstitution of collective identities.

The analyses show, for each of the situations under consideration, that the reality of violence is lived, in the first instance, within the bodies of individuals. For this reason, the process of restructuring must operate at the level of the links between the individual and the social. To Veena Das , 'it is in collective life that the individual tries to understand his or her personal experience and to overcome the traumas he or she suffered'.[25] The reconstitution of a collective identity involves negotiation as well as balancing between on the one hand, the search for an anchor in the past of the communities involved, and on the other hand, the need for a new legitimacy that will reposition the relationships to power within a society. This repositioning, ideally, should emerge from an exercise of rebalancing individual and collective social relations in a society. This process, ultimately, will be carried out with the guidance of third parties (NGOs,[26] international institutions,[27] mediators, etc). It is society as a whole that is involved, that is, its elites — new and old — as much as those who will eventually be persuaded to recognise their authority and obey them.

Will the equilibria studied here prove to be stable? We do not yet have, of course, the historical perspective from which to agree upon the strengths of the analyses presented here. Time is needed to reply to the question of how exactly the work of the anthropologist, facing contemporary violence, can help refine the scientific exploration of the conditions for success of the different mechanisms for restoring peace that have been tried out, as illustrated in this volume. We have not dealt here with events from our own history, such as Guernica, or Nuremberg, or those further back in time but nevertheless at the heart of the history of violence in Europe, such as the revocation of the Edict of Nantes. This does not mean that by choosing to concentrate on contemporary conflicts, by practising a sort of anthropology of the immediate, we have produced a work that therefore is to be called ahistorical. The task of typology undertaken, for instance, by Dieter Neubert, as well as by Wilhelm Möhlig and

---

Society, 55–71. L Huyse (1998), *Young Democracies and the Choice Between Amnesty, Truth Commissions and Persecutions*. Polity Study on Development and Cooperation. (Leuven: Law & Society Institute).

[25] V Das, above n 3, 619.
[26] See for example R Rotberg (1996), *Vigilance and Vengeance: NGOs preventing Ethnic Conflict in Divided Societies*. (Washington/Cambridge: Brookings Institution Press).
[27] See for example T Howland (1999), 'Mirage, Magic or Mixed Bag? The United Nations High Commissioner for Human Rights' Field Operation in Rwanda,' *Human Rights Quarterly*, 1: 1–55.

Rüdiger Köppe, takes a step back from the present, which is necessary in order to formulate comparisons. The work of Jakob Rösel also is basically a comparative study, based on a historical perspective.

The studies presented here lay the foundations for a work of clarification which, in time, will have to prove itself, whether we are dealing with Mali, South Africa, Mauritania or with the Indonesian archipelago.

Printed in the United Kingdom
by Lightning Source UK Ltd.
102188UKS00003B/52-102